CONSUMERS AND ENERGY CONSERVATION

CONSUMERS
AND ENERGY
CONSERVATION

International Perspectives on
Research and Policy Options

Edited by
John D. Claxton
C. Dennis Anderson
J. R. Brent Ritchie
Gordon H. G. McDougall

PRAEGER

PRAEGER SPECIAL STUDIES • PRAEGER SCIENTIFIC

Library of Congress Cataloging in Publication Data

Main entry under title:

Consumers and energy conservation.

Based on papers presented at the First Interna-
tional Conference on Consumer Behavior and Energy
Use, held in Banff, Sept. 1980.
 Bibliography: p.
 1. Energy consumption—Congresses. 2. Energy
conservation—Congresses. 3. Consumers—Congresses.
I. Claxton, John D. II. International Conference
on Consumer Behavior and Energy Use (1st: 1980:
Banff, Alta.)
HD9502.A2C654   333.79'16   81-10626
ISBN: 0-03-059659-9   AACR2

Published in 1981 by Praeger Publishers
CBS Educational and Professional Publishing
a Division of CBS Inc.
521 Fifth Avenue, New York, New York 10175 U.S.A.

© 1981 by Praeger Publishers

123456789   145   987654321

Printed in the United States of America

CONTENTS

vi

PREFACE

Increasing international concern about energy has been paralleled by increasing attention to energy-related consumer research. Evidence of this concern was reflected in one of the first national conservation efforts, Britain's "Save-it" campaign, launched in January 1975 and subsequently evaluated by a series of consumer research studies.[1] In the United States the first national household energy consumption survey was a study sponsored by the Ford Foundation, and reported in The American Energy Consumer.[2] One of the first national research programs in the area of consumer energy research was the Canadian program initiated in 1978 through the combined efforts of the Departments of Consumer and Corporate Affairs, and Energy, Mines and Resources. This program has been an important stimulus for consumer energy research in Canada. In addition, it has provided initial support for the Banff Conference which in turn culminated in the present volume.

In early 1979 plans were initiated for an international conference that would bring together researchers and policy makers concerned about consumer energy conservation. Although there had been sessions dealing with this topic at meetings of the Association for Consumer Research, there had not been a forum to attract researchers from the numerous disciplines and countries involved in consumer energy research. With financial backing from the Canadian government and Esso Resources, plus encouragement from the Journal of Consumer Research, plans were formalized to overcome this deficiency. These plans eventually led to the International Conference on Consumer Behavior and Energy Use, Banff, September 1980.

Our efforts to publicize the conference produced a gratifying response. We received in excess of 160 abstracts and several hundred other enquiries about the conference. From the initial set of abstracts, the review process led to the selection of the 29 studies presented at Banff. The 70 conference participants represented consumer energy researchers and program managers from 10 countries (Belgium, Brazil, Canada, Denmark, France, Germany, the Netherlands, Sweden, the United Kingdom, and the United States).

---

[1]Nicolas Phillips and Elizabeth Nelson, "Energy Savings in Private Households: An Integrated Research Program," Journal of the Marketing Research Society (October 1976), 180-200.

[2]Dorothy K. Newman and Dawn Day, The American Energy Consumer, Cambridge, Mass.: Ballinger Publishing Company, 1975.

The final step was the transformation of conference papers into the papers in this volume. Our intention was to produce a volume that would provide a comprehensive summary of the complete set of Banff papers. This involved editing the papers to a common concise format. With the cooperation of the conference contributors, this process has yielded a set of papers that we feel will serve readers well.

In summary, it is our hope that the present format will provide readers with (1) a summary of a major set of behavioral energy research studies, and (2) as desired, the opportunity to obtain more detail by direct contact with the researchers listed at the end of the volume.

With the encouragement of the 1980 conference participants, plans are under way for the Second Triannual Banff Conference on Consumer Behavior and Energy Use. We hope that this volume will help to stimulate further research and understanding in this important field, and that similar volumes will provide state-of-the-art reviews in the future.

J.D.C.
C.D.A.
J.R.B.R.
G.H.G.M.

ACKNOWLEDGMENTS

The International Conference on Consumer Behavior and Energy Use, and the subsequent development of this volume, have had the support and encouragement of a number of people and organizations. It is with pleasure that we take this opportunity to formally acknowledge this support.

Major financial support was received from the Canadian government through the Department of Consumer and Corporate Affairs, and from the private sector through Esso Resources (Canada). Both these organizations place a high value on the role of consumer energy research. Without their commitment the dialogue provided by the conference and by this volume would not have been possible. Additional financial and administrative support was provided by the University of Calgary, the University of Manitoba, Wilfred Laurier University, and the University of British Columbia.

Several individuals deserve special recognition. Geoff Hiscocks and Lee McCabe of Consumer and Corporate Affairs provided continuing encouragement through their involvement on the conference planning committee·and their assistance in evaluating the papers submitted for review. We are pleased to acknowledge their important contribution.

From as early as October 1978, Robert Ferber, editor of the Journal of Consumer Research, provided guidance that helped convert our preliminary ideas into viable conference and publication plans. William Wells, also representing JCR, served on our conference planning committee. His efforts during the final rather arduous stage of the review process were particularly welcome. In addition to these direct contributions, the JCR involvement gave us confidence that our efforts were well directed. We are particularly pleased to have had their support.

Finally, we appreciate the work of the authors of the 29 papers. They met deadlines, followed format recommendations and more important, provided the high quality research critical to the success of the conference and this volume. We thank them for their cooperation, and look forward to hearing about their future consumer energy research efforts.

CONSUMERS
AND ENERGY
CONSERVATION

INTRODUCTION

Dramatic energy-related events during the past decade have had worldwide economic impact. Political manipulation of oil supplies, predictions of both national and international energy shortages, and major energy price increases have combined to cause major shifts in industrial advantage, international trade, and international balance of payments. The result of this new economic order has been a response by nations to develop strategies leading to new energy supplies and/or reduced energy demand. The supply response has resulted in major increases in fossil fuel exploration and in substantial expenditures on alternative energy technologies. The demand response has resulted in conservation campaigns, price increases, and energy usage constraints.

The focus of this volume is on the latter strategies designed to reduce energy demand. In particular, interest here is on one specific area of energy demand, the consumer sector. The fundamental question underlying every study reported in this volume is: What will motivate consumers to use less energy or to use energy more efficiently?

In many countries preliminary efforts to achieve consumer energy conservation has centered on mass media campaigns. Seen in retrospect it is not surprising that these efforts have had little impact on generations raised with the view that "consumption is good." In conjunction with the initial conservation efforts were research studies on consumer attitudes and self-reported energy conservation behavior. While these studies had good intentions, the results often offered little of practical value for policy-makers. Generally, it was found that most consumers held positive attitudes toward energy conservation and usually reported that they were engaging in a number of actions to conserve energy. If these self-reported behaviors were true, substantial reductions in energy consumption should have occurred. Yet this apparently has not been the case. In summary neither the initial conservation programs, nor the initial consumer research appears to have had much impact on energy consumption.

The purpose of this preamble is to recognize the complexity of achieving consumer energy conservation and to suggest the difficulty of designing and executing consumer research that will help guide future conservation efforts. The following discussion introduces consumer energy research by (1) providing a brief description of the field, (2) suggesting the rationale for this area of study, and (3) providing an overview of prior research.

2 Introduction

Consumer Energy Research

Several major research works underscore the growing attention that has been focused on household energy consumption and conservation. In 1977 Cunningham and Lopreato annotated some 50 studies in the area, while in 1979 Joreges listed over 500 studies. An annotated bibliography by Anderson and McDougall (1980) covered over 400 consumer energy studies. Ellis and Gaskell (1978) provided one of the first major literature reviews of the area. More recently Stern and Gardner (1980) have referred to more than 130 studies in their thoughtful review. Although this line of research essentially began in 1973 (Newman and Day 1975), it is clear that in less than a decade interest and concern have become well established.

A primary purpose of this body of research is to understand the factors influencing energy consuming behavior. While the purpose is clear, the task of understanding energy consuming behaviors presents substantial complexity. The complexity involves identifying the set of factors which influence energy consuming behaviors and determining the nature of each influence. The potential factors include climatic conditions, house/product/vehicle characteristics, household demographics, and attitudinal variables. The nature of influence includes relationships that predispose, circumscribe, enable, or mediate energy consuming behaviors. For example, positive attitudes toward energy conservation would be expected to predispose lower energy consumption. On the other hand, climate would circumscribe the extent to which energy conservation is practical, while income would enable the extent to which energy conserving capital investments are possible. Furthermore, there are household decisions, such as family size, that mediate energy consumption in the sense that although they are decisions that influence consumption, they are made with no direct consideration of energy consumption consequences. Finally, other factors exhibit multiple types of influence on energy consumption. For example, the family dwelling circumscribes energy consumption due to the standards of construction in practice. However, this factor can be altered if family values result in retrofit activities.

In summary, a number of factors that might influence energy consuming behaviors can be identified. Furthermore, several types of influence can be suggested. The research reported in this volume follows a growing body of literature aimed at developing an understanding of these complexities.

Rationale for Consumer Energy Research

Current energy conservation programs and policies comprise a range of information programs, insulation subsidies, energy efficiency regulations, and energy price increases (McDougall

and Ritchie 1979; Stern and Gardiner 1980).   From a policymaker's perspective a major consideration in the evaluation of
conservation program alternatives is an assessment of the
probable magnitude of energy savings.   This includes consideration of both <u>potential</u> energy savings in a technical sense, and
<u>probable</u> energy savings in a behavioral sense.   For example,
technical analysis could be used to calculate the potential
energy savings that would occur if all drivers slowed from 60 to
55 miles per hour.   However, an assessment of behavioral response would be necessary before probable savings could be
forecasted.   It is this distinction between potential and
probable energy savings that forms the rationale for behavioral
energy research.   In other words, the underlying reason for
research such as the studies reported here is to provide
evidence that can help conservation policy makers clarify
behavioral response assumptions.

Prior Consumer Energy Research

     Although the importance of energy was discussed in
Cottrell's <u>Energy and Society</u> (1955), the first major empirical
study was not done until the spring of 1973 (Newman and Day
1975).   The significant features of this study were (1) the
field work was done prior to the OPEC oil embargo, (2) the data
was based on a multistage area probability sample representative
of U.S. households and (3) in addition to the survey data on
attitudes, house/appliance/vehicle ownership and usage, and
demographics, actual consumption data was obtained from the
utilities serving the sample households.   As a result of these
features, this research remains one of the most extensive
studies of household energy consumption completed to date.   The
resulting publication, <u>The American Energy Consumer</u>, was written
as a primer in the area and provided an historical perspective
on household energy consumption, descriptive statistics of
consumption, and tabulation of consumption by both income and
race.   Multivariate explanations of energy consumption were not
pursued.

     Since this initial study, behavioral energy research has
examined many areas.   There has been a continuous flow of
attitudinal research since the 1973 oil embargo.   Most of these
studies examine consumer views concerning the oil crisis, some
ask for self-reported changes in conservation behaviors.   These
studies have been annotated by Cunningham and Lopreato (1977),
and by Anderson and McDougall (1980).   Reviews by Farhar et al.
(1979), and Stern and Gardner (1980) provide a good summary of
this work.

     Other research has focused on a range of household vari-
ables as possible explanations of energy consumption levels.
For example, a Nevada study (Sierra Pacific Power Company 1979)
considered house descriptors, appliance ownership, and demographics.   Forty-four percent of electricity consumption was

explained by type of hot water heater used, fulltime use of home, type of heating systems, and occupation. Furthermore, 45 per cent of winter gas consumption was explained by type of hot water heater, number of bedrooms and bathrooms, and use of portable heaters.

Morrison and Gladhart (1976) considered the same explanatory variables in a study of households in Lansing, Michigan. In this case income was positively correlated to energy consumption, child-rearing families consumed more energy, but appliance ownership was apparently unrelated. Herendeen, Hannon and Ford (1979) studied U.S. expenditures data and found energy use to be related to expenditure levels and number of household members. Gladhart (1976) found no differences in residential energy consumption between rural and urban households, but found rural families consumed more gasoline.

Finally, a number of studies have focused on various programs for reducing energy consumption. For example, researchers have studied the effects of feedback (Battalio et al. 1979), communications (Craig and McCann 1978), and monetary incentives (Winett et al. 1978) on electricity consumption. There has been research on the effects of feedback on fuel oil consumption (Seaver and Patterson 1976) and the effects of public versus private conservation commitments on total in-home energy consumption (Pallak and Cummings 1976; Pallak et al. 1980).

In summary, this brief overview suggests that consumer energy research can be segmented into two general categories: Research that focuses on describing and understanding consumers' energy-related attitudes and behaviors, and research that focuses on evaluating the impact of various conservation program options. It is this categorization that provides the structure for the research presented in this volume. Part I presents sixteen research studies that center on Understanding Consumers. This section includes papers that (1) analyze total household energy consumption; (2) evaluate consumer energy issues with respect to specific situations; (3) assess the diffusion and adoption process of energy innovations; and (4) discuss a range of research issues confronted by energy researchers.

Part II presents thirteen papers that center on Conservation Program Options. This section includes papers that (1) review the range of existing programs; (2) evaluate various price and control mechanisms; and (3) evaluate alternative information and incentive programs.

REFERENCES

Anderson, C. Dennis and McDougall, Gordon H.G. (1980), Consumer Energy Research: An Annotated Bibliography, Behavioral Energy Research Group, 203-2053 Main Mall, University of British Columbia.

Battalio, Raymond C., et al. (1979), "Residential Electricity Demand: An Experimental Study," Review of Economics and Statistics, 61, 1 (May), 180-189.

Cottrell, F. (1955), Energy and Society: The Relation Between Energy, Social Change, and Economic Development, New York: McGraw-Hill.

Craig, C. Samuel and McCann, John M. (1978), "Assessing Communication Effects on Energy Conservation," Journal of Consumer Research, 5 (September), 82-89.

Cunningham, William H. and Lopreato, Sally Cook (1977), Energy Use and Conservation Incentives, New York: Praeger.

Ellis, P. and Gaskell, G. (1978), "A Review of Social Research on the Individual Energy Consumer," unpublished paper, Department of Social Psychology, London School of Economics.

Farhar, Barbara C., et al. (1979), "Public Opinion About Energy: A Literature Review," a report by the Solar Energy Research Institute, Golden, Colorado.

Gladhart, Peter M. (1976), "Energy Conservation and Lifestyles: An Integrative Approach to Family Decision-making," Occasional paper number 6, Family Energy Project, College of Human Ecology, Michigan State University.

Herendeen, R., Hannon, B., and Ford, C. (1979), "An Energy Conserving Tax: How Large Should Rebates Be?" in Changing Energy Use, eds. R.A. Fazzolare and C.B. Smith, New York: Pergamon Press.

Joerges, Bernward (1979), "Consumer Energy Research, An International Bibliography," Internationalen Institut Fur Umwelt und Gesellschaft des Wissenschaftszentrums, Berlin.

McDougall, Gordon H.G. and Ritchie, J.R. Brent (1979), "Consumer Energy Conservation: A Framework for Policy Research," in Advances in Consumer Research, Vol. 7, ed. Jerry C. Olson, San Francisco: Association of Consumer Research.

Morrison, Bonnie Maas and Gladhart, Peter M. (1976), "Energy and Families: The Crisis and the Response," Journal of Home Economics, (January), 15-18.

Newman, Dorothy K. and Day, Dawn (1975), The American Energy Consumer, Cambridge, Mass.: Ballinger Publishing Company.

Pallak, Michael S., Cook, David A., and Sullivan, John J. (1980), "Commitment and Energy Conservation," in Applied Social Psychology Annual, Vol. 1, ed. L. Bickman, 235-253.

Pallak, Michael S. and Cummings, William (1976), "Commitment and Voluntary Energy Conservation," Personality and Social Psychology Bulletin, 2 (Winter), 27-30.

Seaver, W. Burleigh and Patterson, Arthur H. (1976), "Decreasing Fuel Oil Consumption through Feedback and Social Communication," Journal of Applied Behavioral Analysis, Vol. 9, 2 (Spring), 147-152.

Sierra Pacific Power Company (1979), "Home Energy Survey: Electrical and Gas Analysis: Report No. 4," Reno, Nevada.

Stern, Paul and Gardner, Gerald T. (1980), "A Review and Critique of Energy Research in Psychology," Social Science Energy Review, Vol. 3, 1 (Spring), Yale University.

Winett, Richard A., et al. (1978), "Effects of Monetary Rebates and Daily Feedback and Information on Residential Electricity Conservation," Journal of Applied Psychology, Vol. 63, 1 (January), 73-80.

PART I

Understanding Consumers

- Preview
- Household Energy Consumption
- Consumer Energy: Situational Analyses
- Conservation and Solar Adoption
- National and International Research Issues

PREVIEW

Part I of the book is divided into four sections. The first section, Household Energy Consumption, presents three studies concerning the extent to which household energy consumption can be explained by a variety of descriptor variables. The study by McDougall, Ritchie, and Claxton is based on a national sample of Canadian households and explains electricity, heating fuel, and auto gasoline consumption in terms of house and vehicle descriptors, demographics, attitudes, and reported conservation behaviors. The Spencer study with a sample from the American northwest explains residential electricity consumption in terms of house and appliance descriptors and demographics. The Verhallen and Van Raaij study is based on a sample of Dutch homes, and explains natural gas consumption in terms of house descriptors, demographics, attitudes, and reported conservation behaviors. All three studies were based on actual consumption data obtained through the cooperation of energy suppliers.

The second section, Consumer Energy: Situational Analyses, presents four studies that consider consumer energy issues with respect to specific segments or situations. The study by Graef, Gianinno, and Csikszentmihalyi uses an innovative data collection technique to examine energy consumption associated with a variety of leisure activities. Kushler and Jeppesen explore teenage energy conservation, while Warriner focuses on that of the elderly. Finally, the study by Zimmerman analyses automobile travel patterns by stage in family life cycle.

The third section, Conservation and Solar Adoption, presents four studies that deal with the intriguing problem of understanding the diffusion and adoption process associated with energy-related innovations. Leonard-Barton examines the role of interpersonal communication networks in the diffusion process. Berkowitz and Haines approach the problem from a multi-attribute modeling perspective. The final two papers, by LaBay and Kinnear and by Warkov, attempt to explain differences between adopters and non-adopters in terms of a variety of attitudinal and demographic variables.

The final section of Part I, National and International Research Issues, presents five papers that might have been subtitled, "research experiences of consumer energy researchers." The paper by Carlson, Vagts, Patinkin, and Thompson describes the evolution of residential energy surveys of the U.S. Department of Energy. The paper by Levine and colleagues outlines the research being done by a consortium of research groups and national laboratories, and discusses one aspect of this work, namely the problem of evaluating the implicit discount rate used by consumers making energy-related expenditures.

8

Sorrenti and Petherick discuss efforts by Statistics Canada to develop methods for collecting reliable data regarding auto gasoline consumption and vehicle usage patterns. The study by Allen, Schewe, and Liander helps to identify some of the difficulties associated with cross-cultural attitudinal research. In the last paper of this section, Schipper and Ketoff address the substantial problem of developing an international data base that will allow comparative analysis of residential energy use.

In brief, the first section centers on developing a general understanding of factors influencing household energy consumption. The second section is more specific in that it addresses energy consumption situations. The third section is again more specific in that it addresses one energy research topic, the diffusion and adoption process. The final section offers researchers an opportunity to reflect on methodological issues associated with consumer energy research.

HOUSEHOLD ENERGY CONSUMPTION

- Analysis of Consumer Energy Consumption

- Policy Applications for Utility
  Residential Consumer Surveys

- Household Behavior and Energy Use

ANALYSIS OF CONSUMER ENERGY CONSUMPTION

Gordon H.G. McDougall
J.R. Brent Ritchie
John D. Claxton

Although the importance of energy was discussed in Cottrell's Energy and Society (Cottrell 1955), the first major empirical study was not done until the Spring of 1973 (Newman and Day 1975). The significant features of this study were (1) the field work was done prior to the OPEC oil embargo, (2) the data was based on a multistage area probability sample so as to be representative of U.S. households, and (3) in addition to the survey instrument (which obtained data on attitudes, house/appliance/vehicle ownership and usage, and demographics) actual consumption data was obtained from the utilities serving the sample households. As a result of these features this research remains one of the most extensive studies of household energy consumption completed to date.

Prior consumer energy research has been reviewed earlier in this book. Based on this review it appears that although there have been a great number of consumer energy studies, only a few have included actual consumption data as a dependent variable. Further, those studies that have utilized actual consumption usually focused on a limited subset of potential predictor variables. The focus of the current study was to put into perspective a comprehensive cross-section of predictor variables based on analysis using actual consumption data.

Research Objectives

The research reported here had two general objectives. The first was to provide a baseline description of energy consumption in a cross-section of Canadian households. The second was to assess the relative importance of a range of factors which may explain household energy consumption. These factors were categorized into four classes: (1) climate, (2) house/appliance/vehicle characteristics, (3) household demographics, and (4) attitudinal variables. The focus of this chapter is to summarize analysis that assessed the extent to which each of the four classes of variables was related to in-home and automobile energy consumption. In-home energy analysis was based on data from utilities serving the sample households. The auto energy

---

The financial support for this study was received from the Canadian Departments of Consumer and Corporate Affairs, and Energy, Mines and Resources.

11

was self-reported data. Further details regarding this research
are available from the authors.

FINDINGS

Household Energy Consumption

It was possible to develop an accurate measure of total in-
home energy consumption by combining for each household the
appropriate fuel oil, natural gas, and electricity consumption.
However, it was not possible to develop an accurate measure of
energy consumption by major application (heating, cooling, hot
water, and appliances), since the energy sources were not
metered in that manner.   In other words, while an accurate
measure of home heating energy was possible for households that
use natural gas for the sole purpose of heating, many households
used natural gas for heating, hot water, and possibly clothes
drying and cooking. Thus, home heating energy could not accurately be distinguished.   Although it would be possible to
analyze subsamples with specific energy type by application
combinations for the research reported here, a broadly based
sample was considered important. As a result the analysis that
follows used total in-home energy consumption as one major
focus; gasoline consumption was the second.

Analysis Sequence

Preliminary factor analysis focused on identifying major
factors in the attitudinal data.   This was followed by the
following sequence of analysis for both the in-home energy data
and the auto gasoline data. The sample was divided into three
subsamples, an exploratory sample and two replication samples.
The use of two replication subsamples was seen as consistent
with the caution appropriate with exploratory research. With
the exploratory sample a separate regression analysis was run
with each of the four major subsets of predictor variables. The
variables that indicated explanatory power (<0.1) in these
preliminary regressions were then combined and analysed to form
the "best" exploratory model. Finally, this best model was
replicated with the two replication samples.
It is clear that this sequential process does not maximize
explained variance since it is conceivable that interactions
between variables in different predictor subsets could prove
significant. However, this process was seen as minimizing the
probability of chance associations, and therefore, was considered important for research at this stage of development.

Exploratory Analysis for In-Home Energy Consumption

The results of the regression analyses using the four
predictor subsets are shown in Table 1. The regression model

TABLE 1

IN-HOME ENERGY CONSUMPTION: EXPLORATORY REGRESSION ANALYSES

	Subset A Climatic & Regional Variables	Subset B House & Appliance Variables	Subset C Demographic Variables	Subset D[b] Attitudinal Variables
Variables Significant at α <.10	Degree Days (0.16)[a] Atlantic region (-.13) Quebec region (-.10)	Multiple family dwelling (-.10) Number of rooms (.15) Number of floors (.13) Fireplace (.16) Mean thermostat setting (.21) Electric space heating (-.47) Electric hot water heating (-.24)	Family income (.20) Family size (.18) Age of male head (.21)	(F) Energy conserv. important (-.21) (F) Claimed knowledge (-.17) (M) Individual efforts important (-.13) (M) Business/gov't at fault (-.21)[c] (M) Conservation participation (-.15)
Adjusted R²	0.06	0.44	0.07	0.11
Variables Not Significant at α <.10	B.C. region Ontario region Prairie region	Age of house Attached garage Basement closed in winter Oil space heating Electric Range Electric clothes dryer Thermostat set back when out Index of appliances indicating number of and elec. consumption	Education of male head Single adult family Both parents work Yrs at present address	(F) Individual efforts important (F) Business/gov't at fault (F) Accept restrictions (F) Actual energy knowledge (F) Social participation (F) Conservation participation (M) Energy conservation important (M) Claimed energy knowledge (M) Actual energy knowledge (M) Social participation

a. Numbers in brackets are the partial correlations for the regression equation containing all variables significant at α <.10.

b. The (F) indicates female attitudes; the (M), male attitudes.

c. The negative correlation of "Business/gov't at fault" is the only relationship that was opposite to the sign expected.

that tested climatic and regional variables identified three
significant variables. As would be expected the more severe the
winter temperatures, indicated by degree days, the greater the
in-home energy consumption. Controlling for weather, two
regions, Quebec and Atlantic, appeared to consume less. The
subsequent analysis that included both regions and house variables suggested that regional differences were likely associated
with dwelling size.

The regression model that tested house and appliance
variables identified seven significant variables. Households
living in multiple family dwellings used less. Large dwellings
in terms of number of rooms and number of floors consumed more.
Higher mean thermostat settings was associated with greater
consumption, as was the presence of a fireplace. The use of
electricity for space heating and water heating was associated
with lower consumption. The age of the house, presence of an
attached garage, thermostat set-back when no one home, and
appliance ownership showed no significant association with
aggregate in-home energy consumption.

The regression model that tested demographic variables
identified three significant variables. Family income, family
size and age of household head were all positively related to
in-home energy consumption. Education, number of working
parents, and years at present address did not provide
significant incremental explanation.

The regression model that tested attitudinal variables
identified five significant variables. Two were attitudes
expressed by the female household head, and three were attitudes
expressed by males.

The final step in the exploratory analysis tested the 18
variables that had proven significant in the prior four analyses. As indicated in Table 2, eight of these variables were
significant at α of less than 0.10. In addition, the significance level of the family size variable was only slightly
greater than the cut-off level, and therefore, nine variables
were included for the subsequent replication analyses. It
should be noted that none of the attitudinal variables proved to
be significant in the final exploratory model.

Replication Analyses for In-Home Energy Consumption

Table 2 indicates the results of the final exploration
analysis and replication analyses based on two additional
subsamples. In summary the replication analyses closely matched
the final exploration model. For the three analyses the nine
variables explained 48, 58, and 45 percent of the variance in
in-home energy consumption. Two variables, number of rooms and
family size, were significant in two of the three analyses. All
other variables were consistently significant, and indicated
associations with in-home energy consumption that were consistent in terms of magnitude and sign. Degree days, number of

TABLE 2

IN-HOME ENERGY CONSUMPTION: "BEST" MODEL & REPLICATIONS

Climatic & regional variables	Exploration[b] Subsample	Replication Subsample I	Replication Subsample II
Degree days	0.22[a] (3)[c]	0.36 (3)	0.31 (2)

House & appliance variables			
Multiple family dwelling	-.17 (7)	-.10 (7)	-.12 (8)
Number of rooms	0.16 (2)	0.17 (2)	n.s.
Fireplace	0.17 (4)	0.16 (8)	0.13 (7)
Mean thermostat setting	0.15 (6)	0.16 (8)	0.13 (1)
Electric space heating	-.58 (1)	-.65 (1)	-.59 (1)

Demographic variables			
Family income	0.21 (5)	0.11 (9)	0.13 (6)
Family size	n.s.	0.25 (4)	0.13 (5)
Adjusted R^2	0.48	0.58	0.45
Subsample size	251	242	250

a. Partial correlations of variables significant at $\alpha < 0.10$.
    The exploration regression tested the 18 variables in Table
    1 that were significant at $\alpha < 0.10$.   The partials are based
    on regression equations containing only the significant
    variables.

b. None of the attitudinal variables were significant when
    included with climatic, house/appliance, and demographic
    variables.

c. Numbers in parentheses indicate the order of entry in the
    stepwise regression analysis.

floors, presence of a fireplace, mean thermostat setting, and family income were all positively related to consumption. Living in a multiple family dwelling and use of electric space heating were negatively related with consumption.

Exploratory Analysis for Automobile Gasoline Consumption

The results of the regression analyses using the four predictor subsets are shown in Table 3. The regression model that tested climatic and regional variables identified one significant variable. Living in a city of 30 to 500 thousand was associated with higher gasoline consumption. The other variables that tested for regional differences and impact of winter temperatures were not significant.

The regression model that tested vehicle descriptors identified six significant variables. As might be expected the number of vehicles owned, the amount of commuting to work, and the mean vehicle weight all were positively related to household gasoline consumption. In terms of vehicle age the exploratory analysis indicated that consumption increases with age for vehicles under five years old, and decreased with age for vehicles five years old and over. Automobile air conditioners, mean number of cylinders, usage for work, and ownership of campers and boats did not add significant incremental explanation.

The regression model that tested demographic variables identified four significant variables. Family income, both parents working, and number of driving age family members were all related to greater gasoline consumption. The age of the male household head indicated a negative relationship. Family size, education, and years at present address did not add to the explanatory power of the model.

The regression model that tested attitudinal variables identified only two significant variables: female views that business and government are the causes of the energy problem, and male views that energy conservation is important.   In subsequent analysis that included these two variables with the climatic, vehicle, and demographic variables, the attitudinal variables were not significant.

In the final exploratory analysis the thirteen significant variables were combined. Seven variables continued to indicate significant association with gasoline consumption (Table 4). These seven variables were included in the subsequent replication analyses.

Replication Analyses for Automobile Gasoline Consumption

Table 4 indicates the results of the final exploratory analysis and the two replication analyses. Again the replications closely matched the final exploratory model. For the three analyses the seven variables explained 39, 44, and 38

TABLE 3

AUTOMOBILE GASOLINE CONSUMPTION: EXPLORATORY REGRESSION ANALYSIS

	Subset A Climatic & Regional Variables	Subset B Vehicle Descriptors	Subset C Demographic Variables	Subset D[b] Attitudinal Variables
Variables Significant at α <.10	City size 30 to 500k (.13)[a]	Number of vehicles owned (.55) Weekly miles commuting (.12) Mean vehicle weight (.31)[c] Mean vehicle age (-.09) New car (-.09) Vehicle age of new car (.12)	Family income (.15) Both parents work (.03) Age of male head (-.15) Number of driving age (.21)	(F) Business/gov't at fault (-.11) (M) Energy conservation important (.09)
Adjusted R^2	0.02	0.38	0.10	0.02
Variables Not Significant at α <.10	City size under 1000 City size 1 to 30 k City over 500k Atlantic region Quebec region Ontario region B.C. region Prairie region Degree days	Vehicle air conditioned Mean number of cylinders Vehicle used for work Own a boat Own a camper	Family size Education of male head Years at present address	All other attitudinal variables as listed in Table 1 (14 others)

a. Numbers in brackets are the partial correlations for the regression equation containing all variables significant at α <.10.

b. The (F) indicates female attitudes; the (M), male attitudes.

c. Vehicle age was expected to have a curvilinear relationship with consumption increasing with age for relatively new cars, and decreasing with age subsequently. To test this, three variables were included: 'Mean vehicle age'; 'New car,' a dummy variable to indicate cars less than 5 years old; 'Vehicle age if new car,' indicating age if new car,' indicating age if less than 5 years old.

TABLE 4

AUTOMOBILE GASOLINE CONSUMPTION
"BEST" MODEL & REPLICATIONS

	Exploration[b] Subsample	Replication Subsample I	Replication Subsample II
Vehicle descriptors			
Number of vehicles owned	0.58[a] (1)[c]	0.53 (1)	0.46 (1)
Weekly miles commuting	0.11 (4)	0.21 (4)	0.21 (3)
Mean vehicle weight	0.30 (2)	0.31 (2)	0.24 (4)
Vehicle age if new	0.10 (6)	0.13 (6)	n.s.
Demographic variables			
Both parents work	0.13 (3)	n.s.	0.16 (5)
Age of male head	-.11 (5)	-.28 (3)	-.30 (2)
Number of driving age	0.09 (7)	0.18 (5)	n.s.
Adjusted R^2	0.39	0.44	0.38
Subsample size	326	334	354

a. Partial correlations of variables significant at $\alpha < 0.10$.
    The exploration regression tested the 13 variables in Table
    3 that were significant at $\alpha < 0.10$. The partials are based
    on regression equations containing only the significant
    variables.

b. None of the climate & regional variables nor the attitudin-
    al variables were significant when included with the
    vehicle descriptors and demographic variables.

c. Numbers in parentheses indicate the order of entry in the
    stepwise regression analysis.

Percent of the variance in household gasoline consumption.
Three variables were significant in only two of the analyses
(vehicle age, both parents working, and number of driving age
family members). The number of vehicles owned, the amount of
commuting to work, and vehicle weight were consistently related
to greater consumption. Families where the male head was older
were consistently found to use less.

SUMMARY AND CONCLUSIONS

Attempting to understand aggregate household energy consumption based on a national sample is viewed as a relatively stringent undertaking. Although a greater degree of explanation has been found when the analysis focused on one energy application and a homogeneous housing community (Seligman et. al. 1979), for the present study greater generalization was considered important (in other words, understanding that complexities of household energy consumption could be furthered by analysis of either specific household situations or exploration of a broad cross section of households). While the latter presents a greater array of uncertainties, it was considered to be an important avenue for the current research.

Implications for Conservation Policy

Although conservation policy was not the immediate focus of the present research, the findings indicated several policy implications. First, the analysis identified a number of characteristics of heavy users of energy. Understanding these characteristics is valuable in terms of efficiently aiming conservation programs at specific household types. Second, as numerous earlier studies have indicated, programs that concentrate solely on changing attitudes are likely to have low conservation payoffs. Although mass media advertising aimed at this purpose continues to be a major component of many national conservation campaigns, these efforts on their own are likely to have little impact. In other words, the use of media support for major conservation initiatives may be fruitful, however, the use of media as the cornerstone of a conservation campaign appears to be misguided.

Third, in terms of in-home energy it is clear that a major portion of household consumption is circumscribed by the dwelling, an observation also made by Newman and Day (1975). This suggests that programs aimed at improving the energy efficiency of housing stock should receive top priority.

Finally, in terms of automobile gasoline, vehicle characteristics strongly influence consumption. However the number of vehicles owned and commuting habits are also major determinants. This indicates that programs for vehicle efficiency continue to present important potential for energy conservation. In addition, programs to improve transportation infrastructure should receive priority attention. It seems clear that until consumers have alternative modes more readily available, attempting to change attitudes will have little impact on vehicle ownership and usage patterns.

RELATED RESEARCH

Anderson, C. Dennis and McDougall, Gordon H.G. (1980), Conservation Energy Research: An Annotated Bibliography, Behavioral Energy Research Group, 203-2053 Main Mall, University
of British Columbia.

Antil, John A. and Bennett, Peter D. (1979), "Construction and
Validation of a Scale to Measure Socially Responsible
Consumption Behavior," in The Conserver Society, Henion,
K.E., and Kinear, T.C. (eds.), Proceedings Series, American
Marketing Association, Chicago, 51-68.

Battalio, Raymond C., et. al. "Residential Electricity Demand:
An Experimental Study," Review of Economics and Statistics,
61, 1 (May), 180-189.

Burnette, Paula and Carner, Don C. (1979), "California Residential Energy Consumption Profiles."

Claxton, John D., McDougall, Gordon H.G., and Ritchie, J.R.
Brent, "Annotated Directory of Energy Conservation Pro-
grams," Behavioral Energy Research Group, 203-2053 Main
Mall, University of British Columbia.

Cottrell, F. (1955), Energy and Society: The Relation Between
Energy, Social Change, and Economic Development, New York:
McGraw-Hill.

Craig, C. Samuel and McCann, John M. (1978), "Assessing Communication Effects on Energy Conservation," Journal of
Consumer Research, 5 (September), 82-89.

Cunningham, William H. and Lopreato, Sally Cook (1977), Energy
Use and Conservation Incentives, New York: Praeger.

Farhar, Barbara C., et. al. (1979), "Public Opinion About
Energy: A Literature Review," a report by the Solar Energy
Research Institute, Golden, Colorado.

Gladhart, Peter M. (1976), "Energy Conservation and Lifestyles:
An Integrative Approach to Family Decision-making," Oc-
casional paper number 6, Family Energy Project, College of
Human Ecology, Michigan State University.

Herendeen, R., Hannon, B., and Ford, C. (1979), "An Energy
Conserving Tax: How Large Should Rebates Be?" in Changing
Energy Use, eds. R.A. Fazzolare and C.B. Smith, New York:
Pergamon Press.

McDougall, Gordon H.G. (1979), "Profiling the Socially Responsible Consumer," Working Paper, School of Business and
Economics, Wilfrid Laurier University, Waterloo, Ontario.

McDougall, Gordon H.G. and Munro, Hugh (1980), "Consumer Behavior and Energy: Some Methodological Issues," A.S.A.C.
Conference, Université du Québec à Montréal.

McDougall, Gordon H.G. and Ritchie, J.R. Brent (1979), "Consumer
Energy Conservation: A Framework for Policy Research," in
Advances in Consumer Research, Vol. 7, ed. Jerry C. Olson,
San Francisco: Association of Consumer Research.

McDougall, Gordon H.G., Ritchie, J.R. Brent, and Claxton, John
D. (1979), "Energy Conservation and Conservation Patterns
in Canadian Households: Overview," Behavioral Energy
Research Group, 203-2053 Main Mall, University of British
Columbia.

Morrison, Bonnie Maas, and Gladhart, Peter M. (1976), "Energy
and Families: The Crisis and the Response," Journal of
Home Economics, (January), 15-18.

Newman, Dorothy K. and Day, Dawn (1975), The American Energy
Consumer, Cambridge, Mass.: Ballinger.

Pollack, Michael S., Cook, David A., and Sullivan, John J.
(1980), "Commitment and Energy Conservation," in Applied
Social Psychology Annual, Vol. 1, 235-253.

Pollack, Michael S. and Cummings, William (1976), "Commitment
and Voluntary Energy Conservation," Personality and Social
Psychology Bulletin, 2 (Winter), 27-30.

Seaver, W. Burleigh and Patterson, Arthur H. (1976), "Decreasing
Fuel Oil Consumption through Feedback and Social Communica-
tion," Journal of Applied Behavioral Analysis, Vol. 9, 2
(Spring), 147-152.

Seligman, C., et. al. (1979), "Predicting Summer Energy Consumption from Homeowners' Attitudes," Journal of Applied Social
Psychology, Vol. 9, 1, 70-90.

Sierra Pacific Power Company (1979), "Home Energy Survey:
Electrical and Gas Analysis: Report No. 4," Reno, Nevada.

Stern, Paul and Gardner, Gerald T. (1980), "A Review and
Critique of Energy Research in Psychology," Social Science
Energy Review, Vol. 3, 1 (Spring), Yale University.

Winett, Richard A., et. al. (1978), "Effects of Monetary Rebates and Daily Feedback and Information on Residential Electricity Conservation," Journal of Applied Psychology, Vol. 63, 1 (January), 73-80.

POLICY APPLICATIONS FOR UTILITY
RESIDENTIAL CONSUMER SURVEYS

Robert H. Spencer, Jr.

In 1978 Seattle City Light (SCL), a municipally owned
electric utility serving approximately 250,000 customers in
northwestern Washington, embarked on a residential market
research program to improve its understanding of energy consumption phenomena and strengthen its forecasting and policy
development enterprises. More recently, Puget Sound Power and
Light Company, an investor-owned electric utility serving
approximately 550,000 customers around the city of Seattle, has
begun developing a similar research program. This chapter will
review many of the advantages associated with utility data
collection programs. Although it will focus primarily on issues
related to applied rather than theoretical research of energy
consumption behavior, it is hoped that this perspective may lead
to an advancement in the range and quality of data available for
both theoretical and policy purposes in this field.

THE ADVANTAGES OF ELECTRICAL UTILITY RESEARCH

The major advantage of electrical utility research is
directly related to the use of customer master file records for
sampling and related analytical purposes. Electrical utility
records probably provide the best and most current information
on where the population lives and how long they have resided at
a particular location or at least whether a customer has changed
address within twelve months. In addition, electrical utility
records generally include some billing classification codes
which can provide a preliminary indication of the saturation of
electric space and water heating. Sometimes these classifications include dwelling unit information (e.g., single-family
dwelling with electric space heating). This information can be
particularly useful in preparing samples and identifying possible sources of response bias in mail and other surveys.

Finally, electrical utility records include reliable
consumption data for customers. This information can be applied

The author wishes to acknowledge the contribution of Judith
Viedler at the Educational Assessment Center of the University
of Washington in the execution of the survey discussed in this
paper. The survey was funded in part by the Washington State
Energy Office with a grant from the United States Department of
Energy.

to evaluate the representativeness of survey samples and possible bias related to nonresponse. If a market researcher is seeking opinions from customers on conservation attitudes or other phenomena, it would make sense to relate the findings to actual household electricity consumption. This type of analysis would be useful not only for verifying hypotheses, but also in extrapolating findings to the total population.

PURPOSE AND APPROACH OF THE SCL PROGRAM

Instead of specific problems, the SCL research effort began as follows: to develop a residential customer data base which might be applied in rate, conservation, and forecasting policy analyses, and which could be updated annually using an inexpensive survey approach. An interdisciplinary coordinating committee comprised of engineers, economists, and policy analysts who could be expected to make use of the eventual data base was established. This lead to the identification of approximately 100 items including household demographic, economic, dwelling, and appliance characteristics, as well as monthly electricity consumption and associated billing data that could be obtained from the utility's customer master file. The data items that were identified were generally objective in nature and were believed capable of eliciting highly reliable responses. Due to the desirability of obtaining longitudinal data, especially for forecasting and policy evaluation purposes, a mail survey appeared to be the best method to adopt for the research program. Two techniques were used to develop a research questionnaire: the reviewing of other questionnaires and a pretest of alternatives. A pretest was conducted using a long and short form questionnaire under two mailing conditions. The pretest was administered to a random sample of 500 of SCL's residential customers, 125 of whom were assigned to each treatment condition. Response rates associated with each mailing condition were evaluated and the greatest overall response was obtained using the long form questionnaire, 45.7 percent. Telephone surveys were also conducted with 10 percent of the respondent and nonrespondent pretest sample. The purpose of the telephone surveys was to identify any possible problems in the formulation of the questionnaire items, as well as response biases.

A listing of the items included in the main questionnaire is provided in Table 1. The actual questionnaire also included space for respondents to indicate for each appliance whether new units were obtained during the prior twelve months. This information was important in performing multiple regression analyses of household electricity consumption discussed later in this paper. Where appropriate, respondents were requested to indicate the number of appliances in their homes.

TABLE 1

ITEMS INCLUDED IN SCL QUESTIONNAIRE

Dwelling Items

>Housing type
>Housing ownership
>Number of heated rooms

Conservation Items

>Attic (ceiling, roof) insulation
>Exterior wall insulation
>Floor insulation
>Window, door insulation
>Daytime thermostat settings
>Nighttime thermostat settings

Appliance Items

>Primary space heating
>Secondary space heating
>Water heating
>Cooling
>Refrigeration/freezing
>Dishwashing
>Clothes washing and drying
>Air conditioning
>Television
>Hot tubs

Socio-economic Items

>Numer of ages of occupants
>Annual gross income

SAMPLING AND RESPONSE ANALYSIS

For the main SCL survey, a general random sample of approximately 2 percent of the utility's 245,000 residential customers
was selected.   Once customers who had recently moved were
extracted, the sample included 4,973 households.   A response
rate of 50.4 percent was obtained from two mailings, though the
second mailing was just a follow-up reminder and did not include
a second questionnaire. During a replication of the 1978 survey
in 1979, a second questionnaire was included with the follow-up
letter and a response rate of over 62 percent was obtained.
Several procedures were used to determine the representativeness of the sample.   It was concluded that the sample was

representative in terms of billing classifications and there was
no evidence of any statistically significant bias in either the
sample or respondent populations in terms of consumption.   The
housing characteristics of the respondents were also evaluated.
A response bias existed and this was corrected by proportion-
ately weighting the data collected from each respondent by the
dwelling type reported.   This weighted information was then
reported in all tables prepared, except those pertaining to
average annual electricity consumption.

With recent replications of the SCL residential survey,
follow-up surveys have been used to enhance the data base
itself.   For example, a special telephone survey of 250 respondents was administered in the fall of 1979 to determine why and
how residential householders were making appliance acquisition
decisions.   Similarly, a follow-up personal interview has been
proposed in Seattle to obtain detailed insulation measurements
for 200 respondent dwellings to improve the utility's projections of the local conservation potential.

FINDINGS AND POLICY IMPLICATIONS

Two principal methods were used to evaluate the data.
Cross-tabular analyses, including the review of chi-square
values, were performed to identify unique features in the
Seattle City Light service area and to reveal special consumption and appliance acquisition patterns.   Multiple linear
regression analyses were used to investigate further electricity
consumption relationships in support of special rate-related
policy analyses.

One major contribution of the survey data was to provide a
more exacting picture of the saturation of major electrical
appliances in the city.

For example, 34.5 percent of households in Seattle have
electric space heating compared to 16 percent for the nation as
a whole and 20 percent for the western region (EIA 1980, p. 41).
Similarly, 88.5 percent of the households in Seattle have
electric water heaters and 93.3 percent electric cooking,
contrasted to 33 percent of the nation for electric water
heating and 52 percent for electric cooking (EIA 1980, pp. 35
and 39).   These divergences are likely due to the unavailability
of natural gas in some areas of the city, the low electricity
rates generally and special promotions concerning all-electric
rates.

Cross-tabulations also revealed some anomalies with respect
to electrically heated structures.   Most interesting in this
regard was the finding that an electrically heated single family
home had only 5.6 median number of rooms in contrast to 6.1 for
all single family homes.   A review of the insulation data
collected in the survey indicated a statistically significant
difference between homes with electric space heating and other
fuels; the difference was generally of a magnitude from 8

percent to 20 percent more structures with better insulation
(Spencer 1979). Although this was perceptual data and might be
suspect, the information provided such a strong prima facie case
that the gains from a retrofit insulation program might be
minimal that further analyses were undertaken. Interestingly, a
review of structural audit data the utility had been collecting
substantiated the survey findings.

Two other cross-tabular analyses were prepared which had
obvious policy implications. First, the annual electricity
consumption of owner-occupied dwellings was compared to that of
renter-occupied dwellings controlling for housing types and
major appliances. Generally, owner-occupants consumed approximately 16 percent more electricity than renters. This finding
was particularly alarming since the percent of owner-occupied
dwellings in the utility's service area had increased by 8
percent since the 1970 census to 60 percent in 1978. Although
owner-occupants may be expected to have more appliances, this
group should also be more capable of insulating their structures. Second, an analysis of appliance purchases controlling
for the length of residency was conducted. The findings suggest
that persons who move, especially into single family dwellings,
are two to five times more likely to purchase new major appliances for cooking, refrigeration, dish washing, and clothes
washing. Since the electrical utility will be notified of
dwelling changes, persons who are moving should be an excellent
and receptive audience for appliance efficiency-related information. Such a program could take the form of special brochures
mailed to new and moving customers, alerting them to the existence and importance of energy efficiency information. Special
support through an appliance acquisition or structural audit
program for new residents might also prove effective. Regardless, the data is clearly important for the utility which is
interested in maximizing the effectiveness of its community
outreach efforts.

Multiple linear regression analysis was used in an effort
to segment annual electricity consumption statistically among
various appliances and household factors. While this provided
information which was useful for depicting the use of electricity within the service area, some of the coefficients provided
insight into factors which might require policy attention.

Several procedures were used prior to performing the
regression analysis: (1) in order to reduce the multicollinear-
ity problems, several variables were broken down or dropped from
the analysis; (2) where possible, like variables were collapsed
into a single variable based on relative annual consumption
information available from the Edison Electric Institute (MRI
1979); and (3) relatively high residual (consumption) cases were
deleted from the analysis.

The relative residual deletion procedure assumed that the
regression estimates should be more precise for households with
small consumption than large consumption. By using the relative

deletion criteria, the R^2 of the equation was increased from .65 to .97 by dropping 12 percent of the cases and with no significant change in the mean values of the variables. Implicit in the deletion procedure is that a proportion of the cases will deviate due to behavioral and other factors not included in the survey or analysis. Normally, such deleted cases would constitute an appropriate group for follow-up and more detailed behavioral surveys.

The results of the regression analysis are summarized in Table 2. Perhaps the most interesting variables were those which failed to enter the analysis. Due to the ubiquitousness of electric ranges, the only way this variable could be entered was with a compensating constant with a negative sign. Since a negative constant was undesirable (and nonsensical), the range variable was not forced. Also, it proved impossible to force an insulation variable into the model. While this was disturbing, there was substantial evidence that electrically heated homes are uniformly well insulated.

Of the variables which did enter the analysis, it is interesting to note that the washer/dryer and dishwasher variables are larger than expected. While some analysts have noted similar results and have been led to delete these variables from their analysis (Ebbeler 1980), this temptation should be avoided. Closer examination suggested that electricity consumption related to hot water usage is likely to be included. Applying some simple engineering formulae makes it possible to estimate the annual number of washing loads from these coefficients as a consequence. Interestingly, all of the appliance coefficients correspond remarkably well to national estimates (MRI 1979).

Two findings from the regression analysis which had obvious policy implications were the fireplace and income coefficients. The fireplace variable, included for only electrically heated homes, suggests that the average family home with baseboard heating might lose up to 6 percent of its electricity consumed for heating by using the fireplace. A glass fireplace door or fireplace insert program might obviously be beneficial in reducing waste and improving the efficiency of wood heating.

The income result has proved to be quite controversial, suggesting a very slight, at least short-run, influence on household electricity consumption. This finding, however, has been observed in other studies of a similar sort in the Pacific Northwest (Paglin and Burgess 1976; CH2M Hill 1973). Given the high saturations of major electrical appliances, this finding should not be amazing.

SUMMARY AND CONCLUSIONS

The research experience and results discussed in this paper provide one example of what is possible in the energy analysis field. Already, the efforts of individual utilities are being eclipsed in the Pacific Northwest by regional, cooperative

TABLE 2

SINGLE-FAMILY MULTIPLE LINEAR REGRESSION RESULTS

| INDEPENDENT VARIABLES | Coefficient | COEFFICIENT STATISTICS | | t-Value |
		Standard Deviation	Confidence Interval	
FAMSIZE 1: Persons under 19	1616.73	98.70	±193.45	16.38
FAMSIZE 2: Persons 19-61	1387.32	115.96	±227.28	11.96
FAMSIZE 3: Persons over 61	840.57	138.41	±270.75	6.07
FAMINC: Household income (per thousands of dollars)	43.85	10.92	±21.40	4.01
EBASE: Electric Baseboard Heat (per room)	1608.30	61.90	±121.32	25.98
ECENT: Electric Central Heat	14787.35	667.60	±1308.50	22.15
EWATER: Electric Water Heat	3957.25	244.34	±478.91	16.20
TEMP: Daytime degrees above 65	509.77	87.96	±172.40	5.80
REFRIG: Refrigerators & Freezers	456.73	65.32	±128.03	6.99
WSHDRY: Washer/Dryer Combinations	1365.73	235.52	±461.64	5.80
DISH: Dishwasher	928.83	200.31	±392.61	4.64
COLORTV: Color Television	664.76	142.51	±279.32	4.66
FIRE: Fireplaces & Stoves	355.43	230.02	±450.84	1.55

Equation Standard Error: 2597.32
Equation F Ratio: 2053.11
Equation R^2:   .968

undertakings. Recently a region-wide personal interview survey was completed sponsored by the Pacific Northwest Utilities Conference Committee with the support of the Bonneville Power Administration. Analysis of this data base has already begun with the objective of developing a regional conservation assessment.

Cross-sectional analyses have been undertaken at the local level with individual utilities adopting common survey instruments and pooling their data to investigate economic and conservation phenomena. These efforts are fairly broad in scope and have been expanding to include the sharing of customer load data (i.e., data on consumption occurring during 15-minute intervals). These cross-sectional efforts should enable researchers to delve into additional relationships and phenomena, such as differences in energy consumption in rural and urban areas. To the extent that the cooperation of local governmental agencies can be obtained, such studies might result in a greater consonance between utility and governmental policies to the obvious benefit of society.

Still, much more needs to be done and researchers will have an important role in further developments. To the extent that researchers in the energy field are aware of the data resources available through local utilities, they should be able to strengthen and enhance the applicability of their work. Further, researchers can make important contributions in the expansion of local data collection efforts and analytical debates which are emerging. In this regard, especially, there is need for greater attention to the development of high-quality data and application of analytical techniques such as factor and spectral analyses.

If the industrial societies of the world are to survive the depletion of the world's energy resources, more efficient use of our resources is imperative. The success of research in meeting this challenge will depend in large part on the ability of researchers to make greater use of the data resources and statistical techniques at their disposal. It is hoped that this industry example may serve to stimulate some researchers to exploit the utility data resources available and identify additional energy policy implications.

RELATED RESEARCH

CH2M Hill (1973), Residential Customer Characteristics, Seattle: Seattle City Light.

Ebbeler, Donald H. (1980), An Econometric End-Use Analysis of Residential Sector Demand for Electricity in the Southern California Edison Service Area, San Diego: Southern California Edison Company.

Energy Information Administration (1980), Characteristics of the
    Housing Stock and Households 1978, Washington, D.C.: U.S.
    Department of Energy.

GMA Research Corp. (1977), Profile: A Market Media and Audience
    Home Audit Study, Seattle: The Seattle Times.

Midwest Research Institute (1979), Patterns of Energy Use by
    Electrical Appliances, Palo Alto: Electric Power Research
    Institute.

Pacific Gas and Electric Company, Report on the First Biennial
    PG&E Residential Appliance Saturation Study, San Francisco:
    PG&E.

Paglin, Morton and Burgess, Giles H. (1976), Residential Con-
    sumption of Electricity in Portland, Oregon, and Lifeline
    Electric Rates, Portland: City of Portland.

Spencer, Robert (1980), Lifeline Rate Analysis, Seattle: Seattle
    City Light.

_____, (1979), Residential Customer Characteristics Survey and
    Appendix, Seattle: Seattle City Light.

HOUSEHOLD BEHAVIOR AND ENERGY USE

Theo M.M. Verhallen
W. Fred van Raaij

In the Netherlands, about 75 percent of the energy consumed in the domestic sector is used for home heating, while about 15 percent is used for water heating and 10 percent for appliances and lighting. The home heating area offers great potential both for consumers to save money and for society as a whole to save resources. Consumer travel and transport is another major area for potential savings.

Large differences are observed between households in the amount of energy they use for home heating. Seligman, Darley, and Becker (1978) found differences of 100 percent between identical homes and observed drastic changes in energy use when another family occupied a home. These large differences are related to the behavior, activities, and lifestyle of the household members. The number of household appliances, their usage intensity, thermostat settings during the day and night, and the use of ventilation systems all contribute to energy use in the home.

This study investigates usage-related household behavior and its impact on energy use. Energy-related attitudes, socio-demographic variables, and home characteristics are also included to explain the use of natural gas for home heating.

BRIEF REVIEW OF THE LITERATURE

In many countries, attitude surveys have examined the energy consciousness of consumers. Seligman, Darley, and Becker (1978) studied the attitudes of homeowners in their Twin Rivers study. Four factors emerged in a factor analysis of the attitude statements (a total of 55 percent of the variance in consumption was accounted for): personal comfort and health, high effort/low payoff, individual contribution, legitimacy of the energy crisis.

In another factor analysis, Seligman, Kriss, Darley, Fazio, Becker, and Pryor (1979), found the same pattern and an additional factor: belief in science and technology. Consumers who believe in technological solutions to the energy crisis (nuclear

---

Financial support for this study has been provided by DSM, Gasunie, and Bouwfonds Nederlandse Gemeenten. The questionnaire design and data collection was done by Lagendijk Opinion Research in Apeldoorn (The Netherlands).

power, solar or wind energy) tend to reduce their energy use to a lesser degree than those who do not believe in technological solutions. In both studies electricity consumption for summer air conditioning was is the dependent variable.

In other studies, socioeconomic variables are related to self-reported energy use. Newman and Day (1975) compared the energy use of the "poor" with the usage of the "well off"; the energy use of blacks was also examined. De Fronzo and Workev (1979) studied female-headed households' energy use. Cunningham and Joseph (1978) investigated the price responsiveness for energy price increases of low and high income groups.

In few publications is the actual behavior of the household members the focus of research. Attitudes may not be related to actual behavior for several reasons, e.g. consumers do not know what types of behavior contribute to energy saving; "poor" households cannot reduce their energy use any further; consumers may have energy-conscious attitudes but are unable or unwilling to change their behavior. In the study reported here, the focus is on the behavior of household members, an important determinant of household energy consumption.

METHODS

The objective is to investigate the relationship between energy conscious attitudes, energy-related household behavior, and actual use of natural gas in the household. Included are the socioeconomic characteristics of the households, special circumstances during the investigation period, and home characteristics.

Homes Studied

From November 1976 through November 1977, the energy use of 145 households in Vlaardingen, Holy-North (The Netherlands) was monitored. In the area of Holy-North, there are 157 similar homes, 79 having standard thermal insulation of walls and windows, and 78 having superior thermal insulation.

All 157 homes are basically similar in design, except for home insulation, wind orientation, and position of the home with regard to neighbouring homes. The houses are built in rows, attached to each other. A number of houses have only one attached neighbouring house (semi-attached) and three "free" sides. The other houses have two attached neighbouring houses (fully attached) and only two "free" sides. All homes have similar central heating systems using natural gas as a fuel to heat water pumped through radiators in the rooms. The position and wind orientation for homes with standard and superior thermal insulation are similar.

RESULTS

Preliminary Analysis

Attitudes. At the first wave (November, 1976) of this panel study, the respondents answered eight questions on their energy consciousness, price consciousness, attitudes toward home temperature and draughts, and ecological concern. After a principal component analysis of these questions, three factors emerged which explained 62 percent of the total variance. The factors and the proportion of the variance explained by each are: energy consciousness (28.5%), home comfort (17.1%), price consciousness (16.4%). In the remainder of this study, factor scores on these factors, computed for each of the 145 respondents, are used.

Household Behavior. The respondents reported 17 types of energy-related household behaviors. These were factor analyzed and six factors emerged, explaining 58.2 percent of the total variance. The factors and the proportion of the variance explained by each are: bedroom temperature while sleeping (14.3%), home temperatures during absence from home (11.7%), home temperature while at home (9.4%), use of curtains (8.0%), airing rooms (8.0%), and use of bedrooms (6.3%).

In the remainder of the study, factor scores on these six factors, computed for each of the 145 respondents, are used along with the variables, use of hall-door and switching off pilot flame.

Socioeconomic Characteristics. No significant differences were obtained between households occupying homes with standard and with superior thermal insulation.

Energy Use. On four occasions (November, 1976, January, 1977, April, 1977, and November, 1977) the meters for heating gas were read. Table 1 gives the main results for the three periods in the investigation. Households with superior insulation tend to use less natural gas, especially during winter months.

Explaining Household Behavior

Attitudes and Household Behavior. Three attitude variables, obtained from principal component analysis, are employed to predict eight types of household behavior. Table 2 gives the results of eight stepwise multiple regressions. These attitude measures do not predict household behavior very well, except for three situations. Those who prefer higher home temperatures do not lower their thermostats when they are away from home. Price-conscious consumers do close the curtains and possess

TABLE 1

ENERGY CONSUMPTION DURING THREE PERIODS

| Energy Consumption | Home With: | | |
	Standard Insulation	Superior Insulation	All Homes
Average consumption of natural gas (m^3): ($1m^3$ = 1.31 cubic yards)			
Period 1	1015	897	963
Period 2	831	763	797
Period 3	590	508	555
Total	2436	2168	2315
	N = 76	N = 69	

Note: Period 1: November 1976   to   January, 1977
       Period 2: January, 1977   to   April, 1977
       Period 3: April, 1977   to   November, 1977

longer curtains (to the floor). Energy-conscious consumers tend to use fewer bedrooms.

The attitude-behavior relationships are mainly insignificant. Attitudes predict household behavior up to a maximum of 5 percent. It does not seem to be worthwhile in energy campaigns to change general attitudes because these attitudes are not related to household behavior. Most consumers have rather positive attitudes toward energy-saving and ecological problems but do not behave according to their stated opinions.

Home Evaluations and Special Circumstances. Home evaluations are the household member's evaluation of home comfort, ease of heating the home, evaluation of home insulation, wind evaluation, evaluation of the size of windows, and evaluation of heating problems. Special circumstances include absence during the weekends, absence of wife during the day, the type of former home the household lived in, whether the wife has a full-time, part-time or no paid job outside the home, and shift service of the husband. Home evaluations and special circumstances explain up to 18% of the variance in household behavior. The behavioral factor, "home temperature while at home," is explained particularly well by home evaluations and special circumstances.

Socioeconomic Characteristics. Socioeconomic characteristics of the household have a separate effect on household

TABLE 2

HOUSEHOLD BEHAVIOR EXPLAINED BY ATTITUDES
(beta-weights)

Attitudes	Use of hall-door	Pilot-flame	Bedroom temperature while sleeping (1)	Home temperature during absence (2)	Home temperature while at home (3)	Use of curtains (4)	Airing rooms (5)	Use of bedrooms (6)
Energy consciousness	-.01	-.12	-.02	.01	.04	-.05	.09	-.17*
Home comfort	-.09	-.03	.00	.22**	-.06	-.02	-.04	
Price consciousness	-.05	-.08	-.03	-.07	-.03	.19**	-.10	-.01
Multiple R	.10	.16	.04	.23	.07	.19	.13	.17
R^2	.01	.03	.00	.05	.01	.04	.02	.03

* significant at $p < .05$.
** significant at $p < .01$.

behavior with regard to energy consumption. They explain an average of 9 percent of the variance in household behavior.

Home Characteristics. The characteristics of the home explain an average of 7 percent of the variance in household behavior.

Factors Determining Household Behavior. Combining the effects of a number of these variables explains only an average of 28 percent of the variance in household behavior, a rather low percentage considering that 31 independent variables contribute to this result.

Explaining Energy Use

Household Behavior and Energy Use. Household behavior is represented by the six factors from the principal components analysis and, additionally, the use of the hall-door and the pilot-flame. In order to test which household behavior variables contribute to the explanation of energy use, a stepwise multiple regression was performed, using natural gas consumed as a dependent variable. Table 3 gives the main results. Household behavior variables explain 26 percent of the variance in natural gas use for heating purposes. The major behavioral variables that determine energy use are: home temperature during absence from home, use of pilot-flame, bedroom temperature while sleeping, home temperature while at home (not in Period 3), and the use of the hall-door (not in Period 3).
Recommendations for saving energy, therefore, should emphasize lowering the thermostat when leaving home, turning out the pilot-flame when central heating system is not in use, keeping bedrooms cool while sleeping, not turning the thermostat too high when at home, and closing the hall-door in order to prevent cold draughts from the open front door.

Home Characteristics and Energy Use. Table 4 provides the results of stepwise multiple regression of home characteristics explaining energy use. Home insulation and home attachment (fully attached or semi-attached) are the major factors. Energy use of neighbour contributes only in Periods 1 and 2, the winter periods. Wind orientation contributed depending on the season. The effect of insulation is larger during the winter months.
Twenty-four percent of the variance in energy use is explained by home characteristics only. The 145 homes of this study are very similar in design. It may be expected that for a sample of more dissimilar homes, even a larger percentage of variance in energy use may be explained by a larger set of home characteristics.

Home Characteristics and Household Behavior Explaining Energy Use. Adding home characteristics to the behavioral

TABLE 3

HOUSEHOLD BEHAVIOR EXPLAINING ENERGY USE
(beta-weights)

| Household Behavior | Energy Use | | | |
	Period 1 Nov.-Jan.	Period 2 Jan.-Apr.	Period 3 Apr.-Nov.	Total period
House temperature during absence (factor 2)	.25*	.21*	.34*	.30*
Use of pilot flame	.21*	.17*	.25*	.23*
Bedroom temperature while sleeping (factor 1)	.18*	.21*	.15*	.20*
Home temperature while at home (factor 3)	.15*	.17*	.09	.15*
Use of hall-door	.15*	.18*	.09	.15*
Use of curtains (factor 4)	-.07	-.06	.03	-.03
Airing rooms (factor 5)	-.03	-.05	-.06	-.05
Use of bedrooms (factor 6)	-.02	.05	.03	.03
Multiple R	.47	.45	.49	.51
R^2	.22	.21	.24	.26

* significant at p < .01

variables will increase the proportion of explained variance in energy use. The explained variance rises to 46 percent, using stepwise multiple regressions.

Families use less energy when they live in insulated homes that are fully attached, with a big energy spender as a neighbour, and a south or southwest wind orientation of the front of the home. They also use less when they lower the thermostat during periods of absence, switch off the pilot-flame, shut the hall-door, have relatively low room temperatures.

Summarizing the indirect influences of home insulation via behavioral change on natural gas consumption, two main effects are clear: people in better insulated homes tend to lower their thermostat while at home and during the night which decreases the energy use. They also air their rooms more frequently and leave the hall-door open more frequently which increases their energy use. These two effects seem to compensate for each other.

TABLE 4

HOME CHARACTERISTICS EXPLAINING ENERGY USE
(beta-weights)

Home Characteristics	Energy Consumption			
	Period 1	Period 2	Period 3	Total
Home insulation	-.44**	-.30**	-.24**	-.35**
Home attachment	-.20**	-.28**	-.24**	-.26**
Energy use of first neighbour	-.27**	-.13**	-.11	-.18**
Wind orientation ENE	.06	.14*	.08	.10
Wind orientation WSW	-.07	-.06	-.16**	-.11
Wind orientation S	-.03	-.09	.02	-.05
Energy use of second neighbour	-.11	-.05	.01	.05
Multiple R	.52	.46	.39	.49
R^2	.27	.21	.16	.24

* significant at p < .05
** significant at p < .01

SUMMARY OF RESULTS

The results of the multiple regression analyses are given in Table 5 and 6. Table 5 contains the proportions of variance in household behavior explained by energy-related attitudes, socioeconomic characteristics of the households, special circumstances, home characteristics, and combinations of the above independent variables. Overall, an average of 28 percent of the variance in household behavior can be explained by energy-related attitudes, socioeconomic characteristics, special circumstances, and home characteristics. Special circumstances, especially the proportion of time the wife is not at home, account for about 15 percent of the variance. Attitudes, socioeconomic characteristics, and home characteristics explain less variance. It may be expected that personal and household characteristics have a stronger effect on energy behavior for a more diverse sample of households than the households living in Vlaardingen Holy-North. Consequently, the same will be true for the explanation of energy consumption.

TABLE 5

SUMMARY OF VARIABLES EXPLAINING
HOUSEHOLD BEHAVIOR

	Min R^2	Max R^2	Average R^2
Attitudes (3 factors)	.00	.05	.02
Socioeconomic Characteristics	.05	.12	.09
Special Circumstances	.07	.18	.15
Home Characteristics	.01	.13	.07
Attitudes + Socioeconomic + Home Characteristics	.15	.23	.19
Attitudes + Socioeconomic + Special Circumstances + Home Characteristics	.24	.36	.28

TABLE 6

SUMMARY OF VARIABLES EXPLAINING ENERGY USE

	R^2 Period 1	R^2 Period 2	R^2 Period 3	R^2 Total Period
Household Behavior (6 + 2 factors)	.22	.21	.24	.26
Home Characteristics	.27	.21	.16	.24
Special Circumstances	.13	.04		.11
Socioeconomic Characteristics				.06
Home Evaluation				.08
Household Behavior + Home Characteristics	.47	.38	.36	.46
Household Behavior + Home Characteristics + Special Circumstances + Socioeconomic Characteristics + Home Evaluation + Attitudes	.59	.46	.46	.58

Table 6 and Figure 1 give the proportions of variance in energy consumption explained by household behavior, home characteristics and home evaluation, special circumstances, and socioeconomic characteristics. Household behavior and home characteristics together explain 46 percent of the variance in energy use over the total period. Adding all variables, 58 percent of the variance in energy use can be explained.

IMPLICATIONS FOR ENERGY CAMPAIGNS

The results of this investigation provide clear indications of the types of household energy conservation campaigns that may be considered. Five types of energy campaigns are feasible.

Changing Attitudes and Household Behavior

The traditional campaigns for energy conservation are aimed at changing consumer attitudes and consequently household behavior in an energy-saving direction. From this study, only limited support is derived for this type of campaign. The attitude-behavior relationship proved to be weak in that attitudes explain only about 2 percent of the variance in household behavior. Changes in energy-conscious attitudes are not reflected in energy-saving behavior and a decrease in energy consumption. A better attitude measure may explain more variance in household behavior but no dramatic improvement should be expected.

Factors intervening between attitude and behavior are the acceptance of responsibility and the perceived effectiveness as a consumer. Acceptance of responsibility means that the consumer accepts his responsibility of conserving energy and blaming himself and other consumers (and not the industry, the government, or the ecologists) for energy shortages that may occur. Perceived effectiveness includes the notion of personal efficacy in helping to decrease energy consumption and optimism that these efforts will result in positive outcomes. These factors are related to the perception of internal locus of control.

Changing Attitudes Toward Home Improvement

Another type of attitude change campaign may be directed toward changing consumers' attitudes with regard to home improvement such as home insulation, storm doors or windows, and thermostats that set back night time temperature automatically. However, some indications show that the effects of home improvements may be counteracted by household behavior. People living in an insulated home tend to air their rooms more frequently and open the hall-door more frequently. Home improvements and household behavior may both be the consequence of energy-conscious attitudes. However, energy-saving household behavior

**Figure 1: Explaining Energy Use in the Home.
Numbers are proportions of explained variance.**

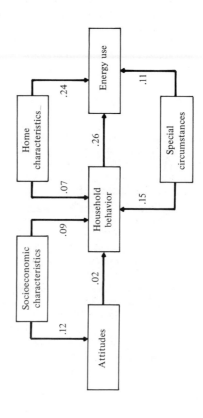

will not automatically be positively influenced by home improvements.

Prescription of Home Improvements

Governmental agencies may prescribe, for new or existing homes, certain standards of energy-saving through the use of insulation materials or other energy-saving devices. This strategy is generally followed for new types of automobiles and industrial heating systems. Again, energy-saving types of household behavior as a consequence of home improvements intervene here.

It should be noted that the variation of the houses in this study is rather small. It may be expected that home characteristics would have a stronger effect on energy consumption for a more heterogeneous set of homes.

Feedback Strategies

Strategies employing individual feedback of information include energy consumption information and its costs provided for households on a weekly or monthly basis. Feedback information may induce changes in household behavior in an energy-saving direction. Consumers observing themselves behaving in an energy-conscious way may infer that they must act that way because they have energy-conscious attitudes. According to self-perception theory (Bem 1967), people infer their attitudes from their behavior, instead of inferring their behavior from their attitudes. For example, a small monetary inducement (4A) may create stable attitudinal change. Changed attitudes may result in ecologically concerned behavior, even in areas other than energy consumption in the home, such as recycling behavior, use of phosphate-free detergents, and increased preference for public transportation. Feedback on energy saving increases one's perception of personal effectiveness in helping to solve energy problems, and this reinforces energy-conscious household behavior.

Changing Household Behavior

The fifth type of energy campaign is aimed at directly changing energy-related household behavior. In this type of campaign, changes in household behavior are recommended to consumers. Table 6 showed that the most effective behavioral recommendations are: turn down the thermostat when leaving home, switch off the pilot-flame when the heating system is not in use, have a low bedroom temperature when sleeping, have a rather low room temperature when at home, and keep the hall door closed as much as possible. The last two recommendations are only effective in the winter months (November through April).

SUMMARY AND CONCLUSIONS

Based on the results of this study, the traditional energy campaigns of changing attitudes and, consequently, household behavior and energy consumption, are debatable. However, it can be expected that including measures of acceptance of responsibility and perceived effectiveness as a consumer may improve the attitude-behavior relationship. Consumers may act according to their attitudes when they feel personally responsible for energy problems and perceive that their personal contribution to energy saving is effective.

Home improvement has a strong effect on energy consumption, either in a direct way or through the home evaluation and household behavior as a consequence of home improvement.

The effects of an energy campaign stressing home improvements may be increased by providing behavioral recommendations with regard to energy use. The effects of home insulation, for instance, are counteracted by the tendency for airing rooms and keeping doors open more frequently. Behavioral recommendations should be accompanied by indications of how much energy one saves by changing one's behavior.

From other studies, it appears that individual feedback information approaches are effective in reducing energy consumption. However, the individualistic character of these approaches will make feedback expensive. Changing attitudes into an energy-conscious direction should be accompanied by changing consumer acceptance of responsibility and perceived effectiveness, and behavioral recommendations of how to save energy. Home improvements should also be accompanied by behavioral recommendations. Information in the form of feedback seems to be very effective to maintain new and stable behavioral patterns and to create energy-conscious attitudes.

RELATED RESEARCH

Bem, D.J.(1967), "Self-Perception: An Alternative Interpretation of Cognitive Dissonance Phenomena," Psychological Review, 74, 183-200.

Cunningham, W.H. and Joseph, B. (1978), "Energy Conservation, Price Increases and Payback Periods," in H.K. Hunt (ed.), Advances in Consumer Research, Vol. 5, Chicago: Association for Consumer Research, 201-205.

De Fronzo and Workev, S. (1979), "Are Female-Headed Households Energy Efficient: A Test of Klausner's Hypothesis among Anglo, Spanish-speaking, and Black Texas Households," Human Ecology, 7, 191-197.

Hayes, S.C. and Cone, J.D. (1977), "Reducing Residential Electrical Energy Use: Payments, Information, and Feedback," *Journal of Applied Behavior Analysis*, 10, 425-435.

Kohlenberg, R., Philips,T. and Proctor, W. (1976), "A Behavioral Analysis of Peaking in Residential Electrical-Energy Consumers," *Journal of Applied Behavioral Analysis*, 9, 13-18.

Newman, D.K. and Day, D. (1975), *The American Energy Consumer*, Cambridge: Ballinger.

Palmer, M.H., Lloyd, M.E., and Lloyd, K.E. (1977), "An Experimental Analysis of Electricity Conservation Procedures," *Journal of Applied Behavior Analysis*, 10, 655-671.

Russo, J.E. (1977), "A Proposal to Increase Energy Conservation through Provision of Consumption and Cost Information to Consumers," in B.A. Greenberg and D.N. Bellenger (eds.), *1977 Combined Proceedings*, Chicago: American Marketing Association.

Seligman, C., Darley, J.M. and Becker, L.J. (1978), "Behavioral Approaches to Residential Energy Conservation," in R.H. Socolow (ed.), *Saving Energy in the Home*, Cambridge: Ballinger, 231-254.

Seligman, C., Kriss, M., Darley, J.M., Fazio, R.H., Becker, L.J. and Pryor, J.B. (1979), "Predicting Summer Energy Consumption from Homeowners' Attitudes," *Journal of Applied Social Psychology*, 9, 70-90.

Weigel, R.H. and Newman, L.S. (1976), "Increasing Attitude-Behavior Correspondence by Broadening the Scope of Behavioral Measure," *Journal of Personality and Social Psychology*, 33, 793-802.

CONSUMER ENERGY: SITUATIONAL ANALYSES

- Energy Consumption in Leisure and Perceived Happiness

- Teenage Consumers and Energy Conservation

- Electricity Consumption by the Elderly

- Household Travel Patterns by Life Cycle Stage

ENERGY CONSUMPTION IN
LEISURE AND PERCEIVED HAPPINESS

Ronald Graef
Susan McManama Gianinno
Mihaly Csikszentmihalyi

The common sense assumption is that the ability to control and use physical energy is a "good thing." Yet the production and consumption of energy are not in any sense valuable by themselves; they are means that must be evaluated in terms of some end. The bottom-line criterion is whether energy use contributes to the long-range net satisfaction of people; if it does not, it must be seen as a hindrance to be removed rather than a value to be increased.

This lack of correlation between energy use and happiness has been noted by many. Linder (1970) and Scitovsky (1976) have suggested that as productivity increases, more and more time has to be devoted to maintaining and consuming energy-intensive goods. Because time itself is the most scarce resource, these demands reduce the satisfaction one can derive from experience, with the paradoxical result that material goods end up impoverishing instead of enriching life. The message that many writers see in the present situation is that unless we change from a society of consumers into a society of conservers, we shall squander the energy reserves on which life depends (Schumacher 1975; Gardner 1976; Robertson 1976).

Given the seriousness of these issues, it is interesting that no one has tested the assumption that an energy-intensive lifestyle is in any measurable sense "better" than one low in energy consumption. It is not known what advantages, if any, a high energy consumption lifestyle brings to the quality of human experience.

In the present study a measure of individual energy use in leisure activities will be compared with a measure of individual happiness. Two null hypotheses will be tested: a) Leisure activities that require more energy will not produce higher levels of happiness than leisure activities requiring less energy; and b) People who consume more energy overall in their leisure activities will not have a higher level of happiness in either their leisure activities, or over their lives as a whole.

The energy use of daily leisure activities will be expressed in terms of Btu requirements, according to Fritsch's (1974) specifications in his Lifestyle Index. This was a first attempt to index energy usage and provided approximations that allow

The research reported here was partially supported by PHS Grant #RO 1 HM 22883-01-04, National Institute of Mental Health.

47

comparisons of leisure activities. For example, it is estimated that downhill skiing consumes more resources than cross-country skiing, that reading a newspaper is more energy intensive than reading a book, or that playing baseball in a local school yard requires fewer natural resources than attending a professional game especially at night in an air-conditioned stadium. Accurate comparisons must wait until more precise estimates are developed.

The quality of experience or happiness and the level of energy consumption in leisure will be measured with a newly developed Experience Sampling Method (ESM). This technique, which depends on electronically-induced self-reports to random paging in normal daily activities, provides reliable and valid assessments of how people feel about the various things they do in their lives (Larson and Csikszentmihalyi 1978; Csikszentmihalyi and Graef 1980; Graef, Gianinno, and Csikszentmihalyi 1979; Larson, Csikszentmihalyi, and Graef 1980).

METHODS

Full-time employees from five companies in the Chicago area were invited to participate in a study of everyday work and non-work experiences. Four hundred fifty men and women, aged 19 to 63 years, volunteered to participate in the study. Of these, 125 were selected to represent a wide spectrum of urban workers. Eighty-six percent or 107 adequately completed the project.

The Experience Sampling Method (ESM)

The ESM involves the random sampling of people's ongoing daily experience for a given period of time, in this case seven working days during waking hours (8:00 A.M. to 10:00 P.M.). Each participant was asked to carry an electronic paging device and a booklet containing 60 information sheets. When the paging device signalled, emitted a "beeping" sound, participants were to fill out an information sheet. The sheet contained questions about where they were, what they were doing, and how they were feeling. On the average, a sheet takes one minute to complete.

The signalling schedule is randomized within two hour intervals during waking hours over the seven day period. This ensures an even distribution of observations across the recording period while no two days follow the same schedule. According to the signalling schedule, each participant received approximately 56 signals or "beeps" over the week, barring technical failure.

The average number of signals responded to or information sheets completed is 44 or about 80 percent of the signals sent. The range is from 30, a lower limit established at the beginning of the study, to 56 responses. People failed to respond to signals for a variety of reasons, none of which appears to have systematically affected the results.

Variables

There are two primary variables examined in this study: people's leisure time activities converted into energy consumption, and the quality of their overall weekly experience as measured by average happiness ratings.

To approximate leisure energy consumption for each participant, Fritsch's (1974) Lifestyle Index was employed. However, rather than calculate Btu consumption figures for each person, we decided simply to categorize leisure activities into low, medium, and high energy consumption according to Fritsch's Btu estimates. The lifestyle index was not intended to provide a rigorous measure of energy consumption but a model for estimation. Once leisure activities are categorized into level of energy consumed, it is an easy step to generate an energy consumption score for each participant based on the percentage of low, medium, and high energy consuming activities they engage in during their leisure.

The energy consumption categories, the leisure activities that compose each of them, and the occurrence for each activity for both males and females are shown in Table 1. There are numerous leisure activities not included in the table; because they do not occur often in people's daily lives or because they were not sampled by the method. In general, the activities listed in Table 1 constitute the usual range of daily leisure activities engaged in. About equal amounts of leisure fall into the low and high categories. People engage much less frequently in those leisure activities defined as medium energy consumption activities.

The quality of experience is measured by how happy the participants rate themselves each time they are signalled. The happiness item on the information sheet is a 7-point semantic differential from "very sad" (-3) to "very happy" (+3). Happy-sad is one of 13 mood items included on the information sheet and is highly correlated ($r > .75$) with other mood items: cheerful-irritable, friendly-hostile, tense-relaxed, and satisfied-dissatisfied. The mood items are scored each time the pager signals in response to the instruction: "describe the mood as you were beeped."

RESULTS

The first hypothesis states that leisure activities requiring more energy consumption, i.e., energy-intensive activities, will not produce higher levels of satisfaction or happiness than leisure activities requiring less energy consumption. Just taking the random observations recorded during leisure time (N=1316, see Table 1) and calculating a mean happiness score for

TABLE 1

A DESCRIPTION OF THE THREE ENERGY CONSUMPTION ACTIVITY
CATEGORIES AND THE DISTRIBUTION OF LEISURE RESPONSES (N=1316)
BY MALES AND FEMALES IN EACH CATEGORY

Leisure Activities by Average Btu Consumption per Year	Males		Females		Percent of Total
	N	%	N	%	
Low Btu Consumption (LOBTU)	173	42.9	489	53.6	50.3
1. Daydreaming	10	2.3	43	4.7	4.0
2. Socializing	119	29.5	323	35.4	33.6
3. Hobbies: artwork, sewing, etc.	7	1.7	23	2.5	2.3
4. Playing a sport or game	25	6.2	36	3.9	4.6
5. Sexual activities	12	3.0	64	7.0	5.8
Medium Btu Consumption (MIDBTU)	26	6.5	97	10.6	9.4
6. Going to a movie	1	0.3	9	1.0	0.8
7. Reading a book	13	3.2	38	4.2	3.9
8. Listening to music	3	0.7	19	2.0	1.7
9. Playing a musical instrument			1	0.1	0.1
10. Entertaining guests at home	2	0.5	12	1.3	1.1
11. Attending a sporting event, concert, club meeting, etc.	7	1.7	18	2.0	1.9
High Btu Consumption (HIBTU)	204	50.6	327	35.8	40.4
12. TV watching	118	29.3	217	23.7	25.5
13. Reading a newspaper or magazine	60	14.9	63	6.9	9.4
14. Shopping (pleasure)	23	5.7	43	4.7	5.0
15. Going to a restaurant, disco, etc.	3	0.7	4	0.4	0.5
TOTAL OBSERVATIONS	403		913		1316

Notes:

Activities in the LOBTU category are those activities for which
Fritsch (1974, pp. 170-172) estimated negligible energy consumption (0 to 5 Btu's consumed per year). MIDBTU activities are
those that range from 5 to 40 Btu's consumed per year on the
average, and HIBTU activities are estimated to be above 40 Btu's
consumed per year.

low, medium, and high energy consuming activities, the hypothesis is supported. In fact, level of happiness is lower during energy-intensive experiences (going to a restaurant is the only exception in the high energy consuming category where the mean happiness is 1.71). These results are shown in Figure 1 for the average ratings in each energy category, and for males and females. The drop in level of happiness is significant overall ($t=1.87$, $p<.05$) and for the females ($t=2.22$, $p<.05$). The males' reported happiness did not differ significantly across levels of energy consumption.

Because the results in Figure 1 are derived from raw observations rather than within person means, it it possible that people are unevenly distributed within the low and high energy consumption categories, thereby confusing the results. In which case, people who engage more frequently in energy-intensive activities might be reporting lower happiness levels even when they are engaging in energy conserving leisure activities. While this result would still support the hypothesis, it implies that less happy people engage more often in energy-intensive activities rather than that energy intensive activities lead to lowered levels of happiness. To test this question of possible cause, we examined the number of times each participant engaged in low and high energy consuming activities and their mean happiness in each category. The results support the latter conclusion that energy-intensive experiences are accompanied by lowered happiness. Ninety-seven percent of the sample have at least one observation in both the low and high energy consuming categories, 85 percent have two or more responses in each category. Of those who have two or more responses, 65 percent have higher happiness means when engaged in low energy consuming leisure activities. Thirty-two percent have higher happiness means during energy-intensive experiences.

The second hypothesis states that people who use more energy overall in their leisure activities will not have a higher level of satisfaction or happiness with either their leisure activities or their lives as a whole. To test this hypothesis, each participant's percentages of activities in each energy category were correlated with his or her mean happiness ratings overall and within obligatory and discretionary experiences. These results are shown in Table 2.

The more energy-intensive a person's leisure experiences the less happy that person tends to be. Thus the second hypothesis is also confirmed. Even during leisure activities, the high energy consuming lifestyle is accompanied by lowered feelings of happiness. However, it is not the case that those who engage more often in energy conserving leisure activities are more happy overall or in their work and leisure situations.

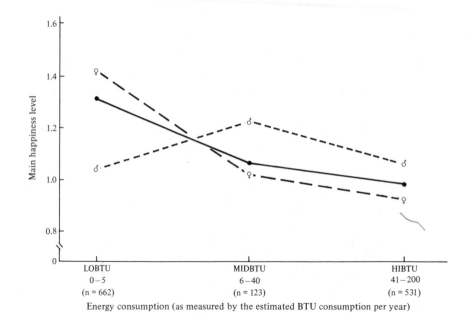

Energy consumption (as measured by the estimated BTU consumption per year)

Figure 1:   The Relationship between Energy Consumption
in Leisure and People's Feeling of Happiness

TABLE 2

THE RELATIONSHIP BETWEEN PEOPLE'S ENERGY CONSUMPTION PATTERNS
AND THE LEVEL OF THEIR HAPPINESS OVERALL AND FOR OBLIGATORY
AND DISCRETIONARY EXPERIENCES
(N = 107)

Percentage Of Energy Consuming Activities	Mean Happiness Ratings		
	Overall	Obligatory	Discretionary
LOBTU	.06	.08	.09
MIDBTU	-.07	-.04	-.08
HIBTU	-.15	-.17*	-.14
Total Energy Intensive Score	-.17*	-.19*	-.16*

Notes:

The percent of LOBTU correlates -.20 (p<.05) with the percent of
MIDBTU and -.64 (p<.001) with HIBTU. The percent of MIDBTU
correlates -.20 (p<.05) with HIBTU. The individual LO and HIBTU
percentages are, of course, highly correlated with the total
energy intensive score (-.70 and .97 respectively).

*p<.05

SUMMARY AND CONCLUSIONS

    In the present study no positive relationship was found
between energy use and happiness. In fact, for the women
sampled there was strong suggestion that happiness was inversely
related to energy use. Comparing happiness ratings in high,
medium, and low energy-intensive leisure experiences, indicated
that happpiness levels significantly lower in high energy-intensive experiences. Moreover, findings suggest that the more
energy-intensive a person's leisure experiences, the less happy
that person tends to be, overall. Other correlates of high
energy-intensive activities included: being older, being married, having a higher income, engaged more frequently in obligatory activities, having lower job satisfaction, and lower self
image.

What has been learned about what contributes to happiness? The key to answering this question rests in understanding more fully the factors which distinguish high and low energy-intensive activities. One clear differentiating factor is the degree of personal involvement required by the activities. The high energy-intensive activities (TV watching, newspaper reading, etc.) are characterized by passive participation in the "process" of the activity. Someone else invests time and energy so an individual can enjoy "the fruits of his labor." In contrast, the low energy-intensive activities involve more active participation in the process of the activity. Such active participation may enhance the intrisic reward potential of an activity, and intrinsic outcomes have been identified as an important component of enjoyment (Csikszentmihalyi 1975).

More systematic analysis of high versus low energy-intensive activities may substantiate this observation and shed further light on why high energy-intensive activities do not yield greater happiness. If the observation here is true, then it may be that in our attempts to make life "easier" through high energy-intensive activities (from electric can openers to speed boats) we have inadvertently taken much of the enjoyment out of life by precluding active involvement on the part of the participant.

RELATED RESEARCH

Csikszentmihalyi, M. and Graef, R. (1980), "The experience of freedom in daily life," American Journal of Community Psychology, 8(4), 401-414.

Fritsch, A.J. (1974), The Contrasumers: A Citizen's Guide to Resource Conservation. New York: Praeger.

Gardiner, W.L. (1976), "The consumer and the conserver," K. Valaskakis (ed.), Values and the Conserver Society. Montreal: GAMMA.

Graef, R., Gianinno, S., and Csikszentmihalyi, M. (1979), "Positive and negative indicators of psychological well-being." Paper presented at the 87th Annual Convention of the American Psychological Association, New York City, September 1979.

Larson, R. and Csikszentmihalyi, M. (1978), "Experiential correlates of solitude in adolescence," Journal of Personality, 46(4), 667-693.

_____, Csikszentmihalyi, M., and Graef, R. (1980), "Mood variability and the psychosocial adjustment of adolescents," Journal of Youth and Adolescence. (in press).

Linder, S.B. (1970), The Harried Leisure Class, New York: Columbia University Press.

Robertson, J. (1979), The Same Alternative, St. Paul, Minnesota: River Basin Publishing Co.

Schumacher, E.F. (1975), Small is Beautiful--Economics as if People Mattered. New York: Harper & Row.

Scitovsky, T. (1976), The Joyless Economy, New York: Random House.

TEENAGE CONSUMERS AND ENERGY CONSERVATION

Martin G. Kushler
John C. Jeppesen

In the seven years since the 1973 oil embargo, the need for energy conservation has become painfully obvious to policymakers and concerned citizens alike. As we enter the 1980s there can be little doubt that the need to conserve energy is one of the most crucial challenges facing the United States. Fortunately, the potential contribution of conservation in solving the energy problem is great. Indeed, experts have recently estimated that the United States could reduce energy consumption by 30 to 40 percent and suffer no decline in standard of living (Stobaugh and Yergin 1979).

TEENAGE YOUTH AS A TARGET POPULATION FOR ENERGY CONSERVATION

One group that offers potential is the adolescent consumer. There are several reasons for targeting energy conservation efforts in this area. First, this age group presents the possibility for an immediate energy savings impact, both in terms of their own increasing opportunities for consumption decisions, as well as through actions they might influence their families to take. Second, efforts targeted at students prior to their assumption of full adult roles and responsibilities could help instill an "energy ethic" which could have a lasting impact in terms of wise future decisions concerning energy use. Third, and perhaps most importantly, there appears to be a substantial need in this area as it has been found that America's students are lacking in knowledge of basic energy facts, and expect to be able to continue to depend on high energy use, and further, appear to be obtaining what information they do have about energy from the media rather than through schooling (National Assessment of Educational Progress [NAEP] 1978).

Unfortunately, additional information about the energy conservation attitudes and behaviors of youth is somewhat scarce. Although a fair amount of study of environmental attitudes has occurred, relatively little research has been

---

This paper was prepared in part with the support of the U.S. Department of Energy, Grant No. EC-77-G01-5092. However, any opinions, findings, conclusions, or recommendations expressed herein are those of the authors and do not necessarily reflect the view of the U.S. Department of Energy. The authors wish to thank Dr. William Stevens and Mary Durkee for their valuable assistance with certain components of the research discussed in this chapter.

published concerning the attitudes of youth toward energy and energy conservation.   Those studies that have been reported, although somewhat limited in scope, are useful to consider (Ayers 1977; Fazio and Dunlop 1977; Collins et al. 1979; Kuhn 1979).

In summary, with a few exceptions, there is a general lack of information about the energy conservation attitudes and behaviors of an important energy consuming group--the American teenager.   The data that is available tends to show that much more could be done to help assure that this consuming group uses energy more wisely.   It is hoped that this chapter will contribute to the base of information about this age group as well as suggest ways that energy conservation attitudes and behaviors might be improved.

BACKGROUND: THE MICHIGAN ENERGY EXTENSION SERVICE PROJECT

In August 1977, the Michigan Department of Commerce, through the Michigan Energy Administration, received a $1.1 million grant from the U.S. Energy Research and Development Administration.   The Youth component of this grant made Michigan's proposal unique among the ten states selected for such awards. One of the major objectives of the Youth Project was to create an "energy conservation ethic" in 50,000 high school age students.   More specifically, the Michigan Energy Extension Service (EES) Youth Project has also attempted to examine the relative effectiveness of various strategies in terms of influencing attitude change and energy consumption.

In the three years since the founding of the Michigan EES Youth Project, several large scale research efforts have been conducted which have attempted to examine the energy conservation attitudes and behaviors of teenage youth.   The intent of this chapter is to present the results of this on-going program of research.

The Youth Energy Survey (YES) Questionnaire

In planning for the implementation of the EES youth program, the staff was faced with the very fundamental question of how to evaluate the effectiveness of the program efforts.   One serious constraint that faced the EES staff was the need to develop an evaluation strategy that could be utilized with tens of thousands of students.   Given this necessity for large numbers of participants (mandated in the federal funding), it became obvious that some sort of self-report questionnaire was the most realistic evaluation device.

A common attitude measure format, that of the Likert-type scale, was chosen as the format of the YES questionnaire. As for content of the questionnaire, a variety of sources were considered including some earlier attempts that others had made to measure energy conservation attitudes (e.g. Rappeport and

Labaw 1975; Olsen and Goodnight 1977). In addition, the literature on psychological measurement, which stresses the importance
of targeting attitudes specifically related to intended behavioral objectives, was particularly useful (Eagly and Himmelfarb
1978). After considering these inputs, the EES evaluation staff
generated a pool of approximately 80 items and pilot-tested them
with several hundred high school students.

Following pilot testing and analysis, utilizing a combination of rational and empirical processes (Jackson 1971), a
45-item attitude measure was constructed. This was combined
with demographic questions and self report questions, and placed
on machine readable survey form. Subsequent use of this instrument during the past three years, with over 100,000 high school
students in nine states, has demonstrated consistent reliability
and very encouraging validity results. (For a more complete
discussion of this instrument, see Stevens and Kushler 1979).

METHOD

Overview: The Michigan Multiple Phase Project

The Youth Project of the Michigan Energy Extension Service
was conceptualized and planned as a longitudinal program of
service and research. As such, several distinct phases of
programming were designed to investigate different aspects of
youth energy conservation attitudes and behavior and how they
might be influenced. Three separate phases of this project have
been completed and form the basis of this paper.

Phase I: Testing a Broad Range of Approaches, The first
phase of the Youth Project was intended to test a wide range of
possible methods for helping to create an "energy conservation
ethic" in high school youth. Four diverse intervention strategies were selected: providing workshops to train teachers to
teach energy conservation; facilitating presentations by students to other students; providing drama (theatre) presentations
to students (e.g. acting out various energy scenarios); and
providing a large scale assembly program ("The Energy Today and
Tomorrow" program developed by Oak Ridge Associated Universi-
ties, Oak Ridge, Tennessee).

Phase II: Testing Strategies for Teacher Training, Based
on the results of the first phase, it was decided to target the
second phase of the Youth Project toward investigating strategies designed to get teachers to include energy conservation in
their classes. Once again, four different strategies were
selected for testing: a "teacher consultation" strategy, where
an extension agent consulted individually with teachers in the
schools; a "committee" consultation strategy, where an extension
agent consulted with teachers and also attempted to get them to
form a conservation committee in their school; a "workshop"
condition, where teachers were invited to attend a half-day
workshop on teaching energy conservation; and a "task-oriented"

workshop condition, where teachers attended half-day workshops which included materials and a presentation on the "task" strategy of having students actually engage in energy conserving behavior as a part of their school assignments on energy.

Phase III: A National Survey of Youth, Based on the results of the earlier Youth Project activities, the U.S. Department of Energy granted additional funds to Michigan to do a survey of a national sample of students. For this study, eight states were selected on a number of criteria to help assure their representativeness of the nation as a whole. Since this project was designed solely as a survey, intended to begin to establish a national youth conservation attitude and behavior data base, no educational interventions were conducted in this project. In all, over 40,000 high school students in 161 high schools across eight states were surveyed.

RESULTS

For the purpose of this chapter, the results obtained from the three studies are divided into two major categories. First, the basic survey results are outlined in terms of existing energy conservation attitudes and behaviors and their relationship to various student characteristics. Following this, project results are described which relate to energy conservation education and its effect on student attitudes and behaviors.

Demographic and Descriptive Variables

One of the most commonly examined demographic variables is that of sex of the respondent. In these studies it was found that females were clearly more positive toward energy conservation than males (Table 1). This was found to be true across all grade levels studied. It is interesting to note that this finding has not only been strongly replicated in all of the student surveys conducted during this project but is also quite consistent with findings from many national surveys of energy conservation and environmental attitudes, in which females are generally found to be more positive than males (Farhar et al 1979).

An interesting finding was the grade level results. When considering these findings, a question naturally arises as to what accounts for the observable trend of higher grades having more positive scores. Is it part of a developmental process; due to increased exposure to the educational system; due to some historical event(s); or a result of some combination of those three factors? These questions are heightened when one also considers the preliminary results of some work EES has done with middle school students. What has emerged is as follows: fifth and sixth graders have attitude scores comparable to the later high school grades, but seventh through ninth graders show

TABLE 1

RELATIONSHIP OF DEMOGRAPHIC AND DESCRIPTIVE VARIABLES
TO ENERGY CONSERVATION ATTITUDES AND BEHAVIORS

| Variables | Significant Findings | | | Comments |
	Phase 1 (Michigan) 1977-78	Phase 2 (Michigan) 1978-79	National (8-States) 1978-79	
Sex	Yes	Yes	Yes	Females consistently more positive toward conservation. Males more positive toward technology and nuclear power, much less positive toward automotive conservation. Behaviors split with males more likely to do mechanically or physically involved tasks.
Grade	Yes	Yes	Yes	Attitudes and behaviors more positive at each successive grade level for grades 9-12. (See discussion for further comments.)
Number of persons in the home.	No	No	No	In study #1, a slight trend was observed toward a larger number of siblings in the home being associated with lower conservation attitudes. No relationship for number of adults in the home. The second and third studies just looked at number of persons in the home and found no significant differences.
Size of home (# of Bedrooms)	N/A	No	No	A slight trend in study #2 toward more positive attitudes for students from larger sized homes. No relationship for behaviors.
Type of home	Yes	No	Yes	Students who live in single family houses are the most positive group, followed by those in apartments or duplexes followed by those in mobile homes. Behaviors are not quite significant.

TABLE 1 CONTINUED

Variables	Significant Findings			Comments
	Phase 1 (Michigan) 1977-78	Phase 2 (Michigan) 1978-79	National (8-States) 1978-79	
Youth ownership of a car	Yes	Yes	Yes	Students who own their own car are less positive toward energy conservation and particularly toward automotive conservation. Trend not quite significant for behaviors (see discussion). Effects persist for both males and females but stronger for males.
Size of car youth owns	Yes	Yes	Yes	Students who own sub-compact cars have the most positive conservation attitudes, followed in direct descending order by owners of compacts, mid-size, and full size cars. Behaviors follow a similar, but not quite significant, trend in all three studies.
Number of cars owned by family	No	No	No	No strong pattern but consistent trend toward families with more than 2 cars being less positive toward conservation.
Size of largest car owned by family	Yes	Yes	Yes	Attitudes revealed the same clear pattern of results as for size of car the youth owns. Behaviors were again in the same trend but not quite significant.
Size of Community	N/A	N/A	Yes	Rural residents scored lowest on both attitudes and behaviors. Suburban residents had the most positive attitudes. City and suburban youth shared the lead in conservation behaviors.
Student's grade point average	N/A	N/A	Yes	Strongly significant linear relationship toward students with high grade point averages having more positive attitudes toward conservation and performing more conservation behaviors.

substantially lower attitude scores.   Much further research is
needed, including repeated surveys over time, before these
trends can be adequately understood.

The finding concerning grade point average is also interesting and is consistent with numerous studies which link higher
educational levels with higher energy awareness and favorability
toward conservation (Farhar et al 1979).   Similarly, both family
socioeconomic status and student IQ have been found to be
positively related to environmental awareness and attitudes
(Horvat and Voelker 1976).

The other significant findings in terms of descriptive
variables primarily revolve around the automobile.   These
differences cannot be explained away by sex differences in car
owners, or by simply looking at the automotive-related items in
the attitude scale.   One further point to consider is that these
findings lend behavioral evidence to the validity of the YES
attitude scale (e.g., persons with more positive energy conservation attitudes drive smaller cars and vise versa).

Finally, there were several demographic and descriptive
variables which were not related to conservation attitudes or
behaviors, including: the number of persons who live in the
home, the size of the home and the number of cars owned by the
family.   There was a slight trend toward students from families
with more cars having lower scores on both energy conservation
attitudes and behaviors.   Unfortunately, it is difficult to
interpret the findings on these items because they are affected
by family income and occupation, two variables on which no data
was gathered.

Exposure to Energy Conservation Education

Table 2 presents the major findings of this study in terms
of the effects of energy conservation education.   The Phase I
results are the least encouraging of the project.   Although only
one example of each broad type of methodology was tested (e.g.,
drama presentation, large scale assembly, etc.) the authors
concluded that it was probably unrealistic to expect such
diffuse, low-contact, large-group methods to change positively
such complex concepts as energy conservation attitudes and
behaviors.

The Phase II results were much more encouraging, particularly in the demonstration of the ability to influence teachers
to teach about energy and energy conservation in their classes.
It was found that this could successfully be done through a
variety of different consultations and workshop approaches.   One
area that was identified for further research, however, was the
issue of how and what to teach to achieve greatest effectiveness.   Many "energy" materials and curricula currently available
were found to have no positive impact on energy conservation
attitudes and behaviors.   The single most promising strategy,
referred to previously, was found to be the "task-oriented"

TABLE 2

RELATIONSHIP OF EXPOSURE TO ENERGY EDUCATION TO
ENERGY CONSERVATION AND BEHAVIORS

| Variables | Significant Findings | | | Comments |
	Phase 1 (Michigan) 1977-78	Phase 2 (Michigan) 1978-79	National (8-States) 1978-79	
Type of communication used to reach students	Yes	N/A	N/A	None of the four strategies used (teacher workshops, student to student presentations, small drama presentations, large scale assemblies) could demonstrate positive impact on students as compared to control groups. The large scale assembly has a slight negative impact. A correlational finding suggested usefulness of more class hours on energy conservation.
Type of intervention to use with teachers	N/A	Yes	N/A	Four different approaches to teachers were tested (see Method section). All four were strongly effective at getting teachers to teach as compared to randomly assigned control group. The teacher workshop with a "task-oriented" approach produced the most positive attitudes and behaviors.
Energy conservation instruction	Yes	Yes	Yes	Students who received energy conservation instruction were more positive in attitudes and behaviors than students who had not received instruction.

TABLE 2 CONTINUED

Variables	Significant Findings			Comments
	Phase 1 (Michigan) 1977–78	Phase 2 (Michigan) 1978–79	National (8–States) 1978–79	
Number of hours of energy conservation instruction	Yes	Yes	Yes	A consistent positive relationship was observed in all three studies whereby more hours of instruction were associated with higher attitude and behavior scores.
Number of courses in which energy conservation was included	N/A	Yes	Yes	Conservation behaviors appear to improve significantly with each additional course exposure; attitudes improve until leveling off after three courses.
Energy conservation "task" assignment	N/A	Yes	Yes	Students who had received an energy conservation "task" assignment from school scored higher on energy conservation attitudes and behaviors.
Number of pages read in past week concerning energy conservation	Yes	Yes	Yes	A consistent positive relationship was observed in all three studies whereby more pages of energy conservation material read was associated with higher attitude and behavior scores.

approach to conservation education. In this approach, the student is asked to engage in an energy conserving behavior and to monitor or discuss the results in terms of energy savings. This strategy combines the best features of the impact of task experienced and self-perception on attitudes (Breer and Locke 1965; Bem 1972), monitoring and feedback (e.g., Seligman and Darley 1977; Becker 1978), and the incremental adoption of new behaviors represented by the foot-in-the-door approach (Scott 1977). For further information the reader is referred to Leedom (1979).

Finally, the results in terms of the four survey variables regarding energy conservation exposure are also very positive. As can be seen in Table 2, the results consistently show that students who receive energy conservation instruction have more positive attitudes and report having performed more energy conservation behaviors. Furthermore, there is a solid indication that additional exposure to energy conservation instruction, both in terms of the number of hours of instruction and in the number of different courses in which conservation topics are taught, will produce additional gains in attitudes and behaviors. Once again, the fact that a student received an energy conservation activity assignment is also related to positive attitudes and behaviors.

An Unintended Benefit of Monitoring Trends Over Time:
Assessing the Impacts of The Three-Mile Island Accident

Significant public events can also contribute energy education effects. It is possible to use the YES to monitor the influence of these events within a framework of periodic assessments. Using this approach, the authors had the opportunity to study the impacts of the Three-Mile Island (TMI) nuclear accident on middle school students in Michigan.

In summary, the results suggested that proximity to a nuclear power plant during the TMI incident was related to the significant shift of student attitudes toward a more pro-energy conservation, pro-solar, and anti-nuclear position. While this post-hoc design lacks the controls of a true experimental design, it does show how the YES, when administered on a periodic basis, can be used to assess the impacts of influential events on student energy attitudes.

SUMMARY AND CONCLUSIONS

The important public policy implications are the findings concerning energy conservation education. The data suggest that energy conservation instruction may be able to change significantly the attitudes and behaviors of high school students. More specifically, the data suggest that a strategy of (a) infusing energy conservation in a number of courses, (b) including several hours of instruction, and (c) assigning actual energy conservation activities to students, has the potential for maximizing the impact on conservation attitudes and behaviors.   These findings are very encouraging and suggest that energy and educational policymakers should seriously consider this area of intervention.   As McClelland and Canter (1979) point out, even small reductions in energy consumption can be very meaningful when aggregated over thousands of households.

RELATED RESEARCH

Aird, Andrew and Tomera, Audrey (1977), "The Effects of a Water Conservation Instructional Unit on the Values Held by Sixth Grade Students," The Journal of Environmental Education, 9, 31-42.

Ayers, Jerry (1977), "Rural Elementary Children's Attitudes toward the Energy Crisis," School Science and Mathematics, 76, 238-240.

Becker, Lawrence (1978) "Joint Effect of Feedback and Goal Setting on Performance: A Field Study of Residential Energy Conservation," Journal of Applied Psychology, 63, 428-433.

Bem, Daryl (1972), "Self-Perception Theory."   In L. Berkowitz (ed.), Advances in Experimental Social Psychology, Vol. 6, New York: Academic Press.

Breer, Paul and Locke, Edwin (1965), Task Experience as a Source of Attitudes, Homewood, Illinois: The Dorsey Press.

Collins, Thomas, Herbkersman, C. Neil, Phelps, Lynn and Barret, Gary (1979), "Establishing Positive Attitudes toward Energy Conservation in Intermediate-Level Children," The Journal of Environmental Education, 11, 18-23.

Darley, John (1978), "Energy Conservation Techniques as Innovations, and Their Diffusion," Energy and Buildings, 1, 339-343.

Eagly, Alice and Himmelfarb, Samual (1978), "Attitudes and Opinions," Annual Review of Psychology, 29, 517-554.

Farhar, Barbara, Weis, Patricia, Unseld, Charles, and Burns, Barbara (1979), Public Opinion About Energy: A Literature Review, Golden, Colorado: Solar Energy Research Institute.

Fazio, F. and Dunlop, D. (1977), "The Development and Use of an Energy Assessment Instrument,"   paper presented at the annual meeting of the National Association for Research in Science Teaching, Cincinnati: (ERIC No. ED 135664).

Ferber, S. (1977), "More on Energy: A Look at Research," American Psychological Association Monitor, April, 1977.

Hounshell, Paul and Liggett, Larry (1976), "Environmental Education One Year Later," Journal of Environmental Education, 8, 32-35.

Horvat, R. and Voelker, A. (1976), "Using a Likert Scale to Measure Environmental Responsibility," Journal of Environmental Education, 8, 36-47.

Jackson, D.N. (1971), "A Sequential Strategy for Personality Scale Development." In C. Spielberger (ed.), Issues in Clinical and Community Psychology, New York: Academic.

Kelman, Herbert (1974), "Attitudes are Alive and Well and Gainfully Employed in the Sphere of Action," American Psychologist, 29, 310-324.

Kuhn, David (1979), "Study of the Attitudes of Secondary School Students toward Energy-Related Issues," Science Education, 63, 609-620.

Leedom, Nancy (1979), A Task-Oriented Approach to Energy Education. Unpublished masters thesis, Michigan State University.

Lissitz, R.W. and Green, S.B. (1975), "Effect of the Number of Scale Points on Reliability: A Monte Carlo Approach," Journal of Applied Psychology, 60, 10-14.

McClelland, Lou and Canter, Rachelle (1979), "Psychological Research on Energy Conservation: Context, Approaches, Methods." In A. Baum and J.E. Singer (eds.), Advances in Environmental Psychology, Volume III: Energy Conservation: Psychological Perspectives. Hillsdale, New Jersey: Erlbaum Associates.

Milstein, Jeffrey (1977), How Consumers Feel About Energy: Attitudes and Behavior During the Winter and Spring of 1976-77, Washington D.C.: Federal Energy Administration.

Mitchell, Robert (1980), "Public Opinion and Nuclear Power Before and After Three Mile Island," Resources, 64, 5-7.

Morrison, Bonnie, Keith, Joanne, and Zuiches, James (1977), "Energy Impacts on Michigan Families," unpublished report, East Lansing, Michigan, Michigan State University.

National Assessment of Educational Progress (1978), Energy Knowledge and Attitudes, Denver: Education Commission of the States.

Olsen, Marvin and Goodnight, Jill (1977), Social Aspects of Energy Conservation, Seattle, Washington: Battelle Human Affairs Research Center (NTIS No. PB-266-29).

Rappeport, Michael and Labaw, Patricia (1975), General Public Attitudes and Behaviors Regarding Energy Saving. Highlight Report, Volume IX, Princeton, New Jersey: Opinion Research Corporation, (NTIS No. PB-244-989).

Scott, Carol (1977), "Modifying Socially-Conscious Behavior: The Foot-in-the-Door Technique," The Journal of Consumer Research, 4, 156-164.

Seligman, Clive and Darley, John (1977), "Feedback as a Means of Decreasing Residential Energy Consumption," Journal of Applied Psychology, 62, 363-368.

Stevens, William and Kushler, Martin (1979), "An Energy Conservation Attitude Questionnaire: Reliability, Validity and Uses," paper presented at the Fifty-first Annual Convention of the Midwestern Psychological Association, Chicago.

Stobaugh, Robert and Yergin, Daniel (1979), Energy Future: Report of the Energy Project of the Harvard Business School, New York: Random House.

U.S. Department of Energy (1977), Energy Conservation in the Home, Oak Ridge, Tennessee.

_____, (1979), Low Cost-No Cost Energy Savers, Washington, D.C.

Winett, Richard (1976), "Efforts to Disseminate a Behavioral Approach to Energy Conservation," Professional Psychology, 7, 222-228.

ELECTRICITY CONSUMPTION BY THE ELDERLY

G. Keith Warriner

With rapidly increasing prices and threatened shortages, there has developed concern that the elderly are being subjected to an undue share of the burden imposed by recent energy problems. Several means have been suggested to assist the elderly in reducing their energy bills or to supplement their incomes to keep pace with the cost of living. These include plans for increasing financial aid to the needy through existing or new Social Security programs, tax breaks for home weatherization or heating stock retrofitting, protection against utility service cutoff during the winter, government and media campaigns to encourage conservation and direct payments or credits to reduce utility bills. Recently Lifeline and other innovative rate structures have been proposed as a means of facilitating the purchase of basic needs for natural gas and electricity by the poor and elderly.

The purpose of this study is to determine the income-related effects, if any, upon residential electricity consumption by the elderly. The relative effects of other factors are also explored. Implications for policy are discussed.

METHOD

Data for this study were collected in conjunction with the Wisconsin time-of-day rate demonstration project (Heberlein, in Part II of this book). This project is a four-year panel study which began in Spring, 1976 and concluded in the Spring of 1980, in which a sample of some 700 homes in northeastern Wisconsin had their electricity consumption monitored by magnetic tape meters which recorded their level of electricity consumption every fifteen minutes. Disproportionate sampling was employed to insure that approximately equal numbers of low, middle, and high consumption consumers would be available for analysis.

During much of this project, homes were subjected to experimental time-of-day rates (for a description of the procedures and results of this phase of the experiment, see

Funding for this research was provided by the Wisconsin Public Service Corporation, Green Bay, Wisconsin. Additional support was provided by the Department of Energy, Washington, D.C., and administered by the Public Service Commission of Wisconsin. The author wishes to thank Dr. Thomas A. Heberlein, University of Wisconsin, for his helpful comments and suggestions on an earlier verson of this report.

Heberlein and Warriner 1980; Caves and Christensen 1979a, 1979b;
Black 1978). During the study's first year (May, 1976 - March,
1977) baseline consumption data were collected. During this
period test households were neither subject to special rates nor
were members aware they had been selected to participate in an
experiment. Hence, during this period, their patterns of
consumption can, for all purposes, be considered normal. These
data are employed here to examine electricity consumption by the
elderly.

Mail Questionnaire

Appliance and demographic data on households were collected
by a mail questionnaire administered in March, 1977. Among the
694 magnetically metered homes, 661 responded, a response rate
of 95.2 percent. Fifty-five returns represented households
whose primary heating fuel is electricity. The latter have been
dropped from the present analysis. Of the 606 remaining residences, 82 (13.5 percent) contain only adults whose average age
is 65 years or older. It is this group relative to the non-
elderly sample of households (N=524) against which comparisons
are made.

Dependent Variables

The primary dependent measure is monthly level of consumption, reported in kWh. An average month's consumption was
calculated based upon six seasonally differentiated months of
the baseline year--July and August, 1976 and January, February,
March and April, 1977--representing the range of climatic
conditions occurring in this region.
As a second dependent measure, average monthly bill was
calculated. The computation of the average monthly bill is more
meaningful than consumption alone in representing the amount
that must be paid by the customer both for the provision of
electric service and their level of consumption, while taking
into account the seasonal diversity in electric rates and
whether the residence is a rural one.

RESULTS

An initial assessment was made of the impact of electricity
consumption upon the elderly and non-elderly. Here the dependent measures of average monthly consumption and the average
bill are being compared, together with several additional
factors. Findings indicate that the elderly use less electricity on the average and, as a result, pay lower monthly bills
per household. However, it is also the case that they pay proportionally more of their monthly income on electricity than
non-elderly households (5 versus 3 percent respectively).
Furthermore, while 81 percent of the elderly's electricity

consumption is used to achieve essential needs relating to lighting, refrigeration, water heating, and cooking, non-elderly households commit only about 54 percent of their consumption to these services. Finally, since their homes contain fewer household members, the elderly use proportionally more electricity per capita than other homes and pay proportionally more on their bills as well.

This analysis suggests that the elderly are in a disadvantageous position relative to other age groups when it comes to using electricity. They consume about one-third less electricity on the average than their non-elderly counterparts but pay only about 26 percent less on their household bill. Per capita they use about 39 percent more, but pay on the average bills which are 51 percent higher. They also pay about 2 percent more of their total income on electricity, while much of this is used to acquire only essential needs. In every comparison between the elderly and non-elderly these differences are significant at the .001 level or better.

Further analysis was conducted to see along what other lines the elderly differ. It is evident that the elderly have substantially smaller incomes than the non-elderly, as well as fewer household members, smaller homes, and less education. The only area in which they do not differ and which might affect electricity consumption is the likelihood of their living in a rural residence.

The elderly own fewer appliances than do other households; however, for most appliances, the lesser likelihood of ownership by the elderly is not all that great. The only major appliances which can be regarded as contributing substantially to the elderly's reduced electricity consumption are the regular freezer, the frost free refrigerator, the electric range, and clothes dryer and even the sizes of these associations are not that large.

All the above factors are likely to be related to level of electricity consumption. To explore this, variables representing the elderly, income, home size, family size, and the appliance index were progressively combined in regression models to predict average monthly consumption. The coefficients obtained represent the relative impact of each factor upon consumption (Table 1).

Single variable models indicate that the appliance index has the largest positive influence upon elderly consumption, followed by home size, family size, and income. When each of these four variables is combined with the variable for older adults (the two-variable models) both factors continue to be influential but the effects of the variable representing the elderly has been considerably reduced from the single variable model, especially when in combination with the family size variable.

TABLE 1

PREDICTING AVERAGE CONSUMPTION FROM AGE, INCOME, AND SOCIODEMOGRAPHIC FACTORS

Type of Model	Adults >65	Family Size	Income	Home Size	Appliance Index	$\bar{R}^{2a}$
Single Variable	$-.29^{b,e}$					.08
		$.42^e$				.18
			$.36^e$			.13
				$.43^e$		.18
					$.65^e$	.42
2-Variable	$-.13^e$	$.37^e$				.19
	$-.20^e$		$.27^e$			.14
	$-.19^e$			$.38^e$		.21
	$-.16^e$				$.64^e$	.46
3-Variable	$-.06^{ns}$	$.35^e$	$.29^e$			.26
	$-.15^e$		$.15^e$	$.31^e$		.21
	$-.12^e$			$.27^e$	$.57e$	.52
	$-.08^c$	$.28^e$		$.28^e$		.25
	$-.05^{ns}$	$.32^e$			$.59^e$	.53
	$-.14^e$		$.18^e$		$.58^e$	.48
4-Variable	$-.01^{ns}$	$.31^e$	$.17^e$		$.56^e$	.56
	$-.03^{ns}$	$.25^e$		$.19^e$	$.57^e$	.56
	$-.10^e$		$.10^d$	$.24^e$	$.56^e$	.52
	$-.05^{ns}$	$.28^e$	$.21^e$	$.21^e$		.30
5-Variable	$-.01^{ns}$	$.26^e$	$.12^e$	$.15^e$	$.55^e$	.57

a. Corrected for degrees of freedom.
b. Standardized regression coefficients.
c. $p < .05$
d. $p < .01$
e. $p < .001$

The three-variable models show that the effects of being elderly have become statistically non-significant in two instances (in combination with family size and income and with family size and the appliance index). In these models the common variable is family size. Thus, it is becoming apparent that a partial explanation of the reason households containing elderly adults consumer less electricity is because they contain fewer household members. However, it is still not clear whether other socio-demographic variables influence the elderly's reduced levels of electricity consumption as well.

Things became a little clearer with the four-variable models. It is becoming apparent that the reasons for the elderly consuming smaller amounts of electricity are because they have smaller homes containing fewer people and appliances. The effect of their having less income to invest in electricity is also important, but only marginally so. This is confirmed in the model containing all five variables.

A final model examining consumption including rural residence and level of education has been included with the other socio-demographic and housing factors to predict electricity consumption. However, the findings from this model in providing an explanation of how electricity is consumed by the elderly do not vary substantially from the five-variable model. Education was not statistically significant and rural residence, although positively associated, added only one per cent to variance explained.

Modelling the Elderly's Electric Bill

Five variables--income, home size, family size, appliances, and whether it is a rural residence--shown to have an effect upon level of consumption in the previous analysis are used to predict the average bill the elderly must pay (Table 2). For both the elderly and non-elderly, the factor most related to the size of their bills is their appliance stock, accounting for 62.2 percent and 54.4 percent of their average bills respectively. Thus even though they tend to own a less extensive appliance stock, the elderly pay a greater proportion of their bill on account of it. Next, for both groups the size of the home is most influential in determining what the bill will be. For the non-elderly, this is followed by family size, income, and rural location, in that order. For the elderly, the least important factor contributing to the size of their bills is income. On the average, this is responsible for only 5.6 percent of their monthly bill, or $1.52. Even if the average elderly household were to receive an income supplement of $100.00 a month, the increase in spending power this would provide would only directly lead to increased electricity consumption and subsequent bill increases in the neighbourhood of $.18 per month. Yet, clearly such minimal increases in the size of the bill against an income supplement of this order

TABLE 2

INFLUENCE OF SOCIO-ECONOMIC AND HOUSING CHARACTERISTICS UPON AVERAGE MONTHLY BILLS

| | Regression Model | | Average Adult Age | | | | | |
| | | | Under 65 | | | 65 and Over | | |
Variable	Unstandardized Coefficient	Standard Error	Mean	Amount	% of Total	Mean	Amount	% of Total
Intercept	-4.01	1.65		-4.01	-10.8		-4.01	-14.6
Family Size [a]	1.78	.20	4.08	7.26	19.5	1.78	3.16	11.5
Income [b]	.00015	.00002	20,187	3.03	8.2	10,140	1.52	5.6
Home Size [c]	1.01	.21	8.55	8.64	23.3	7.24	7.31	26.7
Appliance Index [d]	.025	.001	807.39	20.18	54.4	680.76	17.02	62.2
Rural Residence [e]	6.58	.70	.31	2.04	5.5	.36	2.37	8.7
			Total $37.14		100.1 [g]		$27.37	100.1 [g]
			N 524					82

Squared multiple correlation coefficient ($\bar{R}^2$) [f]   .63

a. Number of people
b. Annual income
c. Number of rooms including baths, half-baths and basements
d. Kilowatt hours
e. Rural = 1; urban = 0
f. Corrected for degrees of freedom
g. Totals may not sum to 100.0 due to rounding

would do much to erase the inequitable position being faced by the elderly in paying a greater proportion of their incomes on electricity than other age groups.

Indirect Effects of Age and Income upon the Size of the Electric Bill

To complete the assessment of the impact of age and income upon the size of the electric bill, the direct and indirect relationships between age and the endogenous, independent variables of income, family size, home size, the appliance index and rural residence were set out in a four-stage causal model (Figure 1). These directed and indirect associations have been calculated and listed in Table 3. As has always been the case in earlier models, age continues to be negatively associated with income and family size. However, it is no longer directly related to home size once these intervening factors have been controlled. The direct effects of all six independent variables upon the size of the bill are unchanged from previous models, with age having no direct effects. Instead, all its effects are mediated by the appliance index, as well as family size, income and home size in combination. The most sizeable indirect effect of age is through family size. The elderly have fewer people in the home and this fact alone largely accounts for their reduced levels of electricity consumption and smaller bills.

While income still maintains some direct influence upon the bill, it also has considerable indirect effects through its associations with home size and the appliance index. This lends support to the contention that income has greater influence in determining the size of the electric bill than what earlier models had suggested. While this is true, it is also the case that even in combination with family size to account for the size of the home, and when combined with rural residence and age to predict appliance ownership, income is able only to account for 29 percent and 14 percent of the variance in these independent variables respectively. Hence, home size and appliances appear to have considerable influence in determining the size of the household electric bill, but for much of these effects income cannot be held responsible.

SUMMARY AND CONCLUSIONS

Investigating the relationship between income and energy consumption is not new. Several studies have shown that a meaningful relationship between the two exist (Morrison 1976; Gladhart, Zuiches, and Morrison 1977; Donnermeyer 1977; Kilkeary 1975; Morrison and Gladhart 1976; Newman and Day 1975; Cunningham and Lopreato 1977). Nevertheless, in drawing conclusions investigators have tended to lump the elderly in with other low income consumers. The present analysis suggests reasons for believing the elderly possess a unique set of

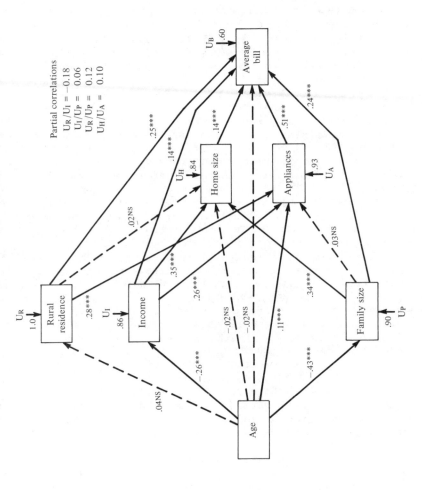

Figure 1: Causal Model of the Effects of Age Upon Average Monthly Electric Bill

Partial correlations
$U_R/U_I = -0.18$
$U_I/U_P = 0.06$
$U_R/U_P = 0.12$
$U_H/U_A = 0.10$

TABLE 3

DECOMPOSITION OF EFFECTS OF FACTORS AFFECTING AVERAGE MONTHLY ELECTRICITY BILL

| Independent Variable | Direct Effect[a] | Indirect Effect[b] Via: | | | | | Total Effect[c] |
		Rural Residence	Income	Family Size	Home Size	Appliances	
Age	$-.02^{ns}$	.00	$-.08^{d}$	$-.12^{e}$	.00	-.06	-.26
Rural	.25				.00	.14	.39
Income	.14				.05	.13	.32
Family Size	.24				.05	.00	.29
Home Size	.14						.14
Appliances	.51						.51

Squared multiple correlation coefficient $(\bar{R}^2)^{f}$ = .64

a. Standardized regression coefficient.

b. Indirect effect = $\Sigma_k \ P_{ij}$, where: i is the affected variable, j is the causal variable, and k varies over all paths leading directly to i.

c. Total effect = direct + indirect effects.

d. -.01 of "income" is tranmitted additionally through "home size"; -.03 is transmitted additionally through "appliances" (see Figure 1).

e. -.02 of "family size" is transmitted additionally through "home size" (see Figure 1.)

f. Corrected for degrees of freedom.

circumstances mitigated by choice and lifespan characteristics which places them in a less disadvantageous position in relation to current energy problems than is often assumed. It appears at best they are not being compelled to consume less electricity than other groups due to economic deprivation. Neither does it appear that improvements in their economic situation will lead to sizeable increases in consumption. This has often been a concern of those evaluating income supplementation strategies or other programs intended to reduce the impact of the utility bill on the elderly. If the elderly had larger incomes or faced a smaller electric bill, it is unlikely we would see much increase in their level of energy consumption either directly, or over the long run through the acquisition of new appliances or larger homes.

All of this does not beg the question that the elderly face disadvantages along several fronts. They pay proportionally more for electricity relative to their incomes, while acquiring amounts which are mainly to achieve essential needs. They have smaller appliance stocks yet pay a greater proportion of their bill on account of this. Per capita they pay more for electricity and since their bill is lower overall, the amount they pay for a fixed charge--which is beyond their control and unrelated to rate of consumption--is proportionally higher.

These inequities could be overcome either by increasing incomes or lowering bills, either by rate reform or by direct payments or energy credits. On the other hand, perhaps the elderly are in an advantaged position in other financial areas. Although having substantially lower incomes than the non-elderly, the elderly may face fewer demands upon that which is available. This is in need of assessment prior to the implementation of new energy programs intended to assist the elderly.

In way of conclusion, it must be admitted that the methodology reported here has been a second best approach. What is needed is a well run, orthogonal experiment testing various policy alternatives and prices, while controlling for age and income. In addition, it is important that studies be conducted to examine the cognitive and behavioral dispositions of the elderly, especially the energy choices they are making and their beliefs and attitudes toward energy. In the absence of these measures, the present study has employed as stand-ins structural factors relating to the elderly's households such as its size, family membership, and appliance characteristics. The impacts of these factors free of the influence of incomes suggest the existence of a social environment which is largely accountable for the elderly's energy behaviors. But this must be assessed more directly if we are to understand it fully.

RELATED RESEARCH

Black, J.S. (1978), "Attitudinal, Normative and Economic Factors in Early Response to an Energy-Use Field Experiment", unpublished Ph.D. dissertation, Dept. of Sociology, University of Wisconsin, Madison.

Caves, D.M., and Christensen, L.R. (1979a), "Residential Substitution of Off Peak for Peak Electricity Usage under Time-of-Day Pricing: An Analysis of the 1976 and 1977 Summer Data from the Wisconsin Experiment," unpublished manuscript, Dept. of Economics, University of Wisconsin, Madison.

_____, (1979b), "Estimating Shifting to Off Peak Electricity Usage Under Time-of-Day Pricing: An Analysis of Monthly Data from the Wisconsin Experiment," unpublished manuscript, Department of Economics, University of Wisconsin, Madison.

Cunningham, W.H., and Lopreato, S.C. (1977), Energy Use and Conservation Incentives, New York: Praeger.

Donnermeyer, Joseph R. (1977), "Social Status and Attitudinal Predictors of Residential Energy Consumption," paper presented at the Annual Meeting of the Rural Sociological Society, Sept. 1-4, Madison, WI.

Gladhart, P.M., Zuiches, J.J., Morrison, B.M. (1977), "Impacts of Rising Energy Prices upon Residential Energy Consumption Attitudes and Conservation Policy Acceptance," paper presented at the Symposium on Social and Behavioral Implications of the Energy Crisis, Energy Institute, University of Houston, June 27-28.

Heberlein, T.A., and Warriner, G.K. (1980), "Attitude, Motive, Ability and Knowledge: Factors Affecting Peak Load Reductions in Consumption of Electricty," paper submitted for presentation at the Annual Meeting of the Rural Sociological Society, Ithaca, New York.

Kilkeary, R. (1975), "The Energy Crisis and Decision Making in the Family," Springfield, Va.: National Technical Information Service, NTIS Report No. NSF-SOS GY-11543.

Morrison, Bonnie Maas (1976), "Residential Energy Consumption: Socio-Physical Determinants of Energy Use in Single Family Dwellings," paper presented at the 7th Annual Meeting of the Environmental Design Research Association, Vancouver, B.C.

_____, and Gladhart, Peter (1976), "Energy and Families: The Crisis and the Response," Journal of Home Economics, January, 15-18.

Newman, D.K., and Day, D. (1975), The American Energy Consumer, Cambridge, Mass: Ballinger.

HOUSEHOLD TRAVEL
PATTERNS BY LIFE CYCLE STAGE

Carol A. Zimmerman

Of all the energy-consuming habits, patterns of personal travel may prove the hardest to change. In an urbanized, post-industrial society such as the United States, a high degree of personal mobility is taken for granted. Most of this mobility is supplied by motor vehicles. In 1977-78 (the most recent period of time for which data are available) households in the United States averaged 4.8 vehicle trips daily and 32 miles of travel per day in vehicles owned or available to the household (U.S. Department of Transportation n.d.). Of the 217.6 billion person trips made over a twelve month period (1977-78), private vehicles were used for 83.9 percent of the trips (U.S. Department of Transportation n.d.).

The purpose of this chapter is to examine one aspect of household travel in the United States and to determine the magnitude of the related demand for energy. To analyze the demand for travel in an energy-short world, a conceptual framework which incorporates both household resources and lifestyle factors is desirable. In the following sections, the life cycle approach is presented as a potentially useful framework for describing the travel behavior of households and for assessing the impact of future energy conditions in the household sector.

A STUDY OF THE VARIATION IN TRAVEL BEHAVIOR AMONG HOUSEHOLDS

The Life Cycle Approach

Over the last few decades the concept of the family life cycle has frequently appeared in the work of economists and marketing specialists (David 1962; Hendricks and Youmans 1973; Wells and Gubar 1966), sociologists (Aldous 1978; Hill and Rodgers 1964), demographers (Glick 1977), and, more recently, historians (Hareven 1977; Modell et al. 1978). Although interpretations vary, the basic thrust of the life cycle notion is that the family unit changes both quantitatively and qualitatively over its life span, from the formation of the family to its dissolution. As the family changes it goes through a sequence of stages, which are differentiated on the basis of significant events in the lives of family members, such as the

The author gratefully acknowledges the technical assistance of the staff of the Planning Services Branch, Federal Highway Administration, Washington, D.C.

birth of the first child, the "launching" of the last child from the home, or the retirement of the breadwinner from the labor force.

With respect to travel behavior, the life cycle approach raises a number of theoretical and practical issues. Perhaps the thorniest theoretical issue is that the family life cycle is based on the assumption that the nuclear family is the typical or ideal family structure. Because many families do not follow the prescribed life cycle pattern, it is argued that the concept is not theoretically sound (Trost 1977). However, Murphy and Staples (1979) have shown that it is possible to adapt alternative family structures to the life cycle framework. A modified version of their approach has been used in the present study.

A second theoretical concern is that even though families do change size, composition, social roles, and other features over time, these changes may not necessitate alterations in travel behavior. Furthermore, household travel patterns may be influenced by factors other than stage in the life cycle, such as socio-economic status, geographical location, or the ethnic background of a family. For this reason, the degree to which travel changes from one stage of the life cycle to the next has been examined.

Among the practical issues involved in life cycle analysis is the problem of identifying stages in the family life cycle. As Wells and Gubar (1966) point out, the criteria used for identifying life cycle stages frequently vary from one study to the next. As there is no standard classification system, every new study is faced with either adding to the list of life cycle schemes or simply adopting a system used elsewhere. This is no less a problem in this study, and as is evident further on, a new classification system has been introduced.

A methodological problem which has received less attention in life cycle studies of consumer behavior is the difficulty of separating life cycle effects from period and cohort effects (Nelson and Starr 1972). As part of the cohort of families in the same life cycle stage, a family may be influenced by some unique aspect of that cohort, such as its size or historical background. The period effect results from a specific historical epoch (eg., the Depression) in which families are studied, such that the observed behavior of families may be different from family behavior at other periods of history. In the study of household travel, the period effect is probably the more problematic, due to the major changes in the American transportation system over the last several decades. Whereas studying stages in the life cycle at one point in the development of the transportation system reduces the cohort effect, extension of the findings very far into the future must be made with caution.

Methodology

The Nationwide Personal Transportation Study (NPTS), a cross-sectional survey of 17,949 households throughout the United States, was used in the empirical analysis of travel behavior by life cycle stage. The survey, conducted for the Department of Transportation by the Bureau of the Census from April, 1977, to March, 1978, employed the stratified multistage cluster sampling technique developed for Census' monthly Current Population Survey (U.S. Department of Transportation 1980). In-home interviews were conducted following a specified travel day. Household members 14 years of age and older were asked to report all trips taken during the designated 24-hour period. A knowledgeable adult household member reported trip information for children between the ages of 5 and 13, and trips for children under 5 were not reported, except when accompanied by another household member. In addition to trip data, other information was obtained about individual members and for the household in general, such as a person's age and marital status, family income, type of residence, and types and number of vehicles. In 13.2 percent of the households, trip information was not collected for one or more persons, so that the total completed sample consisted of 15,579 households.

From the socio-demographic descriptions, each household was categorized by stage in the family life cycle. The classification scheme was based on combinations of the following criteria: age and marital status of the head of household, presence of children of head, age of oldest child, and presence of other relatives and non-relatives. Based on these criteria, five major life cycle patterns were developed: the "typical" family cycle, the single parent cycle, the childless couple cycle, the single person cycle, and the cycle of unrelated individuals. The stages of each of these cycles are described in Table 1.

Variations in travel over the family life cycle were analyzed by comparing measures of travel reported by households in each life cycle stage. Two measures of travel were employed: the average number of trips and the average miles of travel per day. Travel by all modes was included. For each life cycle stage, the travel measures were computed for all trips regardless of purpose and for trips for three specific purposes: earning a living, family business, and social/recreational travel. These categories were derived from groups of 21 trip purposes identified in NPTS. Travel for earning a living consisted of trips to a place of work and trips for work-related business. Trips listed as visits to a doctor or dentist, shopping trips, and travel for family or personal business were classified as family business. Social and recreational travel consisted of seven subcategories: visiting friends or relatives, pleasure driving, sightseeing, entertainment, recreation (participant), vacation, and social. Travel labelled as "all

TABLE 1

DEFINITIONS OF LIFE CYCLE STAGES

Type of Life Cycle

Typical Family	Single Parent	Childless Couple	Single Person	Unrelated Individuals
1. NM <30 na na				
2. MC <30 na na		1. MC <30 na na	1. NB <30 na na	1. NM <30 na UI
3. MC na 0–3 na	1. NM na 0–3 na	2. MC 30–39 na na	2. NM 30–39 na na	2. NM 30–39 na UI
4. MC na 4–6 na	2. NM na 4–6 na	3. MC 40–49 na na	3. NM 40–49 na na	3. NM 40–49 na UI
5. MC na 7–10 na	3. NM na 7–10 na			
6. MC na 11–15 na	4. NM na 11–15 na			
7. MC na 16–18 na	5. NM na 16–18 na			
8. MC na 19–22 na	6. NM na 19–22 na			

TABLE 1 -- (Continued)

Typical Family	Single Parent	Childless Couple	Single Person	Unrelated Individuals
9. MC 50-59 na na		4. MC 50-59 na na	4. NM 50-59 na na	4. NM 50-59 na UI
10. MC 60-69 na na		5. MC 60-69 na na	5. NM 60-69 na na	5. NM 60-69 na UI
11. NM 70-79 na na		6. MC 70-79 na na	6. NM 70-79 na na	6. NM 70-79 na UI
12. NM 80+ na na		7. MC 80+ na na	7. NM 80+ na na	7. NM 80+ na UI

Characteristics of each life cycle stage:

line 1: marital status of head (MC = part of married couple; NM = not married)

line 2: age of head of household (age in years or na - not applicable) (Note: in husband/wife households, husband was designated as head)

line 3: age of oldest child of head (age in years or na - not applicable)

line 4: presence of other relatives of head or unrelated individuals (OR = other relatives; UI = persons not related to head; na = not applicable)

purposes" consisted of these trip purposes and nine other categories used in NPTS.

Consecutive stages of each life cycle were compared to determine the magnitude of difference in travel behavior. The statistical significance of the differences were assessed with a t statistic derived from a test which, owing to differences in the variances of life cycle stages, was adjusted for unequal sample variances (Snedecor and Cochran 1967).

RESULTS

Because of the amount of information for each type of life cycle, the results of the analysis of travel over the family life cycle cannot be presented in complete detail in this chapter.   Instead, most of the analysis focuses on the travel of families in the "typical" life cycle; highlights of travel behavior in the alternative life cycles are presented for comparison.

The Typical Family Life Cycle

The average level of travel by families over the typical life cycle is presented in Table 2, which shows daily number of trips and miles of travel for all purposes and for three specific purposes.   The magnitude of the difference is portrayed graphically in Figure 1, in which the number of trips is shown in cumulative form.

First, looking at travel for all purposes, both Table 2 and Figure 1 reveal that households are considerably more mobile at some stages of the life cycle than at others.   Except for a slight drop in travel in Stage 3 households which have very young children in the home (oldest age 0-3), total travel increases to the end of the child-rearing years at Stage 8 (oldest child age 19-22). After that point there is a sharp, continuous decline in travel through the rest of the life cycle.

In terms of total number of trips, the significance levels lend strong support to the notion that stage in the family life cycle influences the demand for travel.   In terms of distance, the observed life cycle differences appear to be not significant from Stage 3 (oldest child age 0-3) through Stage 6 (oldest child age 11-15), which suggests that the greater level of trip-making is not accompanied by an increase in mileage traveled.

For specific trip purposes, the life cycle effect takes different forms.   In travel for the purpose of earning a living, both the number of trips per day and the distance traveled follow a life cycle pattern similar to that for all travel. That is, following the decline in travel in Stage 3, travel for employment increases as children mature, then drops in the post-parental and retirement stages (9 through 12).   The changes in the travel for work from one stage to the next are statistically significant in all but four cases for trips and distance.

For purposes of family business, the life cycle curve is somewhat flatter than work travel and the differences tend to be not significant in terms of distance.   In contrast to travel for earning a living, the number of trips for family business increases between Stages 2 and 3, and, at the other end of the life cycle, the number of daily trips for this purpose does not exhibit as rapid a decline as trips for work.

TABLE 2

DAILY HOUSEHOLD TRAVEL BY PURPOSE BY STAGE IN THE TYPICAL FAMILY LIFE CYCLE*

Stage in Life Cycle***	Number of Trips				Distance in Miles				No. of Households
	All**	Earn	Fam	Soc	All	Earn	Fam	Soc	
1	4.0a	.8a	.5a	.7	36.1	6.4	4.2b	9.7	653
2	6.0a	1.4a	.9a	.6	61.2a	10.7a	7.0	8.0b	620
3	5.6c	1.1a	1.1b	.6	49.6b	11.7	6.3	5.5b	825
4	6.4a	1.2b	1.1	.6	52.3	13.7	5.9	6.2	636
5	7.2b	1.3b	1.1c	.6b	57.3	14.2c	6.6	6.4	831
6	7.8	1.2a	1.2c	.7	55.5a	11.5c	6.9	6.7a	1096
7	10.1a	1.6a	1.4a	1.1a	73.9a	13.4c	8.5	9.4a	862
8	11.0a	2.0a	1.6b	1.3b	90.2a	16.9b	9.0a	12.8b	590
9	4.5a	1.1a	.9a	.3a	44.1a	13.7a	4.8a	5.0a	838
10	3.5a	.5a	.9	.3a	27.5a	3.7a	5.0	3.9	1070
11	1.5a	.1b	.4a	.2a	11.1a	.2a	1.5a	2.6a	826
12	.9	.0	.3a	.1	2.6	.0	.6	.4a	359

* Figures for this Table are based on tabulations made by the author from the Public Use Tapes of the 1977 Nationwide Personal Transportation Study (U.S. Department of Transportation 1980).

** Trip purposes: All = all purposes   Earn = earn-a-living
                    Fam = family business   Soc = social/recreational

*** Refer to text for definition of stages in the typical family life cycle.

a,b,c Probability levels for test of significance of difference between means of two stages:

           a < 1% level (two-tailed)
           b < 5% level (two-tailed)
           c < 10% level (two-tailed)

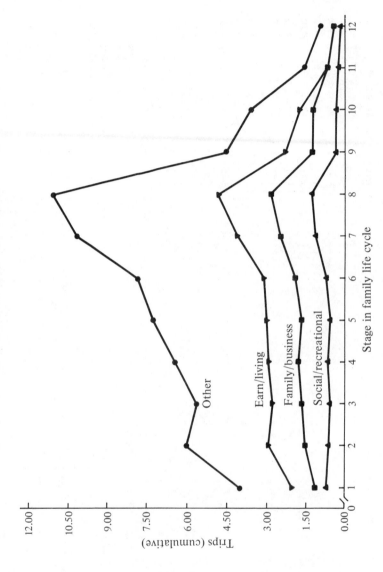

Figure 1: Trips by Stage in the Family Life Cycle

Source: Based on tabulations by the author from the Public Use Tapes of the 1977 Nationwide Personal Transportation Study (U.S. Department of Tranportation 1980).

From Stage 1 through Stage 6 the number of household trips per day for social and recreational purposes remains about the same (.6-.7 trips) until the oldest child is in the late teens and early twenties (Stages 7 and 8), at which point trips increase to over one per day. Afterwards, there is a sharp drop in social and recreational trips. In terms of distance traveled for social and recreational purposes (rather than trips), Table 2 indicates that young households without children travel two to four more miles per day than households with young children, even though the number of trips is the same. Because of the relative invariance in travel for social and recreational purposes across many stages of the family life cycle, only half of the differences between life cycle stages are statistically significant.

From the information on travel behavior in Table 2, it can be concluded that the aggregate level of mobility of households varies considerably over the typical family life cycle. For specific trip purposes, however, stage in the life cycle may be more influential at certain points than at others. For purposes of earning a living each life cycle stage tends to be accompanied by changes in levels of travel. However, travel for family business and social and recreational purposes exhibits sharp differences only in certain phases of the family life cycle. Finally it was observed that changes in household mobility in terms of distance traveled was not necessarily reflected in trip frequency, and vice versa. Thus, the level of demand for travel depends on whether trips or distance is being considered.

As mentioned previously, various information about households surveyed in NPTS was collected in addition to their travel habits. Table 3 presents a number of the characteristics of families in each stage of the typical life cycle. Among the twelve stages major differences exist in several important variables likely to affect household travel. In Stages 7 and 8, the stages where the oldest child is in the late teens and early twenties, there is a peak in family income, family size, number of vehicles, and licensed drivers. Families in Stages 7 and 8 apparently have both the desire and resources available for the average 10 to 11 trips and 74 to 90 miles of travel per day reported in Table 2.

The travel patterns and household characteristics of Stages 7 and 8 contrast sharply with households in Stages 11 and 12 (elderly single person households). At this period in the life cycle, households have meager resources and perhaps little need to travel each day. Single person households at the other end of the life cycle (Stage 1) by comparison are highly mobile, despite their relatively low income.

These examples indicate that changes in socio-economic, demographic, and other household characteristics tend to parallel changes in travel behavior over the typical family life cycle. However, they also suggest that no single variable can sufficiently explain the differences in daily travel patterns

TABLE 3

TYPICAL FAMILY LIFE CYCLE: HOUSEHOLD CHARACTERISTICS, 1977[a]

	Life Cycle Stage[b]											
	1	2	3	4	5	6	7	8	9	10	11	12
Residence												
% Urban	83	73	67	66	63	61	62	68	68	63	73	73
% Single-family detached dwell.	20	48	65	69	78	83	88	86	79	80	54	57
Economic and Demographic Characteristics												
Median family income ($000)	7.5 -9.9	12.0 -14.9	12.0 -14.9	12.0 -14.9	15.0 -19.9	15.0 -19.9	15.0 -19.9	15.0 -19.9	15.0 -19.9	10.0 -11.9	3.0 -3.9	3.0 -3.9
Avg. no. persons	1.0	2.0	3.3	3.9	4.2	4.4	4.5	4.5	2.0	2.0	1.0	1.0
Avg. no. children	na	na	1.3	1.9	2.2	2.4	2.5	2.5	na	na	na	na
Head of household												
Avg. age (yrs.)	24	25	28	31	34	41	46	50	55	64	74	84
% female	39	na	na	na	na	na	na	na	na	na	80	71
% employed	80	89	89	85	87	85	84	78	82	41	7	5
Spouse of head[c]												
Avg. age (yrs.)	na	23	25	28	32	38	43	47	53	61	na	na
% employed	na	69	29	29	34	39	45	41	40	23	na	na
Transportation Resources												
Avg. no. vehicles	1.0	1.8	1.7	1.8	1.9	2.0	2.5	2.9	1.9	1.6	.5	.3
Avg. no. drivers	.9	1.8	1.8	1.8	1.8	1.8	2.5	2.9	1.7	1.6	.5	.3
% within 1/4 mile of public trans.	50	36	29	30	28	24	25	31	30	32	40	41

a. Figures for this table are based on tabulations made by the author from the Public Use Tapes of the 1977 Nationwide Personal Transportation Study (U.S. Department of Transportation 1980).

b. Refer to text for definition of stages in the typical family life cycle.

c. In husband/wife households, the husband was designated as head of household in survey.

over the life cycle. Rather, the level of mobility is more
likely a combination of changes in the needs and wants of family
members as they age and the resources available to the household
to satisfy those demands.

Alternative Life Cycles: Highlights of Travel Patterns

In addition to the typical family life cycle, four alternative life cycles were described in Table 1: the single parent
cycle, the childless couple cycle, the single person cycle, and
the cycle of unrelated individuals. Only highlights of their
travel patterns will be discussed.

In contrast to their nuclear family counterparts, single
parent families, composed of a parent and his or her offspring,
travel considerably less. At every stage, one-parent families
make fewer trips and travel fewer miles per day than two-parent
families. The lower mobility persists even when it is scaled to
account for the smaller size of one-parent families.

The relatively low mobility of single parent families may
be due in part to the fact that such households are generally
poorer (median income $6000 - 7499), more highly urban (78
percent), and have fewer vehicles and licensed drivers (1 per
household) than the average two-parent family. In addition,
with only one adult member, single parent families average half
as many work-related trips, which comprise a sizeable part of
daily travel for most families.

The general pattern of change in travel over the single
parent cycle is similar to the pattern in households where both
parents are present, that is, an increase in trips and miles of
travel as children mature. However, the differences between
stages are not as large and they tend to be less statistically
significant.

The life cycle described as the childless couple cycle,
consists of married couples who have no children in the home.
Households in this cycle were placed in stages according to the
age of the head (husband). With only one exception, the older
the head, the fewer the trips made by households in each stage.
However, between Stages 1 and 2 (head age less than 30 and 30 to
39 respectively) the differences are small and not significant.
And, from Stage 3 (head age 40-49) to Stage 6 (head age 70-79),
there is very little change in the daily number of trips for
family business and for social/recreational purposes. For
work-related travel, trips do not decline until the head is in
his fifties. A similar pattern was obtained for daily miles of
travel, although the differences between stages were less
statistically significant.

Single person households register a dramatic decline in
total mobility over their life cycle. In most cases there is a
significant drop in trip-making as the age of head increases,
for all trips, for trips to earn a living, and for social and
recreational trips as well. On the other hand, travel for

family business remains relatively constant (about .4 to .5 trips per day per household) through age 60 - 69, after which age travel declines. For miles of travel, there is a general decline in mobility through the stages of the single person household, but as with the other life cycles, the changes are generally not statistically significant.

The final life cycle, that of unrelated individuals, probably does not warrant a life cycle status, for most (69 percent) of the 581 households in this category are headed by individuals under age thirty. Nevertheless, it will be briefly described, for it represents an alternative living arrangement which appears to be increasingly popular for some individuals (Glick and Norton 1977). As with the single person and childless couple cycles, overall mobility in households of unrelated individuals declines with increasing age of the household head, from 8.3 trips and 93.3 miles per day in Stage 1 (head less than 30) to 2.0 trips and 3.7 miles in Stage 7 (head 80 or older). With more than 75 percent of households in each stage consisting of only two members, the magnitude of the decline in travel cannot be attributed solely to differences in household size. Rather, differences in mobility are most likely affected by the same forces which contribute to the decline in travel in single person and childless couple households noted above, but also, in this case, by the nature of the relationship between unrelated individuals and the degree to which activities and travel resources are shared.

SUMMARY AND CONCLUSIONS

It should be noted that the life cycle patterns described are based on cross-sectional data, taken at one point in time. Although the analysis of these data has the advantage of not confounding life cycle changes with changes in the transportation system (i.e., the diffusion of private motor vehicles, the expansion of the highway network, etc.), the data do not portray life cycle experiences over time, but represent a synthesis of coexisting families at different stages. Forecasts of travel behavior and personal energy consumption based on cross-sectional data such as these run the risk of assuming greater constancy in behavioral patterns than may exist even within such a well-defined segment of the population as a family life cycle stage. For this reason, the travel patterns of households based on conditions in 1977-78 will probably become less accurate descriptors of behavior over the life cycle as time goes by due to adaptations to energy conditions, social and demographic changes, and other factors which affect daily travel demand. Nevertheless, the life cycle patterns of travel are still valuable indicators of the adjustment made by families in different stages to the transportation environment as recently as 1978.

From the analysis of household travel patterns by life cycle stage, the empirical results and the life cycle approach upon which they are based can be used to assess the energy implications of personal travel as the elements of demand and supply of energy continue to shift. On the supply side, the impact of changes in energy supply due to higher fuel prices or to restrictions such as gasoline rationing can be evaluated from a life cycle perspective. On the demand side, the life cycle approach may be used to forecast the demand for energy for travel as social and demographic trends emerge.

RELATED RESEARCH

Aldous, Joan (1978), Family Careers, Developmental Changes in Families, New York: John Wiley and Sons.

Burch, William R., Jr. (1966), "Wilderness - The Life Cycle and Forest Recreational Choice," Journal of Forestry, 64, 606-610.

David, M.H. (1962), Family Composition and Consumption, Amsterdam: North Holland Publishing Company.

Duvall, Evelyn M. (1971), Family Development, 4th ed., Philadelphia: J.B. Lippincott Company.

Glick, Paul C. (1947), "Updating the Life Cycle of the Family," Journal of Marriage and the Family, 39, 5-13.

_____, and Norton, Arthur J. (1977), "Marrying, Divorcing, and Living Together in the U.S. Today," Population Bulletin, 32, Washington, D.C.: Population Reference Bureau, Inc.

Hareven, Tamara K. (1977), "The Family Cycle in Historical Perspective: A Proposal for a Developmental Approach," in The Family Life Cycle in European Societies, ed. Jean Cuisenier, The Hague: Mouton.

Hendricks, G. and Youmans, K.C. (1973), Consumer Durables and Installment Debt: A Study of American Households, Ann Arbor, Michigan: Survey Research Center, University of Michigan.

Hill, Reuban and Roy T. Rodgers (1964), "The Developmental Approach," in Handbook of Marriage and the Family, ed. Harold T. Christensen, Chicago: Rand-McNally and Company.

Knoke, David and Thompson, Randall (1977), "Voluntary Association Membership Trends and the Family Life Cycle," Social Forces, 56, 48-65.

Lansing, John B. and Morgan, James N. (1955), "Consumer Finances Over the Life Cycle," in Consumer Behavior, Vol. 2, ed. Lincoln H. Clark, New York: New York University Press, 36-51.

Milstein, Jeffrey S. (1980), personal communication.

_____, (1977), "Energy Conservation and Travel Behavior," Washington, D.C.: Department of Energy.

Modell, J. et al. (1978), "Social Change and Transition to Adulthood in Historical Perspective," in The American Family in Social-Historical Perspective, second edition, ed. Michael Gordon, New York: St. Martin's Press.

Murphy, Patrick E. and Staples, William A. (1979), "A Modernized Family Life Cycle," Journal of Consumer Research, 6, 12-22.

Nelson, E.E. and B.C. Starr (1972), "Interpretation of Research on Age," in Aging and Society, eds. M.W. Riley et al., New York: Russell Sage.

New York Times (1980), "Cause and Effect at the U.S. Gasoline Pump," The New York Times, Sunday, March 16, p. E-1.

Norton, Arthur J. (1978), "The Influence of Alternative Life Styles on Traditional Life Cycle Measures," paper presented at the Annual Meeting of the American Sociological Association in San Francisco, Calif., Sept. 4 - 8.

Shonka, D.B. ed., (1979), Transportation Energy Conservation Data Book: Edition 3, Oak Ridge, Tenn.: Oak Ridge National Laboratory.

Snedecor, George W. and Cochran, William G. (1967), Statistical Methods, 6th edition, Ames, Iowa: The Iowa State University Press.

Trost, Jan (1977), "The Family Life Cycle: A Problematic Concept," in The Family Life Cycle in European Societies," ed. Jean Cuisenier, The Hague: Mouton.

U.S. Bureau of the Census (1973a), Family Composition, Subject Report of 1970 Census of Population, Washington, D.C.: U.S. Government Printing Office.

_____, (1973b), Persons by Family Characteristics, Subject Report of 1970 Census of Population, Washington, D.C.: U.S. Government Printing Office.

_____, (1975), <u>Housing of Senior Citizens</u>, Subject Report of 1970 Census of Housing, Washington, D.C.: U.S. Government Printing Office.

_____, (1979a), <u>Marital Status and Living Arrangements</u>, Current Population Reports, Population Characteristics, Washington, D.C.: U.S. Government Printing Office.

_____, (1979b), <u>Household and Family Characteristics</u>, Current Population Reports, Population Characteristics, Washington, D.C.: U.S. Government Printing Office.

U.S. Department of Commerce (19800, <u>1980 Industrial Outlook</u>, Washington, D.C.: U.S. Government Printing Office.

U.S. Department of Transportation (n.d.), "Preliminary National Personal Transportation Study (NPTS) Results."

_____, (1980), <u>1977 Nationwide Personal Transportation Study-Users' Guide for the Public Use Tapes</u>, Washington, D.C.: Federal Highway Administration.

Wells, William C., and Gubar, George (1966), "Life Cycle Concept in Marketing Research," <u>Journal of Marketing Research</u>, 3, 355-63.

CONSERVATION AND SOLAR ADOPTION

- Diffusion of Energy Conservation and Technologies

- Multi-Attribute Analysis of Solar and Other Space Heating Preferences

- Consumer Adoption of Solar Energy Systems

- Adopting Solar and Conservation

DIFFUSION OF ENERGY CONSERVATION
AND TECHNOLOGIES

Dorothy Leonard-Barton

This chapter presents data from three California studies: one study on the acceptance of energy conservation (both behavioral changes and investment in energy-efficient equipment) and two studies on the acceptance of residential solar equipment. The three studies deal with the diffusion of similar energy-conserving innovations among similar but not identical California populations. Specifically, evidence is offered suggesting the important role of interpersonal communication in the diffusion of energy-conserving behaviors and technologies—a role largely overlooked in current diffusion efforts.

SOURCES FOR THE DATA

The Energy Conservation Study (1978)

In Palo Alto, California, in-home (personal) interviews were conducted with 215 homeowners living in three different subdivision tracts. Measures were obtained of attitudes, self-reported behaviors, and of actual gas, water, and electricity usage over a one-year period which coincided with the last year of a severe drought in the region in 1978. The three types of houses in the sample differed considerably in construction and, hence, in degree of energy efficiency. The major dependent variables in the study were (1) adoption of energy-conserving practices and equipment (including solar water heating), and (2) levels of natural gas usage in the home.

The Pilot Solar Study (1979)

In three north California counties around the San Francisco Bay area, in-home (personal) interviews were conducted in Spring 1979 with 215 homeowners, 111 of whom had purchased and installed solar equipment (Adopters) and 104 of whom lived next door

The author gratefully acknowledges the work of numerous colleagues at the Institute of Communication Research, Stanford University, on the three studies reported herein: Everett N. Rogers, Tamar Avi-Itzhak, Ramon Garcia, Eugene Rosa, Ronald Aditikarya, and Ila Patel. The study of energy conservation in Palo Alto was supported by the Institute for Energy Studies, Stanford University. The two solar energy studies were supported by the California State Energy Commission.

or within a few houses of a solar adopter but who had either never considered purchasing similar equipment or who had considered, and rejected, such an innovation (Nonadopters). The nonadopters lived in houses similar to (sometimes identical to) adopters' and were usually of comparably high socioeconomic status. The purpose of this pilot study was to explore at depth the barriers to solar adoption and the experience of solar owners with their equipment as a basis for constructing a questionnaire to be administered state-wide. The major dependent variable was adoption of residential solar equipment.

California Statewide Survey (1979)

In fall 1979, personal interviews were conducted with 812 homeowners who constituted a representative sample of California homeowners. The purposes of the study were to determine the receptivity of California homeowners to solar equipment, including perceived barriers and advantages, to identify communication channels utilized, and to measure levels of awareness, interest, and intention to purchase. Only 21 of the 812 respondents already owned solar equipment. Therefore, the major dependent variable in this study was intention to adopt.

While these three California homeowner populations are certainly distinct, there is considerable demographic, attitudinal, and behavioral similarity among those individuals who ranked high on the conservation-adoption variables used as dependent variables. Moreover, some questions and behavioral indexes were the same in all three studies. While these three studies cannot be treated as one, there is some overlap in measurement and some consistency in the respondent population.

BACKGROUND

The importance of interpersonal communication in the diffusion of innovations has been long recognized. Rogers and Shoemaker (1971) note that while mass media serve to raise awareness of an innovation, interpersonal communication is relatively more important at the "persuasion stage," when potential adopters are making their decision whether or not to try the new product or idea. From this accumulated evidence, it would seem that there is reason to anticipate the flow of information about energy-conserving innovations through interpersonal channels. However, the evidence documenting the role of interpersonal communication has been drawn largely from studies about the diffusion of highly visible innovations such as hybrid corn. Many energy-conserving innovations such as insulation or turning down furnace thermostats are not highly visible. Friends or neighbors might not know that someone near them had adopted, and therefore the "word-of-mouth advertising" might not work well for energy-conserving behaviors.

Although solar equipment is highly visible, there is also reason to question whether it will diffuse by means of interpersonal communication with peers. It is a high risk innovation. Many people perceive solar as technically immature. Therefore, one might expect potential adopters would be more influenced by technical or professional advice than by the advice of friends and neighbors and, consequently, that the "web of word-of-mouth" would be less effective for solar than for less risky innovations.

RESULTS

Networks About Energy Conservation

To take a micro-level view of energy conservation information networks, let us examine sociometric data from one of the three neighborhoods studied in the 1978 Energy Conservation Study. This particular neighborhood is fairly well-defined geographically as three cul-de-sacs, but divided almost in half by a well-traveled street. The respondents are middle-income homeowners, housed in uninsulated, flat-roofed structures with a large proportion of glass in floor-to-ceiling windows and sliding doors. These typical "California-style" houses are extremely energy-inefficient and difficult to retrofit for energy efficiency.

First, we determined usage patterns of natural gas in the neighborhood, comparing this group of homeowners with the entire sample of 215 which had been divided according to gas usage into quartiles (see Figure 1). While a majority of the homeowners in this one neighborhood pictured in Figure 1 fall in the highest gas use quartile for the total three neighborhood sample, several in the upper half of this neighborhood map are in the lowest 25 percentile.

Next, we attempted to identify the opinion leaders on energy conservation in the neighborhood by asking who conserves the most energy and who is the best source of information about energy-conserving practices. Not surprisingly, there was no consensus in the lower neighborhood section about who was the most dutiful conserver, since most of these homeowners were in the upper 25th percentile in gas usage. However, there was more general agreement about gas conservers among respondents in the upper half of the map. Out of four households identified by respondents as energy conserving, three were, indeed, in the lowest 25th percentile of gas usage. The fourth (number 36) was in the upper 50th percentile.

Finally, we mapped the cliques in the neighborhood by determining the linkages among homeowners through the use of a computer program called NEGOPY. Through this program, the researchers can group the respondents and identify both "isolates" (respondents who do not have connections with others in the social network) and "liaisons" (individuals who do not

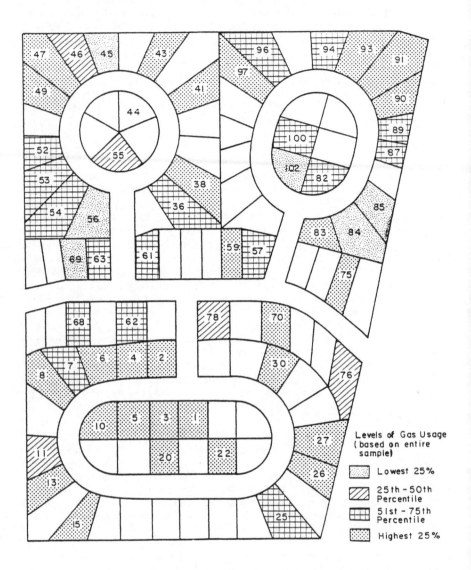

Figure 1: Levels of Household Gas Usage in One Neighborhood

belong to just one clique and who communicate with individuals in two or more cliques). As previous research on social networks showed (Granovetter 1973), such liaisons perform an extremely important function in the transfer of information through "weak links". In this neighborhood, number 46 is a particularly useful individual because he has friends in three of the four cliques which were identified. If one wished to disseminate information about energy conservation in this neighborhood, number 46 would be an excellent choice as an opinion leader and disseminator.

This study established (1) that information about energy conservation and fairly accurate identification of conservers can be transmitted interpersonally through a neighborhood network even when the energy saving innovations are not visible, and (2) that such conservers are regarded as credible sources of information by others in their networks. In short, there are identifiable energy conservation opinion leaders. This Energy Conservation Study did not address the question of how such energy opinion leaders compared in importance with other potential sources of information on energy conservation. In contrast, the two studies on the diffusion of solar equipment did determine the sources of information that respondents considered useful.

Interpersonal Sources of Information

As Table 1 indicates, both the adopters and their nonadopting neighbors in the Solar Pilot Study considered interpersonal sources of information to be the most useful when they were considering the purchase of solar equipment. For adopters, the question eliciting useful information sources referred to those sources actually used in the purchase decision. In the case of most nonadopters, this was a hypothetical question, although some nonadopters had actually shopped for solar equipment. Nonadopters seemed somewhat less risk-prone purchasers than their early adopter neighbors, in that they depended more upon friends as potentially useful sources on information than upon equipment sales personnel. Adopters, whom one would expect to be less dependent on the opinions of peers in making a purchase decision, found the sales personnel more useful than friends.

The Influence of Present Owners

In the statewide survey of California homeowners, we found that almost one-half of the respondents in the statewide survey had seen some type of solar equipment in place, one-sixth of them in a solar adopter's home. One-fourth of California homeowners know at least one person owning solar. A major question for promoters of solar energy is whether this interpersonal contact is a positive or negative influence on a person's decision whether or not to purchase solar equipment.

TABLE 1

SOURCES OF INFORMATION ABOUT SOLAR EQUIPMENT
SELECTED AS MOST USEFUL BY ADOPTERS AND NONADOPTERS[a]

	Adopters (N=111)		Nonadopters (N=104)	
Rank	Information Source	Mean Score[b]	Information Source	Mean Score[b]
1st	Sellers of solar equipment	3.88	Friends' solar equipment	2.65
2nd	Friends' solar equipment	2.70	Sellers of solar equipment	2.44
3rd	Magazines	2.14	Magazines	2.33
4th	Textbooks	1.53	Demonstrations	2.09
5th	Seminars on solar	1.47	Textbooks	1.83
6th	Newspapers	1.37	Seminars on solar	1.60
7th	Energy fairs	1.21	Newspapers	1.54
8th	Alt. technology groups	1.05	Alt. technology groups	1.43
9th	Utility companies	1.01	Utility companies	1.37

a.   Adopters were asked to select and rank in order of importance those sources of information which had proven most
useful to them. Nonadopter respondents who had considered
purchasing solar equipment were asked what sources had been
most useful. Respondents who had never even considered
solar were asked what sources of information were potentially most useful.

b.   This score reflects frequency of mention weighted by
ranking in importance. Range is 0 to 6, where 0 means not
mentioned, 1 means mentioned but not ranked, and 2 through
6 are rankings from low to high.

In California, the answer would seem to be that it is a positive one.

In fact, as Table 2 indicates, the single strongest predictor of intention to purchase solar equipment is the number of owners a potential adopter knows. Evidently, potential adopters are being motivated to adopt by present solar owners. Another of the major predictors of intention to adopt is the number of years respondents believe it would take for solar equipment to pay for itself in utility bill savings (see Table 2). Some people's perceptions of payback may be affected by their experience with solar equipment, for there is a negative relationship between the number of solar owners a person knows and the length of the payback period he/she is likely to figure on ($r = -.14$, $p < .001$). That is, respondents who know solar owners tend, like the owners themselves, to calculate shorter payback periods for solar equipment. It should be noted that economic payback is also a function of income (because of the tax credit) and of the size of the respondents' utility bills.

TABLE 2

MULTIPLE REGRESSION OF INDEPENDENT VARIABLES
PREDICTING INTENTION TO PURCHASE SOLAR EQUIPMENT[a]

	Multiple R	R^2	R^2 Change	B	Beta	F
Index of voluntary simplicity behaviors	.38	.15	.09	.2878	.1350	11.58
Attitude toward solar equipment	.44	.20	.05	.1350	.1333	11.82
Number of solar owners known by respondent	.67	.45	.25	.6047	1.1699	164.83
Number of years respondent believes solar equipment takes to pay back	.68	.46	.02	-.2348	-.1186	9.38

a. Nine other variables were entered into the regression equation but the F statistic associated with each failed of significance at the .05 level, and all nine were therefore dropped: (1) awareness of tax credit, (2) socioeconomic status, (3) respondent's age, (4) probability of moving, (5) perceived effect of solar equipment on house resale value, (6) mechanical ability, (7) expectations about future energy cost increases, (8) utility bill, and (9) attitude towards the energy crisis.

A third significant predictor, the attitude toward solar equipment, was measured by three questions dealing with respondents' perceptions of how technically developed the technology is, how desirable solar energy is as an energy source for household use, and how practical solar equipment is for the respondent personally. The responses suggest that perceptions of how personally practical the purchase of solar equipment would be are highly influenced by the experience of peers with the equipment. Respondents who know solar owners are no more likely than those who do not to believe that solar energy is a desirable energy source for household use, and are actually very slightly more skeptical about the technical maturity of solar equipment than are people who know no solar owners. However, respondents who know solar owners are almost twice as likely as those who do not to believe that solar equipment is personally practical.

Finally, the index of voluntary simplicity behaviors, which had been developed during the three studies reported herein, measures the respondents' level of participation in the 18 activities which decrease consumption (of various kinds) or which increase self-sufficiency (Table 3). In the Energy Conservation Study and the pilot study of solar adopters and nonadopters, this index was found to correlate significantly with interest in energy-conserving investments such as insulation, and with adoption of solar water heating. The voluntary simplicity index also correlates ($r=.29$, $p<.001$) with the number of solar owners known by the respondent in the statewide study. That is, people who recycle, buy secondhand goods, exchange services with others, bicycle, garden, etc., are more likely than their peers to know solar owners.

All of the variables which are significantly related to the intention to purchase are also related to knowledge of solar owners. This finding adds support to the assertion that interpersonal communication is very important in the diffusion of solar technology.

IMPLICATIONS FOR SOLAR MARKETERS AND FUTURE RESEARCH

Interpersonal contacts are probably being underutilized in most present efforts to diffuse solar technology. Mass advertising may not address some of the very real hesitations people have in purchasing a technology which is perceived as being novel. While cost is a major deterrent, so is the idea that such equipment is simply impractical, for one reason or another.

The findings in these studies suggest that a credible source of information about residential solar equipment is a person who embodies "safety" credibility, rather than "professional" credibility. That is, potential adopters appear to desire and seek information from solar owners, people who are "like me."

TABLE 3

ITEMS IN THE VOLUNTARY SIMPLICITY INDEX
IN ORDER OF THE RATE OF ADOPTION (N=812)[a]

Scale Item (Abbreviated Version)	Number of Respondents Giving a Positive Response	Percentage Of All Respondents
1. Make gifts instead of buying	557	71.9
2. Eat meatless main meals	566	70.8
3. Change oil in car	557	69.8
4. Get instruction to increase self-reliance	518	65.3
5. Recycle newspapers	500	62.3
6. Make clothes or furniture	475	59.5
7. Recycle cans	434	54.2
8. Recycle glass	424	52.9
9. Grow vegetables	406	50.7
10. Bike for exercise	398	49.9
11. Buy at garage sales	386	48.4
12. Exchange goods or services	352	44.3
13. Contribute to ecology organizations	262	33.1
14. Buy clothing secondhand	255	32.1
15. Bike of errands	215	26.8
16. Have compost pile	158	20.3
17. Bike to work	74	9.1
18. Belong to a cooperative	60	7.6

a. These numbers represent the total number of positive responses, including all responses ranging from tentative
positives (e.g., "sometimes," or "a few items") to a strong
affirmative (e.g., "always do," or "all items").   Answer
categories ranges from one (low) to five (high) for all
items in the scale; category labels differed among the scale
items.

At present, active solar collectors to heat the home or water appear to have greatest appeal for certain types of people--well-educated individuals of fairly high income. Potential adopters are passing information around among themselves, which should aid in the diffusion of solar technology among this class of people. However, communication theory suggests that such "interlocking" communications are relatively closed systems. Innovations diffuse rapidly within the networks of friends, but pass with greater difficulty to other networks. Of course, if all the well-educated, relatively wealthy individuals in California (let alone the nation) were to adopt solar equipment, the market would be very active, indeed.

If residential solar equipment is to be accepted on the scale desired by government, then so-called "weak links" are needed between the circles of present owners and potential adopters from lower socioeconomic classes. Solar marketers may need to provide mechanisms for the interpersonal transfer of information across neighborhoods and among different types of working people. For instance, solar companies might "break into" new neighborhoods by offering an incentive to the first adopters in that area, with the proviso that such homeowners display their equipment in a certain number of open houses. Even in advertising, current solar owners could be utilized, and video mini-tours could be provided of actual homes in use, rather than of comparatively sterile demonstration models.

Likewise, the relationship between the index of voluntary simplicity behaviors and the intention to purchase solar suggests that interpersonal networks which grow out of cooperatives, gardening groups, and classes in carpentry or car maintenance might be utilized in the dissemination of information about solar. Solar equipment as a means toward self-sufficiency appeals to individuals interested in voluntary simplicity.

If the communicated experience of peers with a new behavior or product is more important to later adopters than to early, then the role of interpersonal communication in the diffusion of energy-conserving behaviors and technologies will increase in importance as these behaviors and technologies diffuse more widely.

RELATED RESEARCH

Arndt, Johan (1967), "Role of Product-Related Conversations in the Diffusion of a New Product," Journal of Marketing Research, IV (August), 291-295.

_____, (1968), "A Cold-Blooded Analysis of Movie-Going as a Diffusion Process," unpublished paper, Graduate School of Business, Columbia University, New York.

Butti, Ken and Perlin, John (1971), "Solar Water Heaters in California, 1891-1930," Co-Evolution Quarterly, Fall.

Coleman, James, Katz, Elihu, and Menzel, Herbert (1957), "The Diffusion of an Innovation Among Physicians," Sociometry, 20, 253-270.

Elgin, Duane and Mitchell, Arnold (1977), "Voluntary Simplicity," The Co-Evolution Quarterly, Summer.

Granovetter, Mark (1973), "The Strength of Weak Ties," American Journal of Sociology, 78, 1360-1380.

Kotler, Philip and Zaltman, Gerald (1971), "Social Marketing: An Approach to Planned Social Change," Journal of Marketing, 35, (July), 3-12.

Leonard-Barton, Dorothy (1980), "Voluntary Simplicity Lifestyles and Energy Conservation," paper submitted to the Journal of Consumer Research.

_____, and Rogers, Everett M. (1979), "Adoption of Energy Conservation Among California Homeowners," paper presented at the International Communication Association meeting, Philadelphia, May 1-5.

_____, and Rogers, Everett M. (1980), "Voluntary Simplicity in California: Precursor or Fad?," paper presented at the American Association for the Advancement of Science, San Francisco, California, January 7.

Midgley, David (1977), Innovation and New Product Marketing, New York: John Wiley and Sons.

Richards, William D. (1975), A Manual for Network Analysis (Using the NEGOPY Network Analysis Program), Institute for Communication Research, Stanford University.

Rogers, Everett M. (1973), Communication Strategies for Family Planning, New York: The Free Press.

_____, and Shoemaker, Floyd (1971), Communication of Innovations: A Cross-Cultural Approach, New York: The Free Press.

Whyte, William (1954), "The Web of Word of Mouth," Fortune, November, 140ff.

MULTI-ATTRIBUTE ANALYSIS OF SOLAR
AND OTHER SPACE HEATING PREFERENCES

M.K. Berkowitz

G.H. Haines

A good in the Lancaster (1971) model is defined by a specific bundle of characteristics. The theory suggests that consumers react in their purchasing decisions not to goods in their own right, but to the inherent package of characteristics embodied in each good. It follows that the utility derived from any good is equivalent to the utility derived from the package of characteristics representing that good if Lancaster's perception of goods is correct. The purpose of this chapter is to examine this relationship with specific reference to home heating modes.

The similarity between the Lancaster model and the model developed by Rosenberg (1956) is readily apparent. The Rosenberg model states that attitude, "defined as a relatively stable affective response to an object" toward the j-th good, A_j, is simply

$$A_j = \sum_{i=1}^{r} \alpha_i X_{ij},\qquad(1)$$

where X_{ij} represents the perceived instrumentality (i.e., the respondent's estimate as to whether, and to what extent, the value in question would tend to be achieved or blocked through use of a particular heating mode) and α_i represents the value importance of the i-th attribute or characteristic (i.e., whether a particular attribute of home heating systems is important to a consumer as a "source of satisfaction").

The Rosenberg relation specified in (1) will be examined to determine if heating mode preferences are formed on the basis of the characteristics embodied in the alternative home heating systems. Four tests are presented: (a) determination of the proportion of respondents within the sample whose attitude score ranked a heating mode highest and that mode was also identified as most preferred by those individuals, (b) regression of attitude score against actual most preferred heating mode, (c) regression of attitude score against actual preferences determined by pairwise mode comparisons, and (d) confusion matrix of heating mode ranked by attitude score versus rank determined by actual preferences using pairwise mode comparison.

Research support for this study was provided by Energy, Mines and Resources Canada. The opinions, as well as errors, are the sole responsibility of the authors.

DATA

A sample of 2109 households across Canada responded to a questionnaire distributed by Market Facts of Canada Ltd. The sample was balanced according to census data for geographic divisions and within divisions by total household income, population density, age, and language preference. Preferences toward four heating modes (gas, oil, electric, and solar) were determined by a series of pairwise mode comparisons and alternatively by a question asking respondents their most preferred home heating mode. Sixteen characteristics were presented to respondents and they were asked to evaluate the value importance of each attribute and, for each heating mode, to estimate the perceived instrumentality of each mode toward the achievement of each value importance goal for each product attribute. The question statements used were based on Hanson's (1972) research, which developed a questionnaire method for eliciting value importance and perceived instrumentality from respondents. Respondents were also asked which characteristics were most important in their purchase decision. Four attributes proved most frequently important: reliability, absence of fumes or odors, safety, and future availability of fuel supply. The attitude measures examined in this study are assumed to be based on these four most important attributes.

RESULTS

Overall, 21.5 percent of respondents stated that they would prefer their homes to be heated by solar energy. When respondents were classified by their level of knowledge about solar heating, of those who felt they knew "quite a lot" about solar heating, 55.6 percent stated they would prefer their homes to be heated by solar energy. The problem, then, is to understand what needs to be done to translate these overall preferences into action on the part of consumers. The relation between overall preferences and heating system attributes or characteristics is one of the crucial links that must be understood to achieve this translation. This is the relation studied in what follows.

Test One

The first test examines the proportion of respondents within the sample whose attitude score ranked a heating mode highest and that mode was also identified as most preferred by those individuals. Since solar heating systems differ from the other three heating modes in terms of the timing of financial outflows, i.e., solar systems have high initial capital costs and low annual charges while the reverse is true for the other modes, initial purchase price and annual operating costs are included as attributes affecting consumer attitudes. While individuals should consider lifetime costs in making their purchase decisions, it is not readily apparent from the data that they do so. Inclusion of these factors in the attitude score enables an analysis of the effect of another character- istic, timing of cash flows, on the formation of preferences to be analyzed. To summarize, the attitude score for the k-th individual is measured in each of the following ways:

$$A_{jk} = \Sigma_i^4 \, \alpha_{ik} \, X_{ijk}$$

(perceived instrumentality times value importance for most impor- tant attributes)   (2)

$$A_{jk} = \Sigma_i^6 \, \alpha_{ik} \, X_{ijk}$$

(perceived instrumentality times value importance for most impor- tant attributes and cost vari- ables)   (3)

The results presented in Table 1 suggests relatively strong predictive ability of the models. Using only the four salient attributes, 50.0 percent of the sample concurred on highest attitude score and most preferred mode with strong relationships exhibited by those respondents preferring solar and electric heating and relatively weak relationships for those preferring oil and gas heating. Once the attitude score is amended so as to include costs, the aggregate predictive ability of the model increases to 52.8 percent. As seen in Table 1, solar heating is relatively unaffected by costs, remaining at about 75.0 percent predictive ability. On the other hand, there is a significant drop in electric heating once costs are included due to the perceived higher costs of this mode outweighing the positive attributes associated with electric heating. The reverse is true for oil and gas heating, the predictive ability doubling in each case with the inclusion of costs.

TABLE 1

PROPORTION OF SAMPLE RANKING A HEATING MODE HIGHEST USING ATTITUDE SCORE AND ALSO SELECTING THAT MODE AS MOST PREFERRED

Heating Mode	Attitude Score Measured by:	
	Equation 2	Equation 3
Oil	20.9%	42.5%
Gas	20.2	40.4
Electric	54.1	43.3
Solar	76.5	74.5
Aggregate	50.0	52.8

Test Two

The second test is a regression of the individual's most preferred heating mode against the attitude score for that mode. Where a mode was selected as preferred by a respondent, the explanatory variable representing that mode was assigned 1 while the remaining modes were assigned 0. Measuring attitude by (2), the estimated equation (with t-ratios in parentheses) is:

$$A_j = 151.422\ X_1 + 149.589\ X_2 + 162.799\ X_3 + 169.963\ X_4$$
$$\quad (71.641) \qquad (82.964) \qquad (117.827) \qquad (119.934)$$

where X_1, X_2, X_3, X_4 refer respectively to oil, gas, electric, and solar. Using (3), the equation is:

$$A_j = 187.299\ X_1 + 196.500\ X_2 + 198.198\ X_3 + 209.651\ X_4$$
$$\quad (47.922) \qquad (58.936) \qquad (77.574) \qquad (80.004)$$

The regression coefficients represent the average attitude score of the most preferred alternative if there was a simple one-to-one correspondence between attitudes and preferences. These results suggest the hypothesis that some attributes may be relevant for respondents in determining attitudes for only some, but not all, heating modes. This is contrary to the usual, and usually unstated, assumption that if an attribute is relevant in determining attitude for one alternative, it is relevant for all alternatives. The alternative hypothesis is that there exists a systematic difference in the value importance associated with the characteristics embodied in alternative heating modes. Because it is not possible to use the same data base to both suggest and test hypotheses, it is clear that further data collection and research are required.

Test Three

While individuals are generally able to discriminate between most preferred and least preferred alternatives, inter-mediate rankings provided by a forced ranking procedure tend to yield ambiguous preference relationships within the intermediate range. In an attempt to overcome this problem, respondents were requested to make pairwise mode preference comparisons. For each individual, a 4 × 4 matrix was constructed where, for example, an individual preferring gas heating to oil heating would have 1 entered in the respective cell and 0 entered in the cell corresponding to oil preferred to gas. Row totals were then calculated yielding a preference value for each mode. Attitude scores were then regressed for each mode against the corresponding preference value for that mode. Irrespective of the manner in which attitude is measured, the coefficients are uniformly significant. Moreover, the coefficients are all positive, implying a direct relationship between the ordinal measured preference values for heating modes and attitudes about the modes based upon characteristics.

Test Four

The final test examined the confusion matrix of heating mode rankings by attitude scores versus the rankings derived from the ordinal measured overall preference values. When ties between the preference values are allowed and A_j is measured using (2), Table 2 presents the corresponding confusion matrix. While the diagonal elements do not uniformly dominate, the extremes of most and least preferred do display the expected dominance.

TABLE 2

CONFUSION MATRIX OF RANKINGS BY ATTITUDE
SCORES AND ORDINAL MEASURED PREFERENCES

		Actual Rank Using Ordinal Measured Preference Values				
		1	2	3	4	n
	1	.41	.22	.24	.22	1223
Predicted Rank Using Attitude	2	.22	.27	.26	.22	999
Scored Measured by 5-a	3	.22	.31	.28	.20	1034
	4	.15	.20	.22	.36	904
	n	1563	907	931	759	4160

Overall percent correct predictions = 34%
Highest and lowest only percent correct predictions = 39%

For the subsample consisting of those respondents exhibiting complete ordering, i.e., no ties between ordinal measured preference values, the overall predictive ability of the model is increased to 37 percent while the predictive ability at the extremes is increased to 45 percent. Again, however, the diagonal elements do not dominate. The inclusion of cost variables reduced the model's predictive ability, both overall and at the extremes.

These results tend to confirm a suspicion that intermediary rankings are ambiguous, even using a pairwise mode comparison approach.

SUMMARY AND CONCLUSIONS

Further details regarding this analysis are available from the authors. The results presented in this paper tend to support the hypothesis that consumer preferences for heating modes can be disaggregated into their preferences for the bundles of characteristics which comprise each heating mode. While heating costs tend to be a significant variable in forming preferences for conventional modes, costs appear to be less relevant to those respondents preferring solar heating. For those respondents, system reliability, safety, absence of fumes and odors, and the future availability of the fuel supply are the primary factors which lead to their strong preferences for solar heating.

The need for both the government and the private sector to increase the level of research, development, and demonstration in the solar area is apparent from this study. It is clear that a more reliable product is required for market acceptability. Such technological advances are not only necessary, they must be demonstrated to market participants as well. A favorable attitude toward solar heating already exists. What is required is the initiative to build a product which will meet the attitudinal expectations of people.

RELATED RESEARCH

Bass, F.M., Tigert, D., and Lonsdale, R.T. (1968), "Market Segmentation: Group Versus Individual Behavior," Journal of Marketing Research, 4, 264-70.

Bass, F.M. and Talarzyk, W.W. (1972), "An Attitude Model for the Study of Brand Preference," Journal of Marketing Research, 9, 93-6.

Crow, R.T., and Ratchford, B. T. (1975), "An Econometric Approach to Forecasting the Market Potential of Electric Automobiles," Proceedings of the Workshop on Energy Demand, W. Nordhaus, editor, International Institute for Applied Analysis, Lexenburg, Austria.

Fisher, B.A. (1950), Statistical Methods for Research Workers, New York: Hafner.

Hanson, F. (1972), Consumer Choice Behavior, New York: The Free Press.

Houthakker, H. (1960), "Additive Preferences," Econometrica, 28, 244-57.

Lancaster, K. (1971), Consumer Demand: A New Approach, New York: Columbia Press.

Robertson, W.H. (1960), "Programming Fisher's Exact Method of Comparing Two Percentages," Technometrics, 2, 103-7.

Rogers, E. and Shoemaker, F. (1971), Communication of Innovations: A Cross-Cultural Approach, New York: Free Press.

Rosenberg, W. J. (1956), "Cognitive Structure and Attitudinal Affect," Journal of Abnormal and Social Psychology, 53, 367-72.

CONSUMER ADOPTION OF SOLAR ENERGY SYSTEMS

Duncan G. LaBay
Thomas C. Kinnear

Solar energy has been categorized as "the contemporary holy grail... promis(ing) energy salvation but (eluding) capture." (Pertschuk 1978, p. 3). In the past, it has been inefficient and more costly than other energy sources; from an economic viewpoint solar energy was competitive only in certain limited applications. Recent technological changes combined with the increase costs of conventional energy sources are expected to result in solar energy systems contributing a vastly increased percentage of United States energy needs by the year 2000.

Given the current activity and interest in solar energy and the future growth anticipated in this industry, an unusual opportunity exists for the study of the consumer buyer behavior process surrounding solar energy products. Very little is presently known concerning the buying process used by individuals and firms adopting solar energy systems.

Several major research questions are very relevant. First, categorizing those individuals who have already adopted solar energy systems as innovators, how have these people evaluated solar products? Do innovators share common characteristics, in terms of demographics or their perceptions of various attributes of solar energy systems? How do these people differ from those who have considered but not adopted such systems, and from those who have not yet considered solar products? In their evaluation of solar energy systems, what are the relevant factors considered by adopters and non-adopters? Do adopters and non-adopters consider the same or different factors? Are similar factors differentially evaluated by the two groups?

This study focuses on these research questions, presenting empirical results obtained from a sample of: (1) consumers of residential solar heating and hot water heating systems, (2) potential consumers who are aware of and knowledgeable about residential solar systems but who have not installed such a system, and (3) potential consumers who are not knowledgeable about such systems.

The focus of the research presented here is on individuals throughout the adoption process. The inclusion of aware non-adopters as a group worthy of attention, in addition to adopters and unaware non-adopters, represents a departure from traditional research directions. In an effort to assess the importance of product and situation specific variables on existing theory, this research explores the appropriateness of concepts identified in the larger body of adoption-diffusion research to a product category which entails high technology, represents a

115

large financial commitment, and most importantly has overriding lifestyle implications.

HYPOTHESES

In keeping with the focus of innovativeness established in the adoption research, the following hypotheses are proposed to examine demographic characteristics of adopters and non-adopters.

H1   Adopters and non-adopters of residential solar energy systems differ on the basis of selected demographic measures. As compared to non-adopters, adopters are younger (H1.1), more highly educated (H1.2), have higher income (H1.3), are earlier in the family life cycle (H1.4), and have higher occupational status (H1.5).

H2   Adopters and non-adopters differ on the basis of their perceptions of certain systems. As compared to non-adopters, adopters rate such systems as greater in relative advantage over other energy sources (H2.1), lower in financial risk (H2.2), and social risk (H2.3), lower in complexity (H2.4), more compatible with their personal values (H2.5), more highly observable by others (H2.6), and more possible to try on a limited basis (H2.7).

H3   No differences exist between adopters and aware non-adopters in the product-related, economic, or social factors of importance considered in the residential solar energy system adoption decision.

H4   No differences exist among adopters of residential solar energy systems dependent upon time of adoption in either demographic characteristics (H4.1) or attribute perceptions (H4.2).

H5   Attribute perceptions of residential solar energy systems are more effective than demographic characteristics in predicting an individual's category membership as an adopter, or non-adopter.

METHODS

The data for analysis were collected through a mail survey of 631 individuals in three subsets of the general population of Maine: adopters of solar home heating or hot water heating systems, non-adopters who were aware of and knowledgeable about such systems, and unaware non-adopters. Three questionnaires, each sharing certain common sections, were developed for use with the three population groups. Table 1 summarizes the information areas addressed by the survey.

Various bivariate and multivariate techniques were utilized in analyzing the data. Bivariate crosstabs were used to evaluate the findings related to personal characteristics, attribute perceptions, factor ratings, and differences dependent upon time of adoption. For each of these cases, chi-square testing was used to evaluate the relevant hypotheses, H1 through H4. Multivariate techniques, specifically multivariate nominal scale analysis (MNA) and dummy variable multiple discriminant function analysis (MDF), were employed to evaluate H5 concerning the importance of attribute perceptions and demographic characteristics in determining adoption. Given the explanatory nature of this study, MNA was chosen as the primary analysis technique.

RESULTS

Demographic Findings

Comparing the adopters with the general population, all of the H1 demographic hypotheses, H1.1 through H1.5, are supported. The adopter is younger, more highly educated, higher in income, earlier in the family life cycle, and higher in occupational status than the general population.

Very few differences are apparent between the adopters and aware non-adopters. Education, income level, and occupation status appear remarkably similar. In age, adopters appear more concentrated around age 35, that is, with less divergence from the categories 26-45. Perhaps reflective of this, there are relatively less single people among adopters, and a larger percentage in the early married stages. These trends are not strong. In general, the adopter and aware non-adopter appear to be very similar, yet very different from the general population.

Attribute Perceptions

Comparing the perceptions of adopters with the perceptions of the general population sample, adopters find solar energy systems to offer greater advantages over other energy sources. Additionally, they evaluate solar systems to be less financially risky, less socially risky, less complex, more compatible with their personal values, and less observable by others.   These results support hypotheses H2.1 through H2.5 concerning innovation perceptions.   The original hypotheses regarding observability, H2.6, and trialability, H2.7, are rejected.

The same direction of results is found when comparing adopters with aware non-adopters. Adopters perceive somewhat greater relative advantage, less risk, less complexity, greater compatibility, and less observability than do aware non-adopters. However, with the exception of complexity and observability, these differences are not statistically significant.

TABLE 1

SURVEY INFORMATION AREAS AND SAMPLE RESPONSE RATES

	Adopters[a]	Aware Non-Adopters[b]	Controlc Group
INFORMATION AREAS			
Perceived characteristics of solar energy systems (relative advantage, complexity, compatibility, perceived risk, observability, trialability)	x	x	x
Economic, social, and product-related factors considered in evaluation	x	x	
Date of adoption	x		
Demographic characteristics (age, education, income, occupational status, family life cycle)	x	x	x
SAMPLE RESPONSE RATES			
Total mailing (n=1018)[d]	147	396	475
Usable returns (n=631)	102	300	229
Response rate (%)	69	76	48
Usable returns by actual category[e]	170	232	229

a. Sampled from lists of known installations obtained from solar dealers, installers, and the Maine Office of Energy Resources.
b. Sampled from lists of unsuccessful applicants for solar hot water tax grants, membership of Maine Solar Energy Association, and registrants from several alternative energy workshops.
c. Sampled from random selection of households from the total Maine population.
d. Excluding bad addresses.
e. The instrument sent to aware non-adopters was designed to screen for and collect full information from actual adopters. Sixty-eight such individuals were identified.

Factor Ratings

The results obtained regarding factors of importance in the solar energy system adoption decision show that the aware non-adopter generally rates each factor to be of greater importance than does the adopter. This trend holds for each factor with the exception of the two of least importance, aesthetics and status-appeal considerations. For eight of fourteen factors, these differences are statistically significant at a .01 probability level or less. From the ordering of the factors, it is apparent that product-related and economic factors are of the highest concern to both adopters and aware non-adopters. Social factors are uniformly evaluated by both groups to be of far less consequence in the adoption decision process.

On the basis of these results, hypothesis H3, which predicted no differences between experimental groups on factor evaluation, is rejected for both product-related and economic factors.

Differences Dependent Upon Time of Adoption

Information from adopters regarding demographic characteristics and their perceptions of the innovation were analyzed against the year of installation of the solar energy system. Considering demographic characteristics only, no significant differences were found (α=.05). Similarly, a consideration of adopters' perceptions of solar energy systems dependent upon their time of adoption showed that few differences exist. Recent adopters were found to evaluate solar energy systems as significantly more compatible with their value systems (p<.005) and involving less social risk (p=.02) than earlier adopters. Ratings of the other perceptions showed no differences dependent upon time of adoption at the .05 level.

These results generally support hypothesis H4 of no differences among adopters on these characteristics and attitudes dependent upon time of adoption, and confirm that adopters so far are quite similar to one another. Taken together with predictions of large numbers of future installations, these results add support to the contention that those who have adopted solar energy systems to date can be classified as true innovators.

Prediction of Adoption Behavior

The results of a series of predictive models using MNA and MDF indicate some support for the contention that attribute perceptions are more effective predictors than demographics. The MNA generalized R^2 and multivariate theta are both higher for the attribute perception model than for the demographic model; similarly the MDF model F-statistics show the same trend.

However, while the attribute perception models are more successful than the demographics models overall in terms of the total
percentage of individuals correctly classified (62 percent
versus 56 percent for the MNA results and 55 percent versus 47
percent for the MDF models), a comparison of the category-
specific results reveals differences.   The results support
hypothesis H5 concerning the prediction of category membership
as an adopter.   For the remaining population categories, no
general support of hypothesis H5 is found.

SUMMARY AND CONCLUSIONS

Several interesting observations emerge from a consideration of the attribute perception and demographic findings for
each sample group.   In comparing summary statistics on these
measures, for each one except trialability, a continuum can be
defined with adopters as a group at one end, the general population group at the other, and aware non-adopters between and
generally closer to the adopters.

The findings regarding observability and trialability are
particularly interesting.   The further one progresses from being
a member of the general population through awareness of solar
energy systems to adoption, the less observable to others one
perceives such an innovation.   Although the results for trial
show that most individuals perceive it likely that some sort of
trial behavior occurs, it must be recognized that even such a
small scale "trial" represents a major financial commitment and
personal involvement. This is due to the nature of the product
class--a long term commitment with no real possibility for
non-involved, low risk trial.   Trial, short of vicarious trial
through the experiences of others, is not an applicable concept
for solar energy systems.

This forces reconsideration of traditional adoption models,
such as that advanced by Robertson (1971), when dealing with a
product representing such a major commitment.   Specifically, it
is likely that for this type of product, legitimization of the
product by the potential buyer would be followed directly by
adoption, with no intervening "trial" stage.

The level of commitment involved in the solar energy system
adoption decision is also evident from the ratings of factors of
importance by both adopters and aware non-adopters.   Economic
and functional considerations are clearly of major concern.

The generally higher evaluations of product and economic
factors by aware non-adopters is also of interest.   Several
possible explanations for this trend exist.   Individuals, having
adopted, may find that their solar systems work to their highest
expectations.   As they become more satisfied and have more
experience with solar systems, each of these factors becomes of
less concern.   Aware non-adopters, on the other hand, lacking
this experience, are more wary and skeptical.

Limitations and Future Directions

In designing a study to provide an in-depth analysis of individuals in one geographic region, there are limitations to the generalizability of results. Further, some bias due to sampling techniques and non-response errors is likely due to the methodology employed.

Insights regarding both adopters and non-adopters of solar energy systems are provided by the current research. It would be beneficial to further study these groups beyond the descriptions presented here, in order to better understand the purchase process involved. The most appropriate extension of the current study is a longitudinal design which tracks the future diffusion of solar energy technology in Maine. Solar energy systems represent an ideal class of products with which to conduct such a study, given their current relative newness and expected continued growth in acceptance. The present study forms a baseline against which changes in adopter and non-adopter profiles and decision making can be measured.

RELATED RESEARCH

Cesta, J.R. and Decker, P.G. (1978), "Speeding Solar Energy Commercialization: A Delphi Research of Marketplace Factors," Journal of Business Research, 6, 311-328.

Gitlow, H.S. (1979), "Discrimination Procedures for the Analysis of Nominally Scaled Data Sets," Journal of Marketing Research, 16, 387-393.

Pertschuk, M. (1978), Welcoming Remarks to the Symposium on Competition in the Solar Energy Industry, Sponsored by the Bureau of Competition of the Federal Trade Commission, Washington, DC, December 15, 1977, in The Solar Market, Washington, DC: Government Printing Office.

Robertson, T.S. (1971), Innovative Behavior and Communication, New York: Holt, Rinehart, and Winston.

_____, and Myers, J.H., "Personality Correlates of Opinion Leadership and Innovative Buying Behavior," Journal of Marketing Research, 6, 164-168.

Rogers, E.M. (1962), Diffusion of Innovations, New York: Free Press.

_____, (1976), "New Product Adoption and Diffusion," Journal of Consumer Research, 2, 290-301.

_____, and Shoemaker, F.F. (1971), Communication of Innovations, New York: Free Press.

Ryan, B. and Gross, N.C. (1943), "The Diffusion of Hybrid Seed Corn in Two Iowa Communities," Rural Sociology, 8, 15-24.

Sparrow, T. (1977), "Socio-economic Factors Affecting the Adoption of Household Solar Technology: Preliminary Findings," paper presented at the Symposium on Social and Behavioral Implications of the Energy Crisis, Woodlands, Texas.

Zaltman, G., and Lin, N. (1971), "On the Nature of Innovations," American Behavioral Scientist, 14, 651-673.

ADOPTING SOLAR AND CONSERVATION

Seymour Warkov

The retrofitting of housing constructed in an era of inexpensive heating fuels represents a major investment for all high energy societies, yet household decisions concerning conventional residential conservation measures versus active solar systems have not received consideration in the burgeoning research literature on "soft paths" (Cunningham and Lopreato 1977; Olsen and Goodnight 1977; Warkov 1978).

How households arrive at a commitment to engage in either or both approaches to achieving reductions in energy consumption is timely. The Windfall Profits Tax Bill was passed by the U.S. Congress on 4/27/80 and signed into law by President Carter on 5/2/80. This bill offers a new residential tax credit of 40 percent on the first $10,000 invested in active solar equipment, photovoltaics, etc. for installation at the principal residence of the tax payer. This paper examines certain relationships between residential energy conservation behavior and adoption of solar heaters as of May, 1979 and November, 1979.

METHODS

A two year study of the HUD Solar Hot Water Program in the State of Connecticut is the basis for this investigation (Warkov 1979). In Spring, 1977, the mass media disseminated information about the availability of 750 four hundred dollar grants for home owners who meet eligibility requirements for solar hot water systems. By September, 1977, some 2200 Connecticut households contacted State energy officials administering the program for additional information; over 900 completed the page application forms and 750 received conditional approval subject to various program requirements. By January, 1978, follow-up contacts determined that 550 were still pursuing the grant; as of June, 1978, only 150 households had provided documentation required to qualify for this subsidy. Applicants dropping out of the program were replaced by households on the wait list. Widespread defection prompted the Northeast Solar Energy Center to commission a household telephone interview survey of program applicants. During Spring, 1979 a random sample of 215 households was contacted to acquire systematic information about factors contributing to this decision. Interviews were completed with some 82 percent of this sample. In each instance contacts were made with the household member signing the application form. A key finding was the following: 61 households had purchased a solar hot water system as of May, 1979; 121 did not acquire solar systems despite their initial interest in the program.

Six months later, telephone contact was achieved with 102 (85 percent) of the 121 households identified as solar non-adopters. By November, 1979, a total of 4 had purchased solar, 68 still considered solar a possibility, while 30 now rejected active solar as a viable retrofit strategy. A complete description of all variables employed in the analysis to predict solar adoption is reported elsewhere (Warkov 1979). Brief descriptions are provided in Tables 1 and 2. In addition, all households were asked whether they considered 10 information sources to be reliable or not (RELIAB).

RESULTS

Energy Conservation Behavior and Solar Adoption

Table 1 displays the mean and standard deviation for each variable, the base case prior to adjustment for non-responses, zero-order correlations with solar adoption, and standardized regression coefficients. A correlation of .12 (p < .05) or higher would be considered statistically significant, but correlations of this magnitude "explain" very little. A preliminary assessment of these correlations suggests that the social environment of prospective adopters as indexed by the volume of encouragement they received from significant actors, perception of solar system advantages that could be classified as "private" rather than "public" benefits, the configuration of the roof and finally, perception of eventual global depletion of fossil fuels comprise the four dimensions of the adoption process for which empirical verification might be possible on the basis of these results. On the other hand, the measure tapping perceived social benefits in the form of preservation of natural resources, national independence from OPEC and the like shows very little effect (r = -.05). More surprisingly, a measure reflecting private economic benefits (fuel savings, insurance against rising fuel prices, eventually save money) did not correlate significantly with household solar adoption (r = .11).

Finally, it is evident that household energy conservation behavior represented by conservation under I and II does not have any bearing on propensities to acquire active solar during the eighteen month interval or more spanning the official date of program initiation through Spring, 1979. For this special population of households ranking well above the State population median on household income and educational attainment, the two "soft paths" evidently are independent means for achieving reductions in natural gas, petroleum, and electrically heated domestic hot water (r = .092, r = .041).

Table 1 also displays the results of a multiple regression analysis representing the "best" set of predictors of household

TABLE 1

CORRELATES OF HOUSEHOLD SOLAR ADOPTION,
MAY, 1979, AMONG HUD SOLAR GRANT PROGRAM PARTICIPANTS

VARIATE		UNADJUSTED N	MEAN	S.D.	r (with soluser)	b	p
(1)	ENCOURIN	159	3.55	2.29	.323	.242	<.01
(2)	SOLPREBN	165	4.78	2.23	.284	.168	<.01
(3)	ROOFIN	176	2.04	.91	.193	.158	<.01
(4)	SOLSAVIN	178	5.19	1.23	.113		
(5)	SOLINSUR	178	4.26	1.59	-.055		
(6)	SHORT	175	2.28	.89	.159	.165	<.01
(7)	CONSVIN5	172	4.61	1.85	.092		
(8)	CONSVIND	172	5.37	2.48	.041		
(9)	SOLUSER	178	1.32	.47			

(1)   Encouragement index is based on the series of items concerning communications with various "change agents."

(2)   Roof index is based on three items concerning shade and rating of layout of roof.

(3)   Private benefits of solar is based on four items from a battery concerning advantages associated with solar system.

(4)   Savings associated with solar based on three items: major advantage in fuel savings, insurance against rising fuel prices, and it will eventually save money.

(5)   Protection based on three items concerning advantages associated with energy independence, preservation of natural resources, and protection against shortages.

(6)   Fossil fuel depletion based on an item concerning global depletion of fossil fuel supplies.

(7)   Conservation index I is based on eight items concerning what people had done in the past five years to conserve energy in the home.

(8)   Conservation index II is based on the same eight items as variate 7 but asks if respondent had ever taken these actions.

(9)   Solar user is based on whether the household adopted solar or not.

solar adoption. In brief, households initially interested in receiving an HUD grant to install solar hot water systems were more likely to acquire this technology when they encountered a supportive social environment, perceived non-economic or only secondary economic benefits to be associated with solar, resided in housing displaying the appropriate siting and building configuration, and attribute a serious energy shortage to declining world fossil fuel supplies. Self-reported residential energy conservation practices, however, are not part of the process facilitating household solar adoption.

Conservation Behavior and Perceived Barriers to Solar

Barriers perceived by a majority of program participants for dropping out of the HUD program by May, 1979 are economic-- price of solar, payback period, and size of the grant. A second category of reasons mentioned by 30 to 40 percent of these prospective adopters include some 3 in 10 who judged that they "could get the same benefits by spending the money on home insulation or other energy conservation measures."

Energy Conservation Information Sources

About 7 in 10 respondents consider the magazines they read, newspapers and government sources (Federal, State Energy Office) to be reliable channels of information concerning energy con- servation; slightly under half consider national and local television and radio as "reliable." On the other hand, only 1 in 4 attribute reliability to energy conservation information offered by a fuel oil dealer or an insulating contractor. With one exception, attributions of reliability to any of the infor- mation sources are unrelated to past or recent residential conservation activity on the part of these households. The exception is instructive and is counter to expectations: Household scores on both measures of residential energy conser- vation are negatively related to perceived reliability on energy conservation if the source is the "State Energy Office" ($r = -.19$, $p < .01$; $r = -.18$, $p < .01$) despite the fact that 3 out of 4 respondents rated this source to be "reliable." In other words, households taking a substantial number of conservation measures tend to distrust or simply are uncertain about this source of information.

In overview, the findings for this study population indi- cate that attributions of reliability to various sources of energy conservation behavior are inconsequential for understand- ing residential behavior designed to reduce energy consumption. Age and educational attainment of household head and household income do not shed light on this null finding. Whether it be the knowledge base concerning the status of solar technology or program deficiencies in disseminating information, it is evident that households already taking measures to conserve were especially critical of the State as a purveyor of energy conservation information. On the other hand, trust in the mass media and in other sources of information reported here was an irrelevant factor in the search for an explanation of household conservation actions taken by Spring, 1979.

Readiness to Adopt Solar, November, 1979

To appraise the results displayed in Table 2 the reader will find it noteworthy that a preliminary analysis of all Spring, 1979 reasons for not buying solar treated as predictors of November, 1979 solar plans yielded the following: with the exception of the reason concerning energy conservation (REASCONS) all "reasons" correlated with ADOPSTAT were essentially zero. Reasons for dropping out of the program, with the exception of energy conservation, have no direct bearing on willingness to consider the purchase of solar six months later. Also, the Spring, 1979 telephone survey found that 40 percent of the non-adopting households were not prepared to acquire solar at that time even if the tax credit and the HUD grant were available in concert with a "steep" rise in heating fuel prices.

Table 2 displays the zero order correlations with ADOPTSTAT. The sole predictor of willingness to consider solar in November, 1979 consists of household appraisals of the benefits of conventional conservation: those who claim that they "could get about the same benefit by spending the money on home insulation or other energy conservation measures," reported six months later that they were not considering the acquisition of active solar hot water heating. However, it is the perception of the benefits of residential conservation, and not reported conservation behavior, that constitutes a "barrier" to solar market penetration in this study population.

SUMMARY AND CONCLUSIONS

Several policy and program implications of these results warrant consideration. First, households initially expressing an interest in solar but unwilling to purchase the technology should be encouraged to take extensive residential conservation action, if they have not done so already. Second, in principle, Connecticut home owners should undertake comprehensive energy conservation measures before acquiring solar hot water heating. With further rises in the price of home heating fuels very likely during the 1980s, it would optimize the use of societal resources if solar marketing campaigns were aimed at households that have already achieved appropriate standards of ceiling insulation and the like. Third, given the negligible impacts of perceptions of reliability attributed by this study population to various energy conservation information sources, it would be timely to focus on the social context of household decision making concerning energy conservation decisions, in particular,

TABLE 2

CORRELATES OF DROPPING OUT OF THE SOLAR MARKET
NOVEMBER, 1979

VARIATE		N	MEAN	S.D.	r (with ADOPSTAT)	b	p
(1)	REASCONS	86	.104	.307	.260	.24	<.01
(2)	CONSVIN5	86	4.546	1.712	-.040	-.06	---
(3)	LEASTIT	86	.395	.491	.170	.12	---
(4)	ADOPTSTAT	86	.314	.466	---	---	---

(1) Benefits of conventional residential conservation mentioned as a major reason for dropping out of the HUD program, May, 1979.

(2) See Index 7, Table 1.

(3) Responsiveness to solar incentives based on tax and cost incentives.

(4) Solar adoption plans, November 1979 based on whether or not considering solar at that time.

the place of social networks in mobilizing household resources on behalf of energy conservation. Finally, both solar and residential conservation decisions appear to be responsive to certain fear appeals. While the traditional use of fear appeals to market various products is inherently problematic, the linking of such appeals, i.e., the world is running out of fossil fuels, to a sense of obligation to future generations deserves consideration (Warkov 1980).

To undertake properly an investigation that addresses the research issues posed here entails access to a randomly selected population of homeowners prospectively or retroactively engaged in retrofitting of residential housing. The key issue should be posed as follows: do households currently deciding between residential conservation and solar heaters perceive the superior advantages of conservation or solar and then proceed to take appropriate action? The research design, the special attributes of the study population, and phrasing of items concerning residential conservation did not allow for rigorous testing of this question. The findings of this study seem to justify further research on this issue.

RELATED RESEARCH

Cunningham, William H., and Lopreato, Sally C. (1977), _Energy Use and Conservation Incentives_. New York: Praeger.

Farhar, Barbara C., Wells, Patricia, Unseld, Charles T., and Burns, Barbara (1979), _Public Opinion About Energy: A Literature Review_. Golden, Co.: Solar Energy Research Institute.

Hyman, Herbert and Sheatsley, Paul (1947), "Some Reasons Why Information Campaigns Fail," _Public Opinion Quarterly_, 11, 412-423.

Olsen, Marvin E. and Goodnight, Jill A. (1977), _Social Aspects of Energy Conservation_, Northwest Energy Policy Project Report for Pacific Northwest Regional Commission, Portland, Oregon.

Stobaugh, Robert and Yergin, Daniel, eds. (1979), _Energy Future_. New York: Random House.

Warkov, Seymour, ed. (1978), _Energy Policy in the United States: Social and Behavioral Dimensions_, New York: Praeger.

_____, (1979), _Solar Adopters and Near Adopters: A Study of the HUD Solar Hot Water Grant Program_. Report for Northeast Solar Energy Center, Cambridge, Mass.

_____, (1980), "Attitudes Toward the Future: Their Impact on Present Decisions," paper presented at Meetings of American Association for the Advancement of Science, San Francisco, January 6, 1980.

NATIONAL AND INTERNATIONAL RESEARCH ISSUES

- Residential Energy Surveys by the U.S. Department of Energy

- Economic Analysis of Consumer Energy Decisions

- Canadian Passenger Car Fuel Consumption Survey

- Cross-Cultural Comparisons of a Conservation-Orientation Model

- Residential Energy End Use: Developing an International Data Base

RESIDENTIAL ENERGY SURVEYS
BY THE U.S. DEPARTMENT OF ENERGY

Lynda T. Carlson
Kenneth A. Vagts
Lynn D. Patinkin
Wendel L. Thompson

In the United States, the Office of the Consumption Data System, Energy Information Administration is charged with the responsibility of designing, developing, and implementing ongoing data collection programs to obtain data on energy consumption and the behavioral and structural components affecting energy consumption in the residential, transportation, commercial, and industrial sectors. This paper concentrates on the household and transportation panel surveys underway to determine the energy consumed in the residential sector.

In 1976, the National Academy of Sciences established a committee to examine the policy needs for energy consumption data, evaluate alternative data collection mechanisms, and develop recommendations on the types of energy consumption related to monitoring, modeling, and policy development. The Office of the Consumption Data System has begun to implement many recommendations in the report as well as needs expressed by many of the program and policy offices within the Department of Energy (National Academy of Sciences 1977). The basic philosophy in designing the data collection program is that the actual consumption data is needed as well as information on the stock of energy-consuming goods and behaviors to understand the consumption.

THE RESIDENTIAL ENERGY CONSUMPTION SURVEYS

In late 1976, design and development of the Residential Energy Consumption Survey was started. In addition to meeting the wide range of user needs for baseline data, modeling, and policy evaluation, a major constraint was to obtain the most accurate data possible on consumption and expenditures. The core data set was to be information on the housing unit, energy related characteristics, household vehicles, household characteristics, and the energy consumption and energy expenditures of the household. The household would be requested to sign waivers so that actual consumption and expenditures data could

---

The opinions and conclusions expressed herein are solely those of the authors, and should not be construed as representing the opinions or policy of any agency of the United States Government.

be obtained from the energy suppliers.   For each household, the
data provided by the utility company would be linked to the
actual degree days for the billing period covered.

To provide data on the quality of the housing stock, an
energy assessment of the housing unit was required which would
involve metering the major appliances to determine end use
consumption.   In a second subsample the plan was to collect
detailed energy-related characteristics; specifically, square
footage, insulation, appliances, air infiltration, and furnace
efficiency. To verify the data on gasoline consumption, expenditures and miles traveled provided by household recall, it was
intended to have households maintain transportation diaries
which recorded consumption and expenditures for fuels.   It was
hoped to have a subsample of households maintain trip logs so
that the trip patterns of a household would be known.   The trip
logs were dropped early in the design stage due to their complexity, but may be reinstated.

The consumption, transportation, and energy assessment data
were originally designed to provide a means of verifying the
data collected from the households.   However, through research
and interim data collections, this verification function evolved
from verification to an integral part of the data collection.

In the planning, the initial design and development was to
take three years and then a large data collection was to occur
once every two years.   However, during the design period, the
United States had experienced a period of rapidly rising energy
prices, gas lines, coal strikes, fuel oil, and natural gas
shortages.   These crises have led to continual demands for
timely data on consumption and behaviors in the residential
sector.   The demands were and are for descriptive information on
energy consumption patterns in the sector.   For example, what
changes were and are taking place in the existing housing stock;
how much energy is being consumed by households; how much
consumption and conservation is taking place by households in
apartment units; what is the inventory and storage tank capacity
of fuel oil households; and how are households responding to
rising energy costs.   Because of this multitude of issues, it
became evident that the only way to continue the development
work for a large residential energy consumption data collection
program was literally to launch one or more interim, small scale
surveys.   Concurrently, these interim surveys would also serve
as substantial pretests for the large scale data collection and
meet the need for timely data on residential section energy
consumption.   The interim surveys (National Interim Energy
Consumption Survey--"NIECS") were limited in data elements and
sample size, but included all the basic design components--a
personal interview collecting basic housing unit and household
data, an energy supplier data collection, a transportation
panel, and a means of obtaining detailed data on the physical
characteristics of the housing unit.   Figure 1 indicates the
present survey design.

Figure 1: Residental Energy Consumption Survey Structure

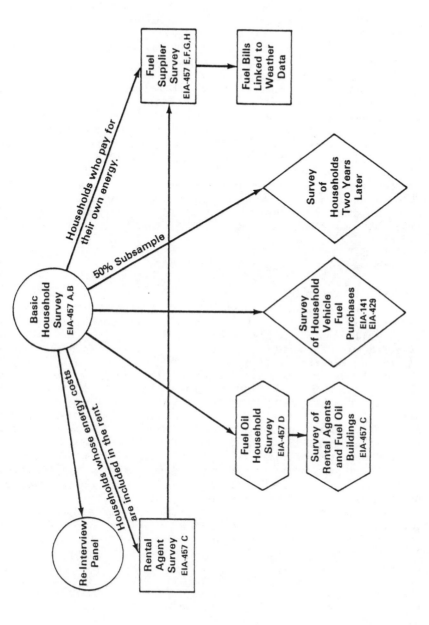

THE NATIONAL INTERIM ENERGY CONSUMPTION SURVEY (NIECS)

The initial household contacts for NIECS began in October 1978.   In a 44-minute interview, data on the housing unit, household and transportation patterns, and vehicle uses were collected. At the conclusion of the interview, respondents were asked to sign waivers authorizing the researcher to obtain their records of fuel consumption from their energy suppliers.   The NIECS sample is a representative probability sample consisting of 103 primary sampling units. A total of 4849 housing units were drawn into the sample, of which 4507 were eligible units. Ultimately, interviews were collected from 4181 households for a final total response rate of 90.5 percent. This high response rate is due to: cash incentives (each respondent was given two "Susan B. Anthony" coin dollars), and a multi-wave, multi-contact approach (three personal interview attempts were made and for unsuccessful personal interviews, a mail questionnaire with the cash incentive was sent). Finally, aggregate consumption data was obtained from utilities for groups of non-respondents.

The Transportation Panel

NIECS was also used as a large scale pretest for the transportation panel. A sampling design and data collection pattern was devised to pick up accurate annual estimates that would reflect seasonality changes in miles per gallon and miles traveled for household vehicles. To obtain accurate annual estimates, households from the NIECS sample were asked to join the panel for two months. The household kept separate logs for each vehicle for each of the two months. The household then left the panel for four months and was asked to rejoin the sample for the subsequent two months. The seasonality component in vehicle efficiency and driving patterns is captured by this pattern and provides a large enough base of data to develop annual estimates of consumption by vehicle and household.

During the pretests, a major gasoline shortage occurred, with long lines at gas stations, in the number of gallons sold per vehicle, and limited availability of specific fuel types in scattered geographical areas. It rapidly became apparent that the panel, if fielded immediately, could be utilized to provide immediate data for monitoring and policy development.

The panel provided a means of monitoring month-to-month changes in consumption, miles traveled, and miles per gallon. Limited anedoctal data was also collected on the presence of gas lines and types of fuel available. Starting in June late 1979, the transportation panel pretest became an actual data collection with a monthly panel of 500 households. In late 1979, the panel size increased to 1000 households per month.

The Energy Assessment

The third major area in which NIECS was used as a pretest
for the Residential Energy Consumption Survey was to obtain
detailed data on the uses of energy-consuming appliances and the
energy quality of the housing stock. The intent was to use this
information to develop a detailed understanding of the energy
quality of the housing stock and to provide a means to monitor
changes in the quality of the housing stock. It was decided to
develop an "energy assessment" to determine end-use consumption.
The energy assessment is a 90-minute inspection of the housing
unit by a para-professional. The inspection collects: square
footage of the unit; age, make, and characteristics of appliances; insulation characteristics; characteristics of siting and
apertures; and detailed information on the heating and cooling
systems in the unit. Methods are still being perfected to
collect information on the rate of air infiltration in the unit
and furnace efficiency. The method used to test air infiltration involves either releasing "invisible" gas in a house or
placing a reverse blower on the front door which has a tendency
to suck all the soot out of a chimney and deposit inside the
house. The existing tests for air infiltration and furnace
efficiency are not well suited for obtaining respondents' participation in the survey!

The first iteration of the energy assessment was administered to 49 houses in the NIECS sample. The assessment has
produced voluminous data which is now being analyzed. The
present concern is to determine how well the assessment can help
in describing the energy quality of the housing stock and how
useful it can be in providing essential information for end-use
analysis. The data collected in the assessment will also be
used in determining how much households know about their houses
and whether this knowledge increases as the price of energy
rises and as energy conservation becomes more of an acceptable
norm. The knowledge will be evaluated by comparing housholds'
responses to square footage, insulation, appliances, and other
items with the information collected in the energy assessment.

Weather Data

A data base on household energy consumption would be
incomplete without taking into account the effects of the
weather on a household's energy use. Each billing record for a
household was linked to weather data for the period covered by
the bill. Daily temperature information was obtained from the
U.S. National Oceanic and Atmospheric Administration (NOAA).
The household's location was linked to the group of counties
which make up NOAA divisions. A program was devised to convert
the NOAA daily temperatures into heating degree days (HDD) and
cooling degree days (CDD).

FINDINGS FROM NIECS

Detailed findings from NIECS are available from the Department of Energy (1979). To illustrate some of the results to
date, the following information on conservation and consumption
patterns are presented.

Conservation

The data indicate that 41 percent (±2.6 percent, 95 percent
confidence limits) of the NIECS households had storm windows on
all of their windows, 37 percent (±2.4) had storm doors, and 69
percent (±2.2) had some attic insulation. Approximately one-
third of the households had closed off one or more rooms during
the winter. Overall, 41 percent (±2.6) of the housing units had
some or complete storm windows, storm doors, and attic insulation, and 86 percent (±1.8) had at least one of these three
types of insulating materials. The proportion of housing units
having all three types of insulating materials varies substantially by region. Units in the North Central region were three
times more likely to contain storm windows, storm doors, and
attic insulation than were units in the South. The proportion
of housing units in the West having all three types of insulating materials was less than one-quarter of that found in the
North Central region.

Generally speaking, the presence of insulation went up as
family income increased. Fifty-five percent (±6) of the households earning $25,000 or more had storm windows, storm doors,
and attic insulation, while only 20 percent (±6.2) of the poor
households had all three types of these insulating materials.
White respondents were twice as likely as black respondents to
have all three types of insulating items, 43 percent (±2.8)
versus 21 percent (±7.6). Households headed by married couples
had significantly better insulated homes--46 percent (±3) had
all three types--than unmarried household heads. Among those
who were unmarried, there were no significant differences in the
summary statistics between male and female heads of households.

Some sort of conservation-related equipment or insulating
material was added to 50 percent (±2.8) of housing units which
were eligible for an energy tax credit. Most additions were
relatively inexpensive. The most frequent additions were
caulking (25 percent), plastic covering (16 percent), and
weatherstripping (15 percent). Of the eligible housing units,
41 percent made an addition of this type. Expensive additions
of insulating materials or any kind of equipment additions were
undertaken by smaller numbers of respondents. At least one of
the following types of insulation--storm doors, storm windows,
and attic insulation--was added by 17 percent (±2) of the eligible housing units. Eighteen percent (±2) of the households
added expensive insulating material and/or expensive equipment.
Half of the households that added an expensive item also added

an item from the category termed "inexpensive insulation." While inexpensive modifications predominated in 1977 and 1978, approximately 10 percent of the households made at least one relatively expensive addition in each year. Table 1 summarizes the information on the presence of insulating materials in households in 1978.

In October 1979, a second interim survey was conducted in the NIECS secondary sampling units. The results indicated that single family households made conservation additions to their houses, but not in dramatic numbers. Significant conservation changes occurred within households whose primary space heating fuel was fuel oil. Interviews conducted in August 1979 indicated that approximately 7 percent of the single family households that used fuel oil as their main heat source during the 1978-1979 winter heating season had converted to an alternative fuel source. Eight percent of the households had added attic insulation and 7 percent had added insulation in the outside walls in the period from November 1978 to August 1979.

Consumption

The NIECS data set provided data on energy consumption and expenditures for the period April 1978 through March 1979 (Residential Energy Consumption Survey). This was the first time actual consumption and expenditure data by households have been collected for electricity, natural gas, fuel oil, and LPG.

The typical U.S. household spent an average of $724 ($\pm$2 percent) during this period to meet their energy needs. Total energy expenditures for the year came to approximately $55.5 billion ($\pm$6 percent). More than half of all residential energy expenditures, $29.9 billion ($\pm$8 percent), were spent on electricity, which accounted for less than one quarter of the total amount consumed. Natural gas expenditures for the year were $15.3 billion ($\pm$10 percent) or 28 percent of the total. Expenditures for fuel oil and kerosene were 8.6 billion ($\pm$7 percent) and $1.7 billion ($\pm$26 percent) was spent on LPG.

Average household consumption in the Northeast and North Central regions were significantly higher than the national average with 166 ($\pm$8 percent) and 180 ($\pm$8 percent) million Btu per household, respectively. The South, with an average consumption of 99 million Btu per household ($\pm$8 percent), and the West, with 110 million Btu ($\pm$10 percent), consumed significantly less than the national average.

Both consumption and expenditures varied significantly in relation to type of structure. Single-family detached houses comprised 63 percent of the residential housing stock, but consumed 71 percent of the total amount of energy. Single-family attached units accounted for 4 percent of both consumption and housing units. Six percent of all units were mobile homes, which consumed only 4 percent of the total amount of energy.

TABLE 1

PRESENCE OF INSULATING MATERIALS IN OCCUPIED
SINGLE-FAMILY DETACHED HOUSING UNITS (PERCENTAGE
OF TOTAL UNITS IN THE UNITED STATES, EXCLUDING
ALASKA AND HAWAII)

Type of Material	1978 (NIECS)[a]
(Number of Housing Units)	(48,547,000)
Storm Windows	
No Windows Covered	37%
Some Windows Covered	22
All Windows Covered	41
TOTAL	100%
Storm Doors	
No Doors Covered	33%
Some Doors Covered	27
All Doors Covered	40
TOTAL	100%
Attic or Roof Insulation	
No	17%
Yes	77
Don't Know	6
TOTAL	100%
Wall Insulation	
No	29%
Yes	54
Don't Know	17
TOTAL	100%

a. Source: NIECS is the National Interim
    Energy Consumption Survey. Figures are
    found in; Residential Energy Consumption
    Survey: Conservation, February 1980,
    DOE/EIA-0207/3. The survey was conducted
    between October and December 1978.

Multiple family units consumed 21 percent of the total
energy while comprising 26 percent of the units. Since buildings with 5 or more units are usually master-metered at a
commercial rate, the consumption and expenditures for this
segment of the residential sector had been previously unknown.
These units consumed a total of 751 trillion Btu (±26 percent).

Of this total, 42 percent was for natural gas, 34 percent was for fuel oil, and 23 percent was for consumption of electricity.

The average household's consumption of energy generally increased as income increased. Low income households used significantly less energy than the average household. Those earning less than $5,000 in 1977 consumed approximately 22 percent less energy than the average household (108 million Btu $\pm$12 percent versus 138 million $\pm$4 percent). Households classified as "poor" used 14 percent less energy than the average (119 million Btu $\pm$6 percent). On the other hand, households earning $25,000 or more consumed 28 percent more than the average (176 million Btu $\pm$16 percent).

Average expenditures for energy also increased with household income. Consistent with their lower level of consumption, the lowest income group (up to $5,000) spent an average of $522 ($\pm$8 percent) on energy. Energy expenditures for all U.S. households average $724 ($\pm$2 percent) for the year. Households in the highest income group ($25,000 or more) spent the most on energy, $938 ($\pm$6 percent).

SUMMARY AND CONCLUSIONS

The data from the NIECS has been used for a broad range of issues. The initial conservation and fuel oil conservation data were used to determine the types of tax related conservation strategies DOE should sponsor for the residential sector. The fuel oil data were used to alleviate widespread fears on potential fuel oil shortages. The consumption data has been put to a broad range of uses, including:

- Forecasting of potential impacts of natural gas deregulation.

- Sharpening DOE's understanding of the potential for conservation and solar applications in the residential sector.

- Examining the feasibility and potential impacts of requiring existing homes to meet a minimum energy standards.

- As the input data set for an energy demand model to be used to forecast the impact of building standards on energy demand.

- Providing policymakers with basic data on levels and changes in energy related improvements by households.

There are also a series of methodological and substantive issues which will be studied over the next several years to improve the data set. The initial data appears to indicate that a household estimates of the unit's square footage or insulation is unreliable. Therefore, starting with the September 1980 data collection, the interviewer will measure the square footage of the unit and attempt to obtain more detailed information on the insulation characteristics of the unit.   In NIECS, a rental agents survey was pretested to obtain data for households that do not pay their own bills or are in master-metered buildings. Since this procedure proved successful, a rental agents survey will be fielded.   Data on the building's characteristics, the fuels entering the building, and the consumption and expenditures for the building will be obtained.   The data will be used to provide a better method for estimating the consumption and, therefore, conservation potential of households residing in master-metered buildings.

Some other major analytic questions are the ways to determine end-use consumption by households for various uses such as space heating, water heating, and space cooling.   As part of this process, an attempt is being made to develop estimates to Btu consumption per degree day per square foot which will allow us to compare changes in consumption and conservation over time.

A current objective is to examine ways in which behavioral questions can be added to the surveys. Specifically, an attempt will be made to design a series of questions that will help determine what motivates people's energy related behavior and also what kinds of energy related things people are actually doing.

The most important lesson learned from the NIECS surveys is that the energy area is highly volatile, and that policy needs and crises require accurate, timely data.   The design of the residential energy consumption survey has been altered to reflect these needs. The result is smaller surveys, conducted more frequently, which will assist policy makers in their decisions concerning consumption in the consumer/residential sector.

RELATED RESEARCH

National Academy of Sciences (1977), Energy Consumption Measurement: Data Needs for Public Policy, Committee on Measurement of Energy Consumption.

Residential Energy Consumption Survey: Consumption and Expenditures, (April 1978 through March 1979, July 1980), U.S. Department of Energy, DOE/EIA-0207/5.

Single-Family Households: Fuel Oil Inventories and Expenditures (1979), National Interim Energy Consumption Survey, U.S. Department of Energy, DOE/EIA-0207/1.

ECONOMIC ANALYSIS OF CONSUMER ENERGY DECISIONS

Mark Levine
Chris Ruhm
James E. McMahon
Laurel Andrews
Stephen P. A. Brown
John M. Callaway
Kenton R. Corum
Dennis L. O'Neal
Fred A. Reid
Kish Sharma

This chapter describes a study of consumer decision making in the purchase of energy consuming and energy conserving equipment. The study involves a collaborative effort among four National Laboratories and associated consultants. The main components of the study are summarized and then some preliminary findings of the study group are presented. Before discussing these two areas some of the reasons for the importance of consumer decision making on energy efficiency are described.

It is widely recognized that the United States and many other nations of Western society are under extreme pressure in balancing energy supply and energy demand. Although there is an awareness that the energy consumer can and should reduce his or her energy use, there is little recognition that the purchase of energy using goods exerts an enormous influence over the magnitude of energy use for many years. The focus of this research consists of a quantitative assessment of the manner in which consumers evaluate economic tradeoffs between immediate costs (of generally more expensive energy efficient equipment) and future benefits (in the form of reduced fuel bills). This information will be used to improve the ability to forecast the growth in energy demand and to provide insights into the formulation of policies and programs to encourage consumers to purchase more efficient equipment and cost effective energy conservation measures. In the study design, primary interest is in the area of in residential equipment and energy conservation measures for building envelopes.

OVERALL CONCEPT

The evaluation of the implicit discount rate provides a unifying concept for this investigation. The implicit discount rate describes the rules by which a consumer, knowingly or

The work presented in this paper was supported by the U.S. Department of Energy, Office of Buildings and Community Systems, Systems Analysis Division.

unknowingly, equates costs and benefits that occur over different periods of time. In this framework, the decision to purchase energy conservation measures (either as a separate purchase decision or combined with the purchase of a particular product, as for example a more efficient furnace) is viewed as an investment decision. Three key steps in the evaluation are:

(1) Characterization of the implicit discount rate for a range of energy conservation decisions. Here, the emphasis is on the evaluation of historical data to determine the implicit discount rate and evaluate the degree to which consumers value energy efficiency in consumer products and specific energy conservation measures. Differences in implicit discount rates among different products can indicate the degree to which the products are seen to consume energy by consumers, the availabiity of more efficient products in the marketplace, the importance of energy conservation in the marketing of different products, or a host of other variables. No effort is made to evaluate the causes of the differing implicit discount rates.

(2) Evaluation of the change in implicit discount rates over time. A reasonable hypothesis, which is being tested, is that a threshold exists in the total fuel bill for an energy using device below which the consumer is relatively uninterested in taking the trouble to learn about energy conservation and the purchase of energy conserving products. Under this hypothesis, the implicit discount rate will decrease as energy prices increase, probably in a series of one or a few steps as the effect of the energy prices becomes noticeable and, eventually, painful. This approach provides information on how, but not why, the discount rate might be expected to change with new circumstances. An important use of this analysis is the determination of changes in energy conservation practice in new residential buildings over time. This result will provide the first comprehensive assessment of the relationship between current (and past) energy conservation building practice and DOE's proposed Building Energy Performance Standards.

(3) Disaggregation of the market into different types of consumers and evaluation of their discount rates. Hausman (1979) deduced how the discount rate varies among different income groups. The approach is being extended to consider a wide range of different classes of consumers: single-family, owner occupied housing; single-family, rental housing; multi-family, rental housing; multi-family, owner occupied housing; and mobile homes. These classes can be further subdivided among a variety of categories: age, income group, geographic distribution, and other variables that define segments of the market that are likely to be relatively homogeneous in their decision process.

This "market segmentation" approach has the potential to identify and, within reasonable bounds, quantify some of the factors effecting energy conservation purchase decisions.

SPECIFIC RESEARCH EFFORTS UNDERWAY

A number of distinct research efforts are underway that relate directly to one of the three approaches identified above. These research tasks are summarized briefly below, with the institution at which the work is performed shown in parentheses.

(1) Implicit discount rates for energy conservation in new residential buildings (ORNL,LBL). This work has been completed for houses constructed during 1975 and 1976 by ORNL. Continuing research involves studying the sensitivity of results to key parameters and assumptions (to place error bounds on the results) and extending the work to additional years (1973 and 1979).

(2) Implicit discount rates for energy efficiency in appliances, furnaces, and air conditioners (MSNW, PNL, BNL). Data analysis is taking place on sales of appliances, furnaces, and air conditioners of different efficiencies. These studies will provide both estimates of discount rates and an assessment of the different methods for calculating them.

(3) Segmentation of appliance sales and efficiency data by markets (LBL). A preliminary breakdown of sales data for residential energy using equipment into different market segments has been completed (Reid 1980). Present work is directed at obtaining a quantitative assessment of the energy efficiency purchase decisions in the different market segments.

(4) Implicit discount rates by market segment (LBL, MSNW, PNL, BNL). This involves the use of the data to evaluate implicit discount rates as a function of market segments. If successful, results will be used to provide a basic explanation of the causes of high discount rates in those markets and among those consumers that have low investments in energy conservation (and among consumers who have larger investments in energy conservation).

(5) Assessment of market barriers to energy conservation (BNL). The work completed in this task (Brown, forthcoming) provides an economic framework by which quantitative results of the fourth task can be evaluated.

(6) Satisficing behavior model of consumer purchase decisions (LBL). The analytic work of the first five tasks assumes that the consumer implicitly or explicitly optimizes his or her purchase decision about a mean return on investment (or that the

purchase decision can be adequately simulated by such a model). In this task, a different approach is taken; the consumer is perceived as a decision maker who follows a sequential rather than an optimizing decision path to arrive at a satisfactory rather than optimal purchase decision. The model will provide an independent evaluation of factors influencing implicit discount rates.

(7) Effect of implicit discount rates on residential energy demand forecasts (LBL, ORNL). A study had been completed using the ORNL Residential Energy Demand Model to assess the sensitivity of energy demand projections (with and without federal energy conservation policies) to assumptions about implicit consumer discount rates (U.S. Department of Energy 1980). This analysis indicates the extreme sensitivity of energy demand projections and evaluations of policies to the implicit discount rate.

(8) Case studies (LBL). Case studies are selected in which the possibility of understanding specific elements of consumer decision making on energy conservation is high.

RESEARCH RESULTS TO DATE

Life-cycle Cost Method of
Calculating Implicit Discount Rates

One method of calculating the implicit discount rate is to determine what rate would make empirically observed decisions the least life-cycle cost alternative. O'Neal, Corum, and Jones (forthcoming) used this method to determine implicit discount rates for consumers in ten cities. Their calculated values depend on the parameters in the life-cycle cost equation which include the specified tradeoff between energy use and conservation investment; present fuel prices for heating and cooling; expected price escalation rates for heating and cooling fuels; lifetime of the capital investment; an assumed constant proportion (less than one) by which an investment which reduces heating requirements also reduces cooling needs; and the rate of interest for borrowing in cases where the investment is purchased with financing.

Results vary widely between cities, fuel types, and cases. In general discount rates are higher with financing than without (this will be true wherever the mortgage rate is lower than the consumer's discount rate). Discount rates with rising real fuel prices exceed those for constant fuel prices since future energy costs are higher in the former situation than the latter.

In most cases, the calculated discount rates are much higher than market interest rates for either borrowing or lending (in both cases we are considering real not nominal

rates). This gives verification to the hypothesis that consumers fail to fully consider the benefits of energy savings
when investing in energy saving goods.

Market Segmentation Approach
to Consumer Decision Making

The factors preventing market forces from resulting in
optimal levels of energy conservation need not effect all
segments of the population equally. Fred Reid (1980) has
completed a preliminary disaggregation by examining how different groups are impacted upon by information constraints, imper-
fect markets, inertia, etc. Reid estimates that less than
14 percent of energy use in the United States responds fully to
market factors. Though the percentages can be expected to have
large variances, estimates indicate that more than 25 percent of
energy use is controlled by agents whose decision making process
is completely insensitive to the market. Further research is
under way by Reid and LBL to expand and verify these results.

Sensitivity Analysis Of Energy
Savings Due to Appliance Standards

When the ORNL model was used to analyze the expected energy
savings due to proposed appliance standards, two important
variables that had a large impact of the result were the energy
price escalation rates and implicit discount rates. The results
are expressed as the difference between the case of implementation of the standards as proposed and a base case without
appliance standards. Empirical analyses are under way to
provide better estimates of the implicit discount rates utilized
by consumers purchasing new appliances. It is hoped that the
results of such analyses will enable future estimation techniques to zero in on probable energy futures and policy implications.

SUMMARY AND CONCLUSIONS

This chapter has attempted to detail the diversity of research being undertaken by the national laboratories as it
relates to energy using appliances. Use of the implicit discount rate mechanism, as discussed, provides a method by which
the effectiveness of the market can be evaluated. Consumers use
much higher implicit discount rates than would be expected with
efficiently functioning markets. Assuming that further research
bears out these conclusions, a strong case can be made for
energy efficiency standards.

The magnitude of barriers to market operations at the
present time cannot be confidently specified. Analysis of
implicit discount rates across time and for individual appliances, as well as between segments of a disaggregated market, is

needed to provide answers to this and most of the other unre-
solved areas identified in this chapter.

RELATED RESEARCH

Brown, S.P.A. (forthcoming), "Barriers to Energy Conservation in
the Purchase and Usage of Energy-Using Consumer Durables,"
Brookhaven National Laboratory.

Hausman, J.A. (Spring 1979), "Individual Discount Rates and the
Purchase and Utilization of Energy Using Durables," The
Bell Journal of Economics, Vol. 10, No. 1, pp. 33-54.

Midwest Research Associates, (1978) "Patterns of Energy Use by
Electrical Appliance Study," Final Report to the Electric
Power Research Institute.

O'Neal, D.L., Corum, K.R., and Jones, J.L., (forthcoming) "An
Estimate of Consumer Discount Rate Implicit in Single-
Family Housing Construction Practices," Oak Ridge National
Laboratory.

Reid, F.A. (1980), "Appliance Acquisition Mechanisms and Energy
Consumption Throughout U.S. Housing: A Disaggregate
Probe," Lawrence Berkeley Laboratory.

U.S. Department of Energy, (June 1980) "Energy Efficiency
Standards for Consumer Products," CS-0169.

CANADIAN PASSENGER CAR FUEL CONSUMPTION SURVEY

Ken Sorrenti

Terry Petherick

The recent world-wide focus on energy use and energy resources has generated a requirement in Canada for reliable statistics about energy consumption, particularly in the transportation sector.

In order to design, implement, and monitor an effective conservation program for personal use passenger cars, it is necessary to understand the current and evolving patterns of passenger car usage, fuel consumption, economic cost for gasoline, and average technical efficiencies achieved by this fleet. The actual relationship between these factors is unknown. Currently only estimates of total gasoline sales are known. The oil companies can only provide uncertain estimates as to how many gallons of gasoline are used by trucks and passenger cars. The portion of this estimate used by passenger cars alone is unknown.

SURVEY OBJECTIVES

The objective of this chapter is the establishment of a national data base concerning personal use of the passenger car in Canada which would contain the following information: total distance travelled, total amount of fuel consumed, average distance obtained per unit of fuel, total expenditures on fuel, and seasonal fluctuations in fuel consumption and in distance travelled.

This project will supply essential information to a variety of government and industry organizations for policy formulation and implementation in the energy field. Among the needs to be served by this data base will be the monitoring of passenger car fuel economy standards and the estimation of passenger car fuel requirements in conditions involving fuel shortages.

SURVEY CONCEPTS

Since little research has been done on the usage of passenger cars, it was decided initially to implement a descriptive survey. As the estimates become available, they will be analyzed in relation to the factors mentioned earlier. At the outset of the project certain general hypotheses were assumed. The first hypothesis is that there are seasonal differences in fuel consumption, second, that fuel consumption differs among weight classes of passenger cars, and third, that there is improved fuel economy in newer cars.

147

The target population for this survey is all personal use passenger cars operated in Canada. Passenger cars are defined by body style and personal use is defined by categorization of uses.   Uses excluded are rent-a-cars, taxis, fleet-operated cars, driver training cars, delivery, inspection or protection service cars, antique cars, ambulances, and hearses. The target population includes only cars which will be operated during the survey reference period. The unit of analysis is the personal use passenger car.

METHODS

When the survey was being developed, consideration was given to employing either a household sample or a vehicle sample. A sample of households would be selected from an area frame or a household list frame and a sample of vehicles would be selected from a vehicle list frame.

For a household survey, several frames were available. However, there are some practical problems in selecting samples from these frames. Any sample of households, whether from a list frame or area frame, would require considerable interviewer time to prepare household and passenger car lists in order to select a sample of passenger cars. Approximately 45 percent of the sample must be current model year vehicles in order to produce estimates for this group. For example, 1979 passenger cars comprise 10 percent to 15 percent of cars on the road; consequently, many interviews would have to be conducted to obtain a large enough sample for this model year.

The household sample sizes required would also be higher than for a sample of vehicles due to larger variances. For a household survey, variances increase because stratification of all vehicles in a province is not possible and a clustered sample design is involved. The effects of these problems could be lessened by listing all automobiles driven by all members of selected households, stratifying this list, then selecting a sample of automobiles.   This is an expensive procedure.   A household survey therefore was rejected due to higher costs and more complicated sample design and interviewing procedures.

The provincial motor vehicle registration lists, then, form the sample frame for the survey. The provinces provide updated copies of their files every three months so no additional procedures for updating the frame are necessary. The registration lists also contain a variety of auxiliary information including vehicle descriptions (make, model, model year), owner name and address, vehicle weight, body style, vehicle use, and license number. This information is used to exclude vehicles from the files which do not belong to the target population and to stratify the files to improve the efficiency of the sample design.   These files are also used for tabulations on characteristics of provincial vehicle fleets. All sampling and most

document preparation can then be done centrally, thereby simpli-
fying the field procedures. The major disadvantage of using the
registration lists is that a personal interview cannot be used.
An excessive amount of travel would be required so costs would
be prohibitive. The survey is instead conducted by telephone
and mail resulting in response rates lower than those experienced using personal interviews. Diary kits are mailed after
completion of the telephone interviews; therefore, in addition
to the problems of telephone survey, the problems of mail-
out/mail-back surveys are encountered. The reduction in costs,
more efficient sample design, and information available on the
entire motor vehicle fleet, however, outweighed the consideration of higher nonresponse, thus the provincial motor vehicle
registration lists became the PCFCS sample frame.

Each provincial file is stratified by model year, geographic code, and one of vehicle weight, number of cylinders or
vehicle wheelbase. Vehicle weight is preferred for stratification over cylinders or wheelbase based on research into factors
affecting fuel consumption. In three provinces, however,
vehicle weight is not recorded so the other two related variables are used. Model year is used for stratification because
Transport Canada requires estimates for two model year groups:
(1) 1978 model year cars, and (2) 1977 and previous model year
cars. Various geographic codes are used to form 2 geographic
groups, urban and rural. Cylinders, wheelbase, or weight are
used to form from 3 to 6 groups. The maximum number of strata
for a province is 24 (2 model year groups by 6 weight groups by
urban/rural). With the stratification completed, the frames are
ready for sample selection.

Simple random samples are selected without replacement from
each stratum. This selection is conducted in two stages because
the sample frames contain foreign elements. An initial sample
of 1500 to 2000 vehicles is selected for each province. These
samples are manually screened in order to exclude any vehicles
which are not in the target population. This reduces the
possibility of conducting unnecessary interviews and gives
accurate estimates of the amount of overcoverage of the frames.

Data Collection Instruments

The method of data collection employs a combination of a
telephone interview and a mail-out/mail-back procedure. Once a
car is selected, a Screening Questionnaire is prepared by
indicating on the form the name and address of the registered
owner along with the vehicle description (make, model, model
year, and licence plate number).

This questionnaire is administered during a telephone
interview and serves these functions:

(1)   To trace specific passenger cars selected in the random sample.

(2)   To verify the information about the car as documented in provincial registration records.

(3)   To locate the principal driver of the car.

(4)   To verify that the car is being used as a personal vehicle rather than for business or commercial purposes.

(5)   To recruit respondents for maintaining records of fuel purchases.

(6)   To eliminate vehicles not in the target population which were not identifiable during the sampling procedure.

(7)   To determine if the car will be operated during the survey reference period.

The second instrument used is the Fuel Purchase Diary. This document is mailed to each respondent for recording fuel purchases for the selected vehicle.   In addition, a third document, the Usage Questionnaire, is included which gathers information on travel to work, long distance trips, vehicle maintenance, and personal and household requirements for mobility.

Each month a prepared set of Screening Questionnaires is sent to each of the eight Statistics Canada Regional Offices. There, the interviewers trace the selected vehicle to the registered owner.   If the car has been sold, the interviewer then traces and contacts the new owner.   Through a telephone interview the interviewer verifies the car description, determines if it is a personal use vehicle and whether it will be operated during the diary recording period.   Contact is made with the principal driver and a diary is mailed.

One week before the diary period begins, the interviewer telephones the principal driver to verify that the diary kit was received and to answer any questions that the respondent may have.   If a diary has not been received, another one is mailed out to the respondent.

For a one-month period, the principal driver and any other drivers of the selected car keep a diary of fuel purchases. Each time a fuel purchase is made, the respondent records details of the purchase in the diary.   The principal driver is asked to fill the tank of the car for the first and last purchase.

At the end of the survey month, the principal driver then completes the Usage Questionnaire and mails it, with the completed diary, to a Statistics Canada Regional Office.   The interviewer follows up nonreturned diaries by telephoning the

respondent and encouraging the respondent to return the completed diary. If, however, the diary has not been completed,
the interviewer determines the reason for this type of non-
response. From the Regional Offices, the documents are sent to
Head Office where they are subjected to manual and computer edit
checks. The data is weighted to provincial fleet populations
and tabulations are produced.

One example of the results of the first survey is presented
in Table 1. As shown, average miles per gallon achieved by all
cars was 19.2, with 1978 model cars obtaining 23.3 mpg, and 1977
and older model cars obtaining 18.5 mpg. This type of information will help policy makers determine the impact of new car
purchases on gasoline consumption patterns. Further results can
be obtained from the Special Surveys Group, Statistics Canada,
Ottawa.

TABLE 1

PERSONAL USE PASSENGER CARS OPERATED DURING
JULY, AUGUST, SEPTEMBER 1979

AVERAGE CONSUMPTION RATE (MILES PER GALLON)
BY MODEL YEAR CLASS BY PROVINCE

| Province | Model Year Class[a] | | |
	1978	1977 and Previous	Total
Newfoundland	20.9	16.5	17.1
P.E.I.	24.5	21.1	21.5
Nova Scotia	25.0	19.6	20.3
Quebec	21.1	17.6	18.1
Ontario	24.7	19.3	20.1
Manitoba	21.1	17.8	18.1
Saskatchewan	21.4	16.9	17.3
Seven Provinces	23.3	18.5	19.2

a. For this quarter, 1979 model year cars were not included in
the survey.

SUMMARY AND CONCLUSIONS

This survey methodology has successfully produced estimates
of personal use passenger car characteristics. This survey
vehicle can easily be adapted to satisfy other research requirements in this field. As descriptive data are accumulated, the
survey may become more analytical. The design may be altered to
test various hypotheses concerning factors affecting fuel
consumption and vehicle usage. This information will enable
users to discern those factors which may achieve substantial
fuel savings in Canada.

CROSS-CULTURAL COMPARISONS OF
A CONSERVATION-ORIENTATION MODEL

Chris T. Allen
Charles D. Schewe
Bertil Liander

Consumer researchers have often used cross-cultural analysis as a method for evaluating and recommending public policy
(Andreasen and Manning 1980; Thorelli and Engledow 1980).
Although comparative analysis has been employed in energy
contexts, it has not been used to its full potential in examining consumers' values and attitudes germane to the energy issue.
Comparative analysis focusing on individuals' attitudes and
values was used in this research to provide insights regarding
the cognitive determinants of conservation-oriented consumption.

The comparative analysis was based on a Swedish sample and
an American one. It has been suggested that although the
Swedish government tightly regulates energy consumption, "in the
final analysis, the Swedish people realize it is in their best
interest to use energy wisely and efficiently. In this sense,
conservation is part of the Swedish frame of mind" (Keough 1978,
p. 10). The present study seeks to determine whether there are
differences in the dispositions and values of Swedes and Americans which offer an explanation for the more conservation-
oriented habits of the Swede. Does the individual Swede consciously and purposefully consume in a fashion to conserve
energy? Or is the Swede's energy-conscious consumption more a
function of governmental rules and regulations, and high prices?

A MODEL OF THE CONSERVATION-ORIENTED CONSUMER

The structure that was used in this comparative analysis
was a model of the conservation-oriented (C-O) consumer. The
C-O consumer perceives the energy problem as real and serious,
believes his/her own consumption behavior is linked to the
problem, and thus consumes purposely in a manner to help resolve
the problem. It was proposed that cognitive determinants of C-O
consumption are of two types: (1) general constructs that have
been linked to socially-conscious consumption, and (2) energy

The authors wish to thank the School of Business Administration, University of Lund, for its financial support, and Jan
Persson and Gösta Wijk for their supervision of the Swedish data
collection. A Faculty Research Grant from the Graduate School,
University of Massachusetts at Amherst funded data collection in
the United States. Thanks are also due to Judith D. Wever for
her very capable assistance at various stages in this endeavor.

152

specific constructs involve dispositions expressly germane to an energy consumption context.

Although past research has been dotted with methodological flaws and mixed findings, it does furnish a starting point for proposing a general description of socially-conscious consumers (Henion 1976; Webster 1975). The socially-conscious consumer can be portrayed as a person generally more concerned about ecological issues, more disenchanted or alienated from a heavily consumption-oriented and materialistic life style, and more confident in one's ability to effect solutions to problems with personal actions (i.e. is characterized by a higher degree of internal locus of control). This profile seems highly applicable to the C-O consumer since this person is taking personal action to help out with a societal problem. Examples of items for the general explanatory constructs--ecological concern, consumer alienation, materialism, and locus of control--are in Table 1.

A variety of researchers have attempted to identify the dispositions and beliefs which underlie C-O consumption. One of the factors which apparently accounts for a lack of C-O consumption in the United States and elsewhere is a lack of concern, a deep-seeded cynicism regarding the seriousness of the energy predicament (Milstein 1977; Richman 1979). However, past findings also indicate that concern alone does not produce C-O consumption (Morrison and Gladhart 1976). If individuals blame "big business" or "big government" for the energy problem, then they are not likely to consume in a C-O fashion (Milstein 1977). Rather, they perceive the source of the problem as responsible for its solution. Yankelovich (1974) offers an appealing intuitive argument that concerned individuals are not likely to take socially-responsible actions when their "perceptions of others" are unfavourable; they rationalize a lack of action on the basis of the perception that others are not acting responsibly.

Perhaps the most important explanation for the paradox of concerned individuals unwilling to conserve is found in a construct generally referred to as perceived consumer effectiveness (Allen 1980; Henion 1976; Scott 1977). The individual must perceive a link between one's own consumption behavior and the energy problem for C-O consumption to occur. The C-O consumer believes the energy predicament is his concern and his behavior does make a difference. The linkage between this general feeling of effectiveness construct and socially-conscious consumption has been established in a variety of contexts (see Henion's 1976 review) including the energy context (Allen 1980; Allen and Dillon 1979). "Who To Blame," "Perceptions of Others," and "General Feeling of Effectiveness" are the energy specific explanatory constructs included in the model of the C-O consumer.

TABLE 1

CONSERVATION-ORIENTATION MODEL AND SELECTED FINDINGS

Constructs and Example Items	Hypothesized Relationships	Significant[a] Differences Between Samples	
		No. of Items	Relationship
Locus of Control			
• Peoples' misfortunes result from the mistakes they make.	C-O behaviors positively related to belief in self as locus of control (H_0: S>US)	3	Opposite to hypothesis
Consumer Alienation			
• Most brands are the same with just different names and labels	C-O behaviors positively related to feelings of separation from norms and values of the marketplace (H_0: S>US)	3	As hypothesized
Ecological Concern			
• More time and money should be spent resolving pollution problems	C-O behaviors positively related to feelings of ecological concern (H_0: S>US)	1	As hypothesized
Materialism			
• Buying a gift for another person is a good way of telling them that you like them	C-O behaviors negatively related to materialistic values (H_0: S>US)	1 1	As hypothesized Opposite to hypothesis

TABLE 1 — (Continued)

Constructs and Example Items	Hypothesized Relationships	Significant[a] Differences Between Samples	
		No. of Items	Relationship

General Feelings of Effectiveness
- Energy is not my problem because there is simply nothing I can do about it

C-O behaviors positively related to feelings of individual effectiveness (H_0: S>US)

1 Opposite to hypothesis

Perceptions of Others
- Most people have made changes in the way they live to help reduce the severity of the nation's energy problem

C-O behaviors positively related to belief that others are doing their share (H_0: S>US)

1 Opposite to hypothesis

Perceived Change in Consumption
- I've changed the way I purchase and use products as a result of the nation's energy problem

An example of C-O behavior (H_0: S>US)

2 Opposite to hypothesis

[a] Significant difference between samples at $p < 0.00001$.

THE STUDY

A detailed description of the study is available from the authors. The following provides a brief summary of the major aspects of the research.

Measurement Instruments

Most of the measurement instruments utilized in the study were adopted from previous research; the constructs are described briefly in Table 1. Locus of control was operationalized to gauge the four components of the construct established by Collins (1974) in his work with the Rotter Internal-External scale. Consumer alienation from the marketplace was measured via the thirty-five item scale developed by Allison (1978). The energy specific explanatory constructs were operationalized to be consistent with prior work (Allen 1980; Allen and Dillon 1979). The ecological concern and materialism scales were developed expressly for this project. Ecological concern was a straightforward five item scale dealing with the priority a society should place on environmental protection. Materialism was developed to assess the importance of consumption activities to the individual and included items dealing with: the judgments that can be made about persons based on the products they possess; the use of gift giving as a means of expressing emotions; and the nature of what individuals have a "right to consume."

Data Collection

Data collection took place in Spring, 1979. The cities sampled were Springfield, Massachusetts, and Malmö, Sweden. In both cases questionnaires were mailed to a random sample of households. In Springfield, 235 of 477 were returned, while in Malmö, 320 of 1032 were returned.

Preliminary analysis demonstrated that data collection in Sweden produced a sample highly representative of both Malmö and Sweden in terms of age and educational profiles. The demographic profile of the Springfield sample, however, proved to be somewhat biased. The Springfield sample was older, more educated, and had higher incomes than was typical of either the Springfield metropolitan area or the New England region.

Item analysis was performed with each of the C-O constructs. Alpha coefficients ranged from 0.44 to 0.88 for the Springfield sample, and from 0.44 to 0.85 for the Malmö sample. This suggests at least a minimally acceptable level of reliability for all scales (Nunnally 1967).

Analytical Approach

Two major types of analyses were employed in examining the survey data. First, canonical correlation was employed in assessing the association between C-O consumption and each of the constructs in the model of the C-O consumer. Second, the two sample groups were compared on each model construct. To establish the potential impact of the Springfield sample bias on the between country comparisons, MANOVA's were run with and without age, income, and education as covariates. The inclusion of covariates made very little difference in the findings, indicating that the sampling bias identified by the demographic profiles did not offer a major threat to the validity of these cultural comparisons.

SUMMARY AND CONCLUSIONS

The analysis of major concern here is the cross-cultural comparisons on the various conservation-orientation constructs. Univariate F tests, agree/disagree percentages, and group means were examined for individual scale items in interpreting findings. The results for selected items are shown in Table 1. These particular items were chosen to reflect not only the strong statistical significance in the results, but also what appeared to be the most meaningful difference based upon examination of agree/disagree percentages and cell means. Furthermore, the significance levels for group difference on all items shown in Table 1 were not influenced by the inclusion of age, income, and education covariates in the analysis of variance model.

Inferences can be drawn from these findings regarding differences in the dispositions and values of Swedes and Americans that may in part explain the more energy-thrifty consumption habits of Swedes. However, the notion that Swedes more than Americans consciously and purposefully consume in a fashion to conserve energy is not supported. Although the Swedes were less materialistic than the New Englanders, they were less likely to view their own behavior as effective, and were more skeptical of what others were doing in helping out with the energy problem. Furthermore, in the study's most lopsided finding, the New Englanders' perceptions of "change in consumption" were much stronger than the Swedes. Nearly two-thirds of the Springfield sample perceived they had altered their consumption habits as a result of the national energy predicament, compared to less than one-fourth of the Malmö sample.

In other words, although clear differences on the C-O constructs were identified, as often as not the differences were opposite to those that would be hypothesized by the conservation-orientation model. The two major conclusions that this suggests are, first, explanations for differences in energy

consumption between Swedes and Americans must be sought elsewhere. The differences in dispositions and values studied here
have not provided an explanation. Second, the conservation-
orientation model as tested here requires careful reconsideration. On the basis of this cross-cultural comparison, it is
clear that the strength of the model has yet to be established.

RELATED RESEARCH

Allen, Chris T. (1980), "Self-Perception Based Strategies for
    Stimulating Socially-Conscious Consumption: The Case of
    Energy," Center for Management Research Working Paper
    Series, No. 80-27, University of Massachusetts, Amherst.

_____, and Dillon, William R. (1979), "On Receptivity to Infor-
    mation Furnished by the Public Policymaker: The Case of
    Energy," in 1979 Educators' Proceedings, eds. N. Beckwith
    et al., Chicago: American Marketing Association, 550-556.

Allison, Neil K. (1978), "A Psychometric Development of a Test
    for Consumer Alienation from the Marketplace," Journal of
    Marketing Research, 15, 565-575.

Andreasen, Alan R. and Manning, Jean M. (1980), "Conducting
    Cross-National Consumer Policy Research," in Advances in
    Consumer Research: Vol. 7, ed. J. Olson, Ann Arbor, MI,:
    Association for Consumer Research, 77-82.

Boffey, Philip M. (1977), "How the Swedes Live Well While
    Consuming Less Energy," Science, 196, 856.

Boor, Myron (1976), "Relationship of Internal-External Control
    and National Suicide Rates," Journal of Social Psychology,
    100, 143-144.

Collins, Barry E. (1974), "Four Components of the Rotter Inter-
    nal-External   Scale,"   Journal of Personality and Social
    Psychology, 29, 381-391.

Henion, Karl E. (1976), Ecological Marketing, Columbus, OH:
    Grid, Inc.

Keough, James (1978), "How Sweden Saves So Much Energy," Sierra,
    63, 8-11.

Milstein, Jeffrey S. (1977), "Attitudes, Knowledge and Behavior
    of American Consumers Regarding Energy Conservation with
    Some Implications for Governmental Action," in Advances in
    Consumer Research: Vol. 4, ed. W. Perreault, Atlanta:
    Association for Consumer Research, 315-321.

Morrison, Bonnie M. and Gladhart, Peter (1976), "Energy and Families: The Crises and Response," Journal of Home Economics, 68, 15-18.

Nunnally, John C. (1967), Psychometric Theory, New York: McGraw-Hill.

Richman, Al (1979), "The Polls: Public Attitudes Toward the Energy Crisis," Public Opinion Quarterly, 43, 576-585.

Scott, Carol A. (1977), "Modifying Socially-Conscious Behavior: The Foot-in-the-Door Technique," Journal of Consumer Research, 4, 156-164.

Thorelli, Hans B. and Engledow, Jack L. (1980), "Information Seekers and Information Systems: A Policy Perspective," Journal of Marketing, 44, 9-23.

Verhallen, Theo M.M. and van Raaij, W. Fred (1980), "Household Behavior and Energy Use," Papers on Economic Psychology, No. 7, Erasmus University, Rotterdam.

Webster, Frederick E. (1975), "Determining the Characteristics of the Socially Conscious Consumer," Journal of Consumer Research, 2, 188-196.

Yankelovich, Daniel (1974), "How Opinion Polls Differ From Social Indicators," in Social Indicators and Marketing, eds., R. Clewett and J. Olson, Chicago: American Marketing Association, 54-66.

RESIDENTIAL ENERGY END USE:
DEVELOPING AN INTERNATIONAL DATA BASE

Lee Schipper
Andrea Ketoff

Data on the uses of energy in the residential sector have been particularly difficult to come by, especially in European countries. Because such information is important to understand future demands for energy, opportunities for conservation, the impact of higher energy prices on families, and the possible impacts of sudden shortfalls in supply, this lack of information presents a serious problem. For example, the OECD, and most member countries, as well as the UN, until recently only kept information on the "other" sector, a hodge-podge classification that counted everything not in transportation or industry and often included agriculture. Not surprisingly, most OECD nations found themselves with few ideas for energy saving in the residential sector at the macro level. While a host of technical programs were developed to improve particular components of buildings or appliances, there was little ability to predict the impact of such programs upon future energy consumption.

Recently, however, the Energy Information Administration of the US Dept. of Energy asked the Lawrence Berkeley Laboratory (LBL) to begin assembling data on residential energy use in seven important OECD countries, Japan, Sweden, Canada, West Germany, France, Italy, and the United Kingdom. These countries represent a spectrum of incomes, climates, lifestyles, and fuels used as well as energy efficient technologies. Additionally data has been assembled on several other OECD countries, and on Kenya, Korea, and other developing countries. LBL has also developed a data base on US residential energy use.

An earlier paper (Schipper 1979) described some methodological issues apparent at the outset of the study. The present chapter outlines progress so far in assembling and analyzing data. No attempt will be made to specify all data assembled to date. Rather, the purpose is to show what kinds of factors seem to be important to the historical (1960-1980) development of

Work sponsored by the Applied Analysis Division of the Energy Information Administration, U.S. Department of Energy. This paper is a substantial revision of an earlier LBL report and reflects the opinions of the authors and not the Lawrence Berkeley Laboratory or the U.S. Department of Energy. We acknowledge the helpful comments of Howard Ross (U.S. Dept. of Energy), who reviewed an early version of this manuscript.

energy use. It should be emphasized that this chapter summarizes this work. Further details about this work are available from the authors.

STRUCTURE AND ENERGY INTENSITY

The data base being developed is designed to facilitate the
analysis of structure and intensity (Schipper and Lichtenberg,
1976). Structural issues that may be of concern include factors
such as dwellings per capita, dwelling size, dwelling type,
incomes, penetration of central heating, appliance penetration,
indoor temperatures, and climate. Using data on these structural factors, it is possible to do international comparisons based
on intensity calculations such as electricity or fuel per
capita, per income, per dwelling floor area, per degree day, et
cetera. Table 1 provides examples of the types of international
data that is being compiled. The data sources for energy end
use estimates have been varied. In some countries, government
reports provide extensive data on energy end use while, in
others countries, information is scattered through a variety of
studies. Not surprisingly, other sources had to be pursued,
including oil and gas companies, electric utilities, trade
associations, housing and census bureaus, academic research
groups, and professional societies. Similarly, structural data
have been obtained from housing ministries, census bureaus,
utility surveys, and housing companies.

PRELIMINARY ANALYSIS

What tentative conclusions can be read from the preliminary
data? First, the rapid rise in fuel and particularly electricity use appears to be associated with rising incomes and
increased ownership of energy using devices. However, these
devices are saturating even as incomes continue to rise. Hence
considerably less growth in energy use relative to incomes would
be expected in the future.

Second, comparison across incomes suggests that electricity
prices in particular, which seem to vary more than fuel prices,
are extremely important determinants of consumption. It comes
as no surprise that the Swedes and Canadians consume the most
electricity for appliances in both an absolute sense and relative to income. These countries enjoy the lowest electricity
prices.

Third, because the use of electricity for heating may arise
out of deliberate government policy, it is crucial to separate
this use from other uses of electricity. In Sweden electric
heating comprises a major part of the growth in use between 1972
and 1979. Growth in electric heating has also been dramatic in
France. One issue that arises when aggregated data are examined
is how to segregate the resource energy consumed by electric
heat.

TABLE 1

INTERNATIONAL DATA BASE

The following are examples of the types of data being compiled.
Detailed data can be obtained from the authors.

1.   Residential Energy Use Breakdown
     • for UK, Canada, Germany, Sweden, France, Italy, and
     Japan

     • Heating: Number of dwellings, persons per dwelling,
     dwelling floor area, proportion of centrally heated
     dwellings, total fuel.

     • Hot water: proportions electric and fuel, total energy
     per capita

     • Cooking and appliance energy consumption: total and per
     capita

2.   Degree Day Estimates

     • for Canada, France, West Germany, Japan, Italy, Sweden

3.   Electric Appliance Saturation and Yearly Consumption

     • for Canada, France, West Germany, Italy, Sweden, and UK

     • broken down by cooking, water heating, dish washer,
     clothes washer, refrigerator/freezer, and other appli-
     ances

4.   Domestic Electricity, Gas, and Oil Prices

     • for Canada, France, West Germany, Japan, Italy, Sweden,
     UK, USA

     • for time period 1960 through 1979

     • for heating and non-heating purposes

     Fourth, the prominence of Swedish (and to a certain extent
Canadian) low heat losses is not clear because space heating has
not been disaggregated by dwelling type or age, and presence or
absence of central heating (available data, however, appear to
make this possible for some countries).
     Fifth, the levels of saturation of central heating in most
countries are still growing, suggesting that space heating needs
will continue to grow, although at a reduced rate.

Further, in the area of space heating, increases in central heating point up opportunities to improve building shell charac- teristics in existing homes, and to demand the most effective space heating devices be put on the market. The EEC (Common Market) has considered a nine country wide standard on the nominal performance of space heaters to encourage improvements in efficiency. Official forecasts in Germany, Italy, France, and the UK have avoided making any detailed comments on the prospects for improved weatherization of existing homes or the impact of better built newer homes upon future energy demands. While there are retrofit studies published or underway in each country, for example (Leach et al 1979) only Sweden's Statens Planverk (1977) appears to have had a noticeable impact upon energy planning. No country (except Sweden) has yet tried to analyze the results of public monies or loans handed out to building owners or private families who have made conservation investments. A Swedish study, the "Starre" report (1979), did analyze the grants disbursed in 1977/8 and found less energy saved per unit of investment than hoped. The main problem was that most investment funds flowed towards facade renewal, perhaps a legitimate use of public funds but not the use for which the money had been intended.

One important final lesson is that government authorities responsible for overall energy planning or even residential planning seem very ill informed about the nature of energy use, the state of information, or the dynamics of the last seven years. Such knowledge seems crucial to energy planning in general, to the design of conservation programs and the measure- ment of their success, and to the design of research and devel- opment.

IMPLICATIONS FOR THE STUDY OF BEHAVIOR AND ENERGY

The work thus far leads to certain important ideas about the interaction of consumer behavior and energy use. First, there is an enormous variation in energy use per family for a given end use, a variation too large to be explained by tech- nology alone. It appears that behavior--the way people use hot water, their preference for frozen rather than fresh foods-- plays a key role. But much remains to be quantified.

Another interesting question is the role of energy prices. While formal study of the role of prices and incomes will come later in this work, all indications from present data are that prices are important determinants of energy use and intensities. For example, appliance electricity use is highest in the low electricity price countries and lowest in those countries with high prices. Penetration of central heating seems to depend directly upon income, while heating efficiency depends on price. For example, the Swedes, paying more than the Canadians for heat in comparable climates, live in somewhat more efficient homes.

An additional question that arises is the most effective means for carrying out a conservation program. By 1979 it appeared that new appliances in most countries were beginning to show improved energy efficiencies. Heating use, adjusted for climate, seemed to have stabilized. Were these changes the results of higher prices alone, or were government programs important? How much information were consumers obtaining in their efforts to economize on energy use? Quantification, as done in the present study, will provide some of the answers to these questions by pinning down how consumers have changed their energy use in the face of stiff price increases, new technologies, and more information.

Finally, there is one additional point worth raising. Over the years, there have been many attitude surveys about energy use and conservation, about preferences for one kind of heating over another, or about knowledge of the energy problem in general. Many negative conclusions are drawn, particularly that consumers do not care about energy problems or conservation. A recent Wall Street Journal Article (12 May 1980, Page 1) by J. Kronholz, for example, asserted that drivers in France were paying little concern to energy conservation. The evidence offered was that gasoline consumption in France was 21 percent higher in 1979 than in 1973. Yet buried in the same article were the data that during the same period the numbers of autos had increased by 22 percent, and that miles driven had also gone up steadily. Therefore, gallons/car/year had decreased and miles per gallon, a sure sign of conservation, must have increased. At the same time the growth in autos in France had been cut in half since 1972, and the real increase in prices was only on the order of 20 percent for the 1972-79 period. Given the modest price increased, the reduction in the growth rate of automobile ownership, the increase in miles per gallon, and the still low saturation of cars in France (1 per 3 people by 1980), it seems that the observations are completely consistent with a view that conservation is taking place. The problem is that the measurement of conservation--here measured in terms of intensities (like miles per gallon)--has been overlooked. The popular measure, gasoline consumption, is increasing and this brings "bad tidings." It is likely that this type of measurement problem has in fact hindered many attempts to find out what consumers are up to regarding energy use.

SUMMARY AND CONCLUSIONS

End use estimates for each country have been assembled, with the quality of these estimates varying greatly. Future work includes finalizing these estimates by checking among years for consistency and adding new data now available from fuel suppliers and other analysts. One priority is to be able to improve the estimates for those countries where no studies have been previously performed. A second priority is to study the differences in patterns among types of dwellings, particularly among the various kinds of multi-family and single family dwellings, as well as simply between these two classes.

Additionally the work is at a point where it is possible to begin to compare the importance of lifestyle differences in causing--or resulting from--differences in energy use. In particular the use of the refrigerator and its size, heating habits, and hot water are all important uses of energy in the homes that depend greatly on lifestyles. It is important to make these lifestyle-energy connections quantitative wherever possible.

Another important area for future work is that of economics. To date there have been few studies of the economics of energy end uses in the home, only studies of energy consumption. The current data base will allow careful economic analysis of the major energy uses. Related to this problem is the question of evaluating changes in consumption since 1972 brought about by higher energy prices and in some cases by important end use conservation policies. Few countries have tried to monitor or analyze their own progress. Further international comparisons can help to evaluate the relative impact of alternative conservation initiatives.

RELATED RESEARCH

Anon. (1978). End Uses of Energy in Italy in 1975. Roma, Ente Nazionale Idrocarburi (Special report on "Settore Domestico").

Basile, P. et al, eds. (1977), Workshop on Alternative Energy Strategies: Individual Country Demand Studies. Cambridge, Mass.: MIT Press.

Energisparkomitteen (1979), standing committee in Stockholm publishes quarterly analyses of aggregate and sectoral consumption with some structural data.

Fisk D. (1977), Microeconomics and the Demand for Space Heating. Energy Vol. 2. New York: Pergamon Press.

Griffin, J. (1979), Energy Conservation in the OECD. Cambridge, Mass: Ballinger Books.

Leach, G. et al. (1978), A Low Energy Scenario for the United Kingdom. London: Int'l Inst. for Environment and Development.

Noergaard, J. (1979), Energi og Husholdninger. Lyngby: Danmarks Tekniske Hoejskole.

Pindyck, R. (1978), The Structure of the World Demand for Energy. Cambridge: MIT Press.

Rosenfeld, A. et al. (1980), Building Energy Compilation and Analysis. Energy and Buildings, in press, available as LBL-8912, Lawrence Berkeley Laboratory Report.

Schipper, L. (1979), International Comparisons of Residential Energy Use. Proc. International Conference on Energy Use Management. New York: Pergamon Press.

_____, and Lichtenberg A. (1976), Science 194, P. 1001.   3 Dec. See also J. Dunkerly et al., 1977 How Industrial Societies Use Energy. Baltimore: Johns Hopkins Press.

Starre, G. (1979),   Bostadsstyrelsens Utvaerdering av Energisparstoedet: Del 1: Bostaeder.   (Evaluation of Energy Conservation Subsidies: Part 1, Homes) Stockholm: Bostadsdepartementet (Ministry of Housing).

Statens Planverk (1977), Energibesparing i Befintliga Bebyggelse. Stockholm: Liber Feorlag.

PART II

Conservation Program Options

- Preview
- Conservation Program Overviews
- Prices and Controls
- Information and Incentives

PREVIEW

The papers presented in Part II focus on consumer energy conservation programs. They describe and analyze the impact of diverse programs in a variety of settings. The first two papers, by Cannon and by Gradin and Anderson, provide Conservation Program Overviews. The Cannon paper describes a number of federal and community actions that have been tested in various parts of the U.S. The Gradin and Anderson paper describes a host of existing and proposed energy conservation programs in the 21 member countries of the International Energy Agency.

The second section presents five papers dealing with programs that have direct impact on energy consumption through Prices and Controls. Heberlein, Linz, and Ortiz examine the impact of residential electricity prices that vary by time of day. Pitts, Willenborg, and Sherrell assess the impact of increasing gasoline prices. Van Helden and Weistra evaluate the impact of a progessive rate structure for household electricity. The final two papers, by Corney, Nixon, and Yantis and by Dyer, evaluate consumer reaction to utility control of peak loads via periodic interruptions in residential electricity supply.

The third section of Part II presents six papers dealing with programs that have a more indirect impact on energy consumption through Information and Incentives. Anderson and Claxton use a field experiment to assess the impact of energy labels on consumer appliance purchases. Redinger and Staelin address the same issue in a laboratory setting. Gaskell, Ellis and Pike evaluate the impact on household energy consumption of conservation information and daily consumption feedback. Pitts and Wittenbach assess the impact of the U.S. Residential Energy Tax Credit. Hirst and Lazare evaluate a home energy audit program. Finally, the paper by McNeill and Hutton describes and evaluates a major initiative by the U.S. Department of Energy. In the fall of 1979 a program called the Low Cost/No Cost Energy Conservation Program was implemented in six New England states. The program involved integrated marketing and communication efforts. McNeill and Hutton report the effects of this program.

Clearly, the array of possible energy conservation programs is substantial. Furthermore, the number of options that have been implemented is far greater than the number that have been evaluated. Fortunately the programs discussed here have been subjected to careful evaluation. Review of these efforts can provide valuable insights for the selection and design of future conservation initiatives.

CONSERVATION PROGRAM OVERVIEWS

- U.S. Energy Conservation: Federal and Community Actions

- International Perspective on Energy Conservation

U.S. ENERGY CONSERVATION:
FEDERAL AND COMMUNITY ACTIONS

Lisa Cannon

The United States, in its transition from cheap, abundant
sources of energy to scarcer, more expensive sources, faces
difficult and challenging public policy issues. The basic
policy of reducing oil imports by stimulating domestic production and encouraging conservation involves a commitment to
change not only in federal actions, but also in the daily
decisions and actions of this country's 220 million consumers.

This chapter will examine some of the programs the
Department of Energy (DOE) has launched in its effort to make
energy conservation part of the transition strategy—as well as
a permanent feature of our society. The chapter will also look
at some significant non-federal conservation projects, and try
to identify points at which federal and individual efforts to
achieve conservation might be integrated in the future.

BACKGROUND

The basic tenet of United States energy policy is to make
energy prices reflect the realities of today's energy market.
The phased decontrol of oil and gas prices by 1981 and 1985,
respectively, will bring this reality sharply home to Americans.
However, the change requires more than using the price mechanism
alone. Consumers' habits, lifestyles, economic decisions, and
attitudes are still largely tied to an earlier energy era which
no longer exists. The government is taking additional steps to
help American consumers better understand and act upon today's
necessities.

One of hardest tasks is defining specific conservation
goals and the manner in which these should be achieved. This
policy dilemma is clearly expressed as follows:

Conservation is the most immediate and cost effective
means to deal with the energy problem by reducing the
need for oil imports; mitigating the impact of rising
oil prices; increasing the efficiency of the U.S.
economy; limiting the transfer of wealth to oil producing states and from consumers to producers of
energy; and extending the availability of dwindling
fossil fuels ... Unfortunately, the meaning of "conservation" as used by government policy-makers and as
perceived by the 220 million-odd decision-makers in
the country differs susbstantially (D.O.E. 1980).

Part of the difficulty lies in presenting conservation as an opportunity rather than a sacrifice. People must be convinced that very substantial savings are attainable without lowering the standards of living they have worked hard to achieve. However, doing this requires altering the nature of personal and corporate energy-wasting habits and significantly changing the existing building and equipment stock.

Another difficulty is defining the potential of conservation. Estimates about potential energy savings vary widely. For example, DOE, as recently as 1979, assumed that conservation could save 1.5 million barrels of oil per day by 1990. More recently, the Harvard Business School's Energy Group study suggested that conservation could save 8 million barrels of oil per day by 1990 (Stobaugh and Yergin 1979). These differences illustrate the different assumptions that are being used to predict consumer responses to prices, programs, and incentives, as well as the different assumptions about technical feasibility of new energy supplies and processes.

Current experience suggests that no single approach can drastically reduce energy consumption quickly and painlessly. Rather, conservation will be achieved through an evolutionary process. It is for this reason that United States conservation policy involves a large number of programs and approaches at all levels. Many of these approaches are national in scope and cover all the end use sectors--residential, transportation, commercial, and industrial.

NATIONWIDE PROGRAMS

A national conservation policy that affects nearly all consumers includes a residential tax credit for conservation improvements. The credit permits homeowners to claim 15 percent or up to $300 on their income tax for expenditures on storm windows, attic and wall insulation, weatherstripping, caulking, double and triple glazing, and other measures. For the 20-month period from April 1977 to December 1978, approximately 5.8 million taxpayers (or 7.7 percent of the U.S.) took advantage of the credit, with estimated average expenditures of $700.

The federal government has promulgated proposed national energy performance standards for new residential and commercial buildings, which will require all building designs to be at or below maximum allowable energy consumption "budgets" based on location and use requirements.

The Department has also developed procedures for testing the efficiency of household appliances, and has issued proposed efficiency standards for nine specific products which, if made final, will have to be met by all appliance manufacturers. These standards are complemented by labeling requirements for such appliances, stating for the consumer the expected ratio of useful energy output to energy consumed.

Another national energy policy is fuel efficiency standards for new automobiles (in effect through 1985). Beginning in 1978, the first year the standards were administered, the standard was 18 miles per gallon. The standard for 1980 is 20 miles per gallon; the standard for 1985 is 27.5 miles per gallon. Supplements to the fuel efficiency standards are the "gas guzzler" tax which imposes a tax on manufacturers whose automobiles fail to meet the standards, and automobile fuel economy guides and labels which provide consumer information on expected fuel economies for new cars by model type. Sixteen million fuel economy guides were distributed in 1979 to the public, largely through retail automobile showrooms.

Many other conservation programs are administered at the national level, but rely upon state and local government agencies for implementation. These include:

1.   Energy Conservation Program for Schools, Hospitals and Buildings Owned by Units of Local Government and Public Care Institutions: A $900 million matching grant program which assists institutions in auditing and retrofitting their buildings;

2.   Residential Conservation Service: An audit and information program administered by each state through the regulated utilities, through which every utility customer receives printed conservation materials and the offer to have his or her home individually audited;

3.   Weatherization Assistance Program: A grant program for low-income households to have up to $800 worth of conservation improvements installed;

4.   Public Utilities Regulatory Policies Act: A mandate to public utilities to review the feasibility of changing to more efficient rate designs and developing more hydroelectric resources.

FEDERAL PROGRAMS FOR STATE AND LOCAL GOVERNMENTS

There are a number of federal programs which are specifically designed to enhance the capabilities of state and local governments to play an important role in achieving energy conservation. All of these programs are essentially grant programs which provide federal money and technical assistance to states, with the stipulation that the states fulfill certain specific requirements relating to the establishment of state programs, regulations, and even laws. These programs are considered an especially important part of the United States' energy conservation strategy because state and local governments are by definition closer to consumers and therefore often are better able to design and enforce appropriate conservation

measures, even within the prescriptions of a national law. Two
such programs are described: a grant program and an outreach
program.

The first and most comprehensive conservation grant program
mandated by the Congress and administered by DOE was the State
Energy Conservation Program (SECP) enacted in 1976.   This
program allocated grants to each state ($50 million per year,
total), with the stipulation that each state must put into
effect eight specific conservation measures.   These are:
lighting and thermal efficiency standards for all publicly-owned
buildings; promotion of carpools, van pools and public transportation; mandatory energy efficient state procurement guidelines;
a traffic law or regulation permitting a right turn at a red
stop light; public education programs; energy audits (not
necessarily on-site); and general coordination of energy initiatives statewide. States are also permitted to use grant monies
for other projects as long as all the requirements are fulfill-
ed.   The goal of this ambitious program was to reduce energy
consumption by 5 percent in each state by 1980.   1980 has
arrived, but the 5 percent energy savings goal is uncertain.
The 1978 savings (the last year evaluated) was 747 trillion
Btu's, representing only 13 percent of this goal (USGAO 1980).

In retrospect, it is not difficult to see why the SECP
encountered some difficulties.   The aim of the program was
ambitious; the start-up time necessary to first analyze energy
use within the state and devise a systematic plan for reducing
consumption was underestimated; and the specific measures
mandated may not always have been appropriate to every state.
In almost every state, legislative changes were required relating to lighting, procurement, and building codes, and these
often proved to be obstacles to prompt implementation.   Although
the states had many specific reporting requirements relative to
program progress and energy savings achieved, these requirements
were sometimes beyond the technical capability of some states to
fulfill.   Lack of uniformity in the calculation methodologies
for energy savings resulted in some states submitting savings
figures which were difficult to analyze. For the Department, in
turn, the lack of uniformity meant review of dozens of different
reporting formats. We learned through this experience that
strict regulations need to be promulgated for reporting and
auditing.   Finally, while the SECP program had the very important effect of establishing energy offices of some kind in every
state, its real impact in terms of tangible accomplishments for
the money spent may never be known.

A strong emphasis in all DOE's State Conservation programs
has been information and outreach campaigns.   Currently there
are approximately 75 energy information programs with outreach
components in 13 different U.S. Government agencies, with a
collective 1980 budget of approximately $270 million.   Of this
amount, DOE controls about 70 percent.

The most successful energy outreach program is the Energy Extension Service. This program provides energy savings information, and advice to individuals, small private firms, local governments, architects, savings and loans officers, farmers, tenants, and homeowners. The EES was established by Congress in 1977, and began as a 10-state pilot program now in the process of being made nationwide. The 10 pilot states carried out a total of 72 separate information delivery systems, targeted to residences, small businesses, and public institutions. The programs ranged from intensive on-site audits of commercial buildings to workshops for consumers, and consumer energy-information hot-lines.

The evaluation of the EES was intended to determine which types of service deliveries worked best in terms of actual savings achieved at minimal cost. Some of the key ingredients in the evaluation were monthly status reports by each state; on-site visits by contractor and DOE staff; and an evaluation begun concurrently with program implementation in every case.

There were several interesting findings in the EES evaluation. First, of all the target groups, small business clearly showed the greatest response and the most energy savings. Second, participation by small business was improved by workshop and audit attendees having to pay some participation fee, suggesting that people feel they are getting something more worthwhile if they have to pay something for it. In fact, one of the recommendations of the EES National Advisory Board was that the nation EES program be carried out on the basis of matching grants from state and federal sources (with mandatory pass-through of funds to local units, also).

The two key findings were: (1) the need to deliver outreach services at the local level by credible local institutions; and (2) the need to create consumer awareness of the existence and advantages of available technologies and to respond to the specific needs and problems of the individual consumer. This concept of customized information is fundamental to the Extension Service. The general finding of the EES pilot program was that there seemed to be almost no correlation between changes in general energy knowledge and concrete actions towards energy conservation. Similarly, the primary reasons for the success of the EES are: local delivery, individual design, diversity and flexibility, delegated authority, and one-to-one contact with energy consumers.

The federal government, as these two programs indicate, is clearly not the source from which all energy initiatives should emanate. In fact, some of the most innovative conservation projects have sprung from local inspiration and local necessity, as the following examples will illustrate.

INDEPENDENT APPROACHES

Most of the independent conservation initiatives in the United States today--that is, initiatives taking place outside of any federally-mandated programs--are occurring at the level of local governments and communities. It is estimated that some 400 communities across the country have some kind of energy program in operation. To date, the Department of Energy has interacted only marginally with most of these community projects. Recently, however, the federal government has established a large information network for communities, providing toll-free telephone numbers that community leaders and local officials can call to obtain information about other community and city projects. This network, called the President's Clearing House for Community Energy Efficiency, is located in Washington, D.C., and is staffed not only by DOE personnel, but also by four rotating teams of local officials who spend a month at the Center. The Clearinghouse houses a large archives of printed material on the various community projects around the country, although access to the information is still not as well codified as we would like. Upon request, the Clearinghouse mails out packages to interested local officials who want to read about other community planning and project experiences.

In reviewing local activities, the best of the community programs seem to combine some of the same ingredients, which include:

(1) Broad representation from the community, including elected officials and private citizens: The city of Wichita, Kansas, for example, put together a 10-month energy commission made up of city council members, county commissioners, school board members, one member each from the State House and Senate, and a broad range of small community organizations. A representative of the Governor and the U.S. Congressman for the district are ex officio members.

(2) Substantial self-reliance within the community: Drawing upon volunteer time and organizational skill, as well as local money in some cases. They are never hand-out programs, and nearly always use existing structures.

(3) Leveraging money from several different sources: To put together one integrated conservation program; including federal, state, and private foundation money plus some contributions from local businesses.

(4) Strong consciousness-raising efforts: Including fairs, radio and TV promos, school programs, etc.

Two examples of communities that have used these principles are Portland, Oregon and Fitchburg, Massachusetts.

Portland, Oregon

One of the most successful independent conservation programs initiated by any community is that of Portland, Oregon.
This city of 400,000 located in the American northwest, has a
very strong incentive to develop a strong conservation plan, as
the costs of new power are extremely high. Any future generating capacity will have to come from coal or nuclear plants both
of which create severe economic and environmental burdens. In
order to avoid such a choice the City of Portland managed to
mobilize itself to create and implement an ambitious conservation strategy.

The Portland Energy Conservation Project consists of six
major initiatives which are:

1. Designating specific responsibility to the city
    government for implementing the city's conservation
    programs, including the establishment of a city Energy
    Commission for policy; a city Energy Office for staff-
    ing and implementation; a private, non-profit corpora-
    tion to carry out the actual weatherization programs
    (Portland Energy Conservation, Inc.).

2. A building retrofit requirement for residential and
    commercial buildings which requires audit and weather-
    ization before the building title can be transferred
    (known as the time-of-transfer policy).

3. Future land use policy promoting attached housing and
    close-in housing; reducing the need for travel and
    reducing trip lengths to service (shopping) centers
    and work.

4. Encouraging the use of renewable resources by removing
    administrative obstacles; making tax incentives avail-
    able for solar systems; establishing deed covenants
    for solar easements; proposing waste heat recovery or
    solar systems for whole neighborhoods.

5. Increasing the efficiency of the transportation system
    operating within the city by levying one cent per
    gallon gas tax; modifying parking system; organizing
    car pools, assisting bicycle traffic.

6. Changing city operation and maintenance procedures to
    reduce energy consumption in municipal buildings;
    requiring life cycle costing for procurement and
    construction actions; modification of street lights.

Portland achieved the community's consensus on the Energy
Project as a result of extensive outreach efforts. All aspects

of the plan were discussed in a series of 35 briefings held around the city and in two city-wide workshops and two formal hearings. The plan itself calls for a 35 percent reduction in energy use by 1985. The residential and commercial strategy is to make the home audit and retrofits voluntary for five years, to be followed by implementation of the mandatory time-of-transfer ordinance. At this time, Portland is just about to begin the implementation of its residential and commercial retrofit program, which will include the establishment of a one-stop conservation center and a loan pool to offer low-interest loans. The city will also provide a standard audit methodology to be used for all buildings. The city is using a $3 million grant from the United States Department of Housing and Urban Development for start-up of these services.

Fitchburg, Massachusetts

Secondly, there is the example of a small town in New England--Fitchburg, Massachusetts. This town and its original approach to conservation have become so well known that "Fitchburg" has practically become a generic term in conservation jargon. As a direct result of the experiment this town tried, at least 20 or 30 other communities around the country have done "Fitchburgs".

The background facts about Fitchburg are that its home owners have one of the highest per-household oil consumption rates, averaging 1200 gallons per year; local fuel suppliers no longer supply fuel on credit; and costs are rising every winter. In the face of these cold facts, Fitchburg formed a community project called Fitchburg Action to Conserve Energy (F.A.C.E.). On October 24, 1979, FACE began a three month campaign to "winterize" as many area homes as possible, using only low cost materials than can be installed on a do-it-yourself basis.

The Fitchburg experiment was to launch an intensive 3-week blitz of every neighborhood in the town, using neighborhood centers as the basis for the outreach. At these centers, work shops were held where volunteers conducted hands-on training sessions. These workshops were held six days a week and were completely free. All the labour involved from the training to the crews who actually went to homes were volunteers, with the exception of two federal government employees who helped to organize the campaign. The money used for materials came from the Federal Weatherization Program, because that money had been clogged up in state administrative problems and was going unused. The town received a special waiver to use the federal money in this unique program. For households that didn't qualify for the weatherization money, material kits were available, at a cost of $25.00.

As a result of the winterization campaign, over 3500 people attended training sessions, over 1800 kits were distributed, and 350 requests for crew assistance were received.

Fitchburg marked a very significant point in the progress of the nation's single largest conservation program.   What Fitchburg said to the federal government was, essentially, that the official federal program wasn't appropriate in that particular town, but that the money and technical skills certainly would be. Fitchburg said "let us do it our way," and nearly 500 people volunteered to do something for the campaign.

SUMMARY AND CONCLUSIONS

This overview of federal and independent conservation programs suggests some basic ingredients for future conservation policy. One of the most important requirements is to undertake thorough, detailed evaluations of every federal conservation program to obtain as much data as possible about exactly why certain programs have been more successful than others, and what every program has achieved in both qualitative and quantitative terms, at what cost per unit of energy saved.

To summarize, some of the "lessons" learned after nearly five years of federal energy conservation programs are:

- price alone has not been sufficient to motivate consumers to practice conservation at optimal rates;

- general information is inadequate to affect consumer behavior significantly; customized information is needed on a more individualized basis to help the consumer modify consumption behavior;

- highly prescriptive programs that set precise goals and the specific means of achieving them appear to be less effective that those that permit a high degree of flexibility and variation in local application;

- consumers frequently appear to have more confidence in the outreach extended through trusted local institutions than that administered by federal institutions;

- the role of the federal government in promoting conservation in the future needs to be supportive of local initiatives, fostering innovation and variation.

RELATED RESEARCH

Conservation and Solar Energy Programs of the Department of Energy: A Critique, Office of Technology Assessment Congress of the United States, Washington, D.C., GPO Number 052-003-00757-6.

"Delays and Uncertain Energy Savings in Program to Promote State and Energy Conservation," (June 1980) draft General Accounting Office Report, U.S. General Accounting Office.

Energy Extension Service Pilot Program Evaluation: After One Year (1979), Prepared for presentation to International Conference on Energy Use Management ICEU II, Los Angeles, California.

Evaluation of the Energy Extension Service Pilot Program: The First Year (August 1979), U.S. Department of Energy Assistant Secretary for Conservation and Solar Energy, Office of State and Local Programs, DOE/CS-0100.

Observations and Recommendations on the Future of the Energy Extension Service Program (March 1979), First Report by the National Energy Extension Service Advisory Board, DOE/CS-0075.

President's Clearinghouse for Community Energy Efficiency (1980), Community Energy Efficiency, p. 13.

Ridgeway, James (1979), Energy Efficient Community Planning: A Guide to Saving Energy and Producing Power at the Local Level, Emmans, Pennsylvania: JG Press.

Saint Paul Energy Mobilization: A History (May 1980), Saint Paul Energy Office.

Stobaugh, Robert B. and Yergin, Daniel (1979), Energy Future: Report of the Energy Project at the Harvard Business School, New York: Random House.

The Energy Consumer (February/March 1980), U.S. Department of Energy, Office of Consumer Affairs.

U.S. Department of Energy, Draft Policy, Programming and Fiscal Guidance, January 30, 1980, FY 1982-1986.

U.S. Department of Energy (1980), Comprehensive Program and Plan for Federal Energy Education, Extension and Information Activities, U.S. Department of Energy.

INTERNATIONAL PERSPECTIVE
ON ENERGY CONSERVATION

Rolf Gradin
C. Dennis Anderson

The primary purpose of this chapter is to present an
overview of national energy conservation programs in the 21
member countries of the International Energy Agency (IEA), a
body within the Organization of Economic Co-operation and
Development (OECD). The presentation includes discussion of
program types by sector and, where available, conservation
results. This will familiarize energy researchers and policy
officials with the work accomplished and experience gained in
other countries. Hopefully, this international perspective will
lead to increased information exchange among policy officials on
the cost-benefit of various conservation policy types. Also, it
is hoped that behavioral energy researchers might see opportunities for extending their research to international settings.
The ultimate pursuit is more effective conservation initiatives.

THE IEA AND ENERGY CONSERVATION

The International Energy Agency (IEA) is an autonomous body
established in 1974 within the framework of the Organization for
Economic Co-operation and Development (OECD). Its purpose is to
implement an International Energy Program, a comprehensive
effort to strengthen co-operation on energy policy among participating countries. Twenty-one of OECD's 24 member countries
participate at present: Australia, Austria, Belgium, Canada,
Denmark, Germany, Greece, Ireland, Italy, Japan, Luxembourg,
Netherlands, New Zealand, Norway, Portugal, Spain, Sweden,
Switzerland, Turkey, United Kingdom, and the United States.
This chapter relies heavily on the author's experience as
head of IEA's Energy Conservation Division. It is also based
upon:

- data and descriptions of energy policies provided by IEA
  countries for the review of national energy programs and
  analyses prepared by the IEA Secretariat and IEA's Standing
  Group on Long-Term Co-operation in connection with these
  reviews

- analyses and studies carried out by IEA's Conservation Sub-
  Group, and the five Expert Groups concerned with energy
  conservation in industry, transport, buildings, district
  heating, and public information.

Readers interested in remaining up to date on the details of energy conservation activities in IEA countries are referred to the periodic reviews published by IEA's Conservation Sub-Group, e.g., International Energy Agency (1979).

The basic aims of IEA are:

- co-operation among IEA participating countries to reduce excessive dependence on oil through energy conservation, development of alternative energy sources, and energy research and development

- an information system on the international oil market as well as consultation with oil companies

- co-operation with oil producing and consuming countries with a view of developing a stable international energy trade as well as the rational management and use of world energy resources in the interest of all countries

- a plan to prepare participating countries against the risk of a major disruption of oil supplies and to share available oil in the event of an emergency.

The importance of IEA countries in world energy consumption is illustrated by the fact that together they account for over one half of the world's total energy requirements. An indication of the size and growth rates in consumption of total primary energy (TPE) in member countries is presented in Table 1. As indicated, IEA consumption of TPE in 1977 was 3.349 Mtoe (millions of tons of oil equivalent). Between 1973 and 1977 primary consumption increased at an average annual rate of 0.8 percent compared with an historical growth of 5.1 percent per annum between 1968 and 1973. Since 1973, the slow-down of energy demand growth in IEA countries has been dramatic.

There are many reasons for this development. First, economic recession led to a decrease of gross domestic product (GDP) growth, from 4.5 percent per annum between 1968 and 1973 to 1.6 percent per annum from 1973 to 1977, and higher energy prices have reduced energy demand. Second, many IEA countries have introduced specific energy conservation measures, which further decelerated energy demand.

TPE grew less quickly in relation to GDP since 1973 than in the past, which can be interpreted as an overall improvement in energy efficiency. The TPE/GDP ratio, which increased from 1.45 (toe per thousand 1970 US$) in 1960 to 1.48 in 1973, has declined to 1.41 in 1977. The TPE/GDP elasticity (the annual percent change in TPE for a 1 percent annual change in GDP), which was 1.0 for the period 1960-1973, has dropped to 0.4 for the period 1973-1977. The 0.4 figure, because it reflects the impact of a severe economic recession, cannot be considered indicative of

TABLE 1

HISTORICAL AND PROJECTED TOTAL PRIMARY ENERGY
CONSUMPTION IN IEA MEMBER COUNTRIES

Country	$Mtoe^a$					
	1960	1968	1973	1977^b	1985	1990
Austria	12.38	17.37	23.54	24.80	32.8	38.1
Belgium	25.38	36.42	46.74	44.54	57.0	64.0
Canada	96.05	139.03	185.70	203.36	262.0	297.5
Denmark	8.99	16.34	19.72	19.92	20.7	23.9
Germany	145.78	201.81	265.82	261.82	337.8	371.0
Greece	2.76	6.76	12.24	14.26	24.4	31.7
Ireland	4.24	5.88	7.62	7.59	13.7	17.0
Italy	49.78	94.1	132.69	138.58	193.0	235.0
Japan	94.66	216.73	337.77	350.46	560.5	674.7
Luxembourg	3.27	3.94	4.76	3.84	4.6	5.0
Netherlands^c	21.94	39.47	61.67	63.51	90.1	98.8
New Zealand	5.41	7.42	9.45	11.30	15.4	18.2
Norway	8.98	15.93	19.74	19.82	27.5	31.0
Spain	19.90	36.83	56.61	67.90	94.0	114.2
Sweden	27.24	40.14	47.10	50.30	58.4	63.2
Switzerland	11.80	18.00	23.39	24.50	26.7	30.1
Turkey	9.00	17.80	24.49	32.00	69.4	91.2
United Kingdom	169.69	201.05	223.96	211.50	245.0	269.0
United States	1,014.8	1,412.78	1,744.14	1,799.22	2,263.3	2,605.3
IEA TOTAL	1,731.43	2,527.87	3,247.05	3,349.22	4,396.3	5,078.9

Annual Growth |——— 5.0 ———|— .8 —| |— 2.9 —|
                 |— 5.1 —|——— 3.5 ———|

a.   Mtoe: millions of tons of oil equivalent.
b.   1977 figures are based on the OECD report, Energy Balances in OECD Countries.
c.   The Netherlands has since revised its projected consumption downwards.

NOTE: For the historical development of energy demand up to 1977, OECD Energy Statistics (Energy Balance of OECD Countries) are used; for the projection of energy demand from 1977 to 1980, national data submitted for IEA 1978 Review of National Programmes are used. The 1977 figures do not always correspond to the figures given in the OECD Statistics due to differences, e.g., in conversion ratios and statistical accounting.

SOURCES: Energy Balances of OECD Countries and IEA 1978 Review of National Programmes.

future trends (the ratio is expected to be about 0.8 for 1977–1985). However, it does indicate that IEA countries, by strengthening their conservation efforts, should be able to achieve greater energy savings while at the same time achieving an acceptable level of economic growth.

In general terms it appears that, since 1973, energy conservation has gone from being viewed as short term measures for dealing with temporary supply disruptions to being an important element of a country's overall energy policy. Many conservation initiatives have been implemented which are intended to save energy both in the short term and in the long term. These initiatives vary from incentive programs to voluntary and regulatory measures. Because of the philosophical and social economic differences among member countries, the emphasis on the type of policy instruments used differs. However, some of the most important conservation measures taken to date by most member countries include:

- publicity campaigns informing the public about the need to save energy, motivating them to do so and telling them how to do it

- pricing measures to encourage energy conservation, e.g., taxes on energy and tariff structures for gas and electricity which encourage conservation

- incentive schemes designed to stimulate investments leading to energy conservation

- regulations and standards establishing minimum energy consumption efficiencies, e.g., for cars and new buildings.

NATIONAL CONSERVATION PROGRAMS

This section presents detailed tabulations of conservation policy types in the major consumption sectors of IEA Member countries. As the tables illustrate, the energy conservation policy thrust varies considerably from country to country. Combinations of "sticks" and "carrots" characterize national conservation policies. However, due to differences in underlying philosophies and in the social and structural aspects of their economies, some countries emphasize voluntary measures while others emphasize regulatory initiatives. Yet, despite the relatively broad array of existing and proposed conservation efforts in various sectors of member economies, there is still considerable potential for improvement in energy conservation efforts, as will be discussed in the final section of the chapter.

Industrial Conservation Programs

Industry is the largest and most diversified sector in the
IEA, accounting for around 40 per cent of the total final energy
consumption (TFC). The share of industry in TFC varies, however,
from country to country; in 1977, for instance, it was 23
percent for Denmark and Turkey, 56 percent for Japan and 59
percent for Luxembourg. In 1973, industry in the IEA consumed
984 Mtoe, up from 1960 consumption of 545 Mtoe. During this
period, consumption grew by 4.3 percent annually. In 1977,
following the oil crisis, industrial energy consumption in the
IEA was lower than in 1973.

The measures so far adopted in IEA countries to promote
conservation in industry are presented in Table 2. A brief
discussion of the most important of these measures follows.
Fiscal and financial incentives are designed to encourage
investment in energy saving techniques and to speed up the
marketing of new energy saving equipment. Projects with a
longer pay-back period or a higher risk are generally given
priority assistance. Energy prices and taxes are important
elements of energy conservation programs, because industries are
sensitive to cost increases. However, a certain caution is
exercised in using this instrument, as progressive rates and
high energy taxes could have a negative influence on co-operation between industry and government. Reporting and auditing
schemes are used in about one-half of the IEA countries, usually
in combination with mandatory or voluntary target setting.
Information activities are almost universal and include publications, meetings, and advisory services (for small and medium
sized firms).

All countries emphasize the importance of conservation
awareness as an essential ingredient for the achievement of
industrial energy conservation goals. Experience in many
countries has shown that it is far easier to get results if the
people involved in a project, from management to factory hands,
are aware of the need to conserve and become involved in the
implementation of the conservation measure.

Conservation Programs in Transport

On average among IEA countries, transport accounts for an
average of about one quarter of TFC in IEA countries. The share
is highest in New Zealand at 37 percent, in Greece at 34 percent, and in the United States at 33 percent, and lowest in
Luxembourg at 11 percent. However, during 1960-1973, transport
energy consumption grew fastest in Japan at 9.8 percent per
annum, and slowest in the United Kingdom at 3 percent per annum.
In 1977, transportation energy consumption grew to 670 Mtoe from
617 Mtoe in 1973, an average of 1.9 percent per annum. This
increase is much smaller than before the oil crisis. From 1968
to 1973, average energy consumption in the transport sector grew

TABLE 2

IMPLEMENTATION OF ENERGY CONSERVATION MEASURES IN INDUSTRY

	Financial/Fiscal Incentives			Reporting/Auditing			Information, Advice/Assistance				Other Measures		
	Grant/ Subsidy	Loan	Tax Incentive	Target Setting	Reporting	Auditing	Information/ Publication	Meeting/ Seminar	Advice for small & medium sized firms	Award	Restructure	CHP*	Waste/ Waste Heat
Australia	X	X	X				X*	X	X			P*	X
Austria	X	X	X		X		X	X	X			X	X
Belgium						P	X	X	X				X
Canada	X		X	X	X	X	X	X	X			X	X
Denmark	X	X					X	X	X			X	X
Germany	X	X	X		X		X	X	X			X	X
Greece		X		X	P		X	X	X			P	P
Ireland	X						X	X	X			X	X
Italy	P	P		P	X		X	X	P		X	X	X
Japan	X	X	X	X	X	X	X	X	X	X	X	X	X
Luxembourg													
Netherlands	X	X	X			X	X	X	X			X	X
New Zealand	X	X	X	P		X	X	X	X	X		X	X
Norway	X	X	X		X		X					X	X
Spain	XP	P	P		X	X	X	X	X			X	P
Sweden	X				X	X	X	X	X			X	X
Switzerland	X		X				X		X			P	P
Turkey							X						
United Kingdom	X	X	X	P	X	X	X	X	X	X		X	X
United States	X	X	X	X	X	X	X	X	X			X	X

X : exists, P : in preparation, CHP: combined production of heat and electricity.

by about 5.5 percent per annum. From 1977 to 1985, IEA energy demand in the transport sector is expected to increase by 1.5 percent per annum and by 2.1 percent per annum from 1985 to 1990. Generally IEA countries demand forecasts vary from about 1 to 5 percent per annum.

Table 3 summarizes the energy conservation measures in existence and in preparation in member countries. Not included in the table are taxes on fuel and weight or engine size of vehicle which most countries had in place long before the energy crisis set in.

Mandatory fuel economy standards and energy labelling programs exist in a small number of major auto producing countries, but the latter is under consideration by the European Economic Community (EEC). The proposed EEC labels would present consumption figures related to day-to-day driving conditions (the "Europa test").

Speed limits save energy and increase highway safety, although it is difficult to quantify the magnitude of the savings. All IEA countries adopted strict speed limits for energy saving during the energy crisis. These limits remained in effect after 1974, but were increased to a somewhat higher level at which they would be more readily acceptable to the public. Because of the problems that exist with respect to public acceptance and enforcement, an effective public education program is needed to complement this program. To ensure public acceptance, speed limits must be set at reasonable levels.

A number of countries have implemented car pooling programs despite their apparent drawbacks to travellers (e.g., increased travel time, loss of independence and privacy). These programs tend to concentrate on suburban areas with large industries. Support for mass transit exists in all IEA countries but Turkey. Experience has shown, however, that public transport's share of personal transportation has declined despite substantial public subsidies. The share of public transportation can probably only be significantly increased by restricting private automobile usage. Such restrictions are quite unpopular and are not likely to be introduced on a large scale.

Conservation Programs for the
Residential and Commercial Sector

Since 1973, IEA energy consumption in the residential/commercial sector increased from 810.7 Mtoe (33 percent of the total final consumption, TFC) to 821.7 Mtoe in 1977 (34 percent of TFC). The share of residential and commercial consumption in total final consumption is highest in Denmark (54 percent) and lowest in Luxembourg (18 percent). The growth rate for energy demand in the residential/commercial sector for the IEA was fairly low at 0.4 percent. Eight countries showed a negative

TABLE 3

IMPLEMENTATION OF ENERGY CONSERVATION MEASURES IN THE TRANSPORT SECTOR

	Fuel Economy Standards		Energy Labeling *		Speed Limits km/h Motorways/Roads	Car Pooling	Support for mass transport	Information campaigns
	Mandatory	Voluntary	Mandatory	Voluntary				
Australia					100/60	X	X	X
Austria					130/100	X	X	X
Belgium					120/90/60	P	X	X
Canada	X			X	100/90	X	X	X
Denmark					100/80/60 (from 15 March 1979)		X	X
Germany		X			(130)/100	X	X	X
Greece					100		X	X
Ireland					88/64	X	X	X
Italy					90-140/110-80/50		X	X
Japan		X		X	80-100/40-50	X	X	X
Luxembourg					120/90/60		X	X
Netherlands					100/80	P	X	X
New Zealand					80/50	X	X	X
Norway					90/80/80		X	P
Spain					100/90/80		X	X
Sweden				X	90-100/70	X	X	X
Switzerland					130/100		X	
Turkey					90/80/70	X	P	
United Kingdom			X		113/97	P	X	X
United States	X		X		88	X	X	X

X : exists, P : in preparation, * The European Economic Community is considering adoption of energy labeling for new cars.

growth rate during this time (Belgium, Denmark, Germany, Greece, Ireland, Japan, New Zealand, and Switzerland).

During the period from 1960 to 1973, energy demand in the residential/commercial sector in the IEA increased by an average of 5.0 percent per annum.   Demand increases were highest in Turkey (17.9 percent per annum) followed by Japan (15.0 percent per annum) and lowest in the United Kingdom (0.8 percent per annum).

Energy demand in this sector is expected to increase by only 1.9 percent per annum between 1977 and 1985 and by 1.7 percent from 1985 until 1990.   The share of the residential/commercial sector in total final consumption will decrease from 34 percent (1977) to 32 percent in 1985 and to 30 percent in 1990.

Although public awareness of energy conservation measures is recognized as being vital to the success of an effective energy program in this sector, information alone is often not enough to motivate the consumer to conserve energy.   Financial or fiscal incentives including tax credits or refunds, subsidies, grants, or loans are provided in most countries.   Programs vary considerably in scope and funding from country to country (Table 4).

Subsidies and grants are provided by 13 countries.   Grants and subsidies vary in their scope from limited budgets and small incentives to large levels of public funding (e.g., in Denmark, Germany, the Netherlands, Sweden, and the United Kingdom).   In some countries (e.g., Canada, Germany, Sweden, and the United States), similar incentives are provided to promote the use of renewable energy such as solar collectors and heat pumps.

Loan schemes are employed by about a third of the IEA countries.   The payback period for loans typically ranges from four years interest-free for the purchase of appliances to 15 to 20 years with an interest rate of about 4.5 percent for longer term projects.

Tax credits or discounts on taxable income for the purchase of energy conserving equipment or insulation materials are, in general, preferred to a direct tax applied to high energy consuming appliances or equipment.   However, New Zealand has levied a direct tax on high energy consuming equipment, i.e., a 30 percent tax on air conditioners which incorporate refrigeration units, and a 20 percent tax on domestic clothes dryers.

Building codes are very commonly applied on the construction of new homes in the IEA.   The codes generally apply to insulation of outer ceilings, outer walls, ground floors, and windows.

Information by means of labelling of household appliances, air conditioners, etc., encourages both consumers to buy energy efficient products and, indirectly, producers to manufacture efficient appliances.   Energy conservation labels should, however, be based on adequate internationally tested methods which measure performance under agreed standardized conditions.

TABLE 4
IMPLEMENTATION OF ENERGY CONSERVATION MEASURES IN THE RESIDENTIAL AND COMMERICAL SECTOR

| | Fiscal/Financial Incentives | | | Building Codes | | | | Prohibition of bulk metering | Efficiency Labelling for Appliances* | | Information Auvice |
| | Discount on Taxable Income | Subsidy Grant | Loan | New Buldings | | Existing Buildings | | | | | |
				Mandatory	Voluntary	Mandatory	Voluntary		Mandatory	Voluntary	
Australia	P	X		P					P		P
Austria		X		P	X				P	X	X
Belgium		X		P		P			X		X
Canada	X	X	X	X		X			P		X
Denmark	P	X		X		X			P		X
Germany	X	X	X	X		X		P	P	X	X
Greece	X		P	X		P			P		X
Ireland	X	X		X			X		P		X
Italy				X		X		X	X		X
Japan			X	P		P		X	X		X
Luxembourg	P	X		X		P			P		X
Netherlands		X		X		X			P		X
New Zealand	X	X	X	X		X			P		X
Norway			X	X		X			P		X
Spain	X			X				P	X		X
Sweden		X	X	X		X			X		X
Switzerland	X			X		X			P		X
Turkey		P		P		P			P		X
United Kingdom	X	X		X					P		X
United States	X	X	X	X					X		X

X : exists, P : in preparation, * The European Economic Community has approved the introduction of energy labels for major appliances.

Energy efficiency labelling for consumer appliances is mandatory in four countries. In four others, labelling on a limited number of electrical appliances has been carried out on a voluntary basis. The EEC has approved the introduction of energy consumption labelling for a range of household appliances. In addition, Sweden plans on introducing a similar program beginning in 1980. Also, a number of countries have or are considering direct action on product design via minimum efficiency standards for major appliances (e.g., United States, Denmark, Germany, Greece, Italy, the United Kingdom).

Another program summarized in Table 4, combined production of heat and electric power (CHP), is identified in the IEA as a measure for energy conservation and also for fuel switching away from oil in the heating sector. District heating and CHP have so far received significant government attention, incentives, or encouragement in only a few IEA countries (e.g., Denmark and Sweden). In other countries the concept of district heating has been viewed as a violation of personal independence, especially if combined with measures for mandatory connection of buildings to the district heating network. Left on their own, consumers tend to favor individual heating, preferably oil. The interest in district heating and CHP has been stimulated by a joint IEA project where the Danish experiences were demonstrated to the other countries.

Finally, many countries offer financial incentives for the development and adoption of such renewable energy sources as solar energy. This is particularly the case for solar and heat pump sources as supplements to conventional space heating modes. For example, Australia has eliminated sales taxes for solar installations; Austria has tax incentives for the introduction of heat pumps; the U.S. Administration has proposed extensive tax credits for the use of renewable energy and establishment of the Solar Bank to provide interest subsidies for home improvement loans and mortgages to finance the purchase and installation of approved solar energy systems; the Canadian Federal Government has launched a major program designed specifically to expand the use of solar and biomass; and the Japanese "Sunshine Project" includes incentives for solar energy.

Thus, renewable energy policy seems to be moving out of the strictly research, development, and design program stage to include measures to accelerate their application. However, the experience to date of many IEA countries shows that the economics of many conventional conservation measures are, for the time being, better than the economics for renewables. In the short term, therefore, the potential for energy savings through the implementation of renewable energy seems limited. In the long term, with the successful completion of these programs, renewables are expected to make a significant contribution to the energy balance of member countries.

In summary, a wide array of specific conservation policies and programs exist or are proposed for the major sectors of many

IEA Member countries. Energy conservation is a serious matter for all countries and the incidence, scope and funding of such programs is likely to increase in the face of the tight energy supply conditions envisioned for the 1980s.

PUBLIC INFORMATION, EDUCATION, AND MOTIVATION CAMPAIGNS IN IEA

As evidenced in the tables, information campaigns are frequently used as a conservation initiative in the IEA. The consensus resulting from the work of IEA's Sub-Group on Information/Education and Motivation is that specific energy saving measures must be supported by efforts to bring about and to maintain high consumer awareness of the need to conserve energy, particularly oil. Without exception, IEA Member countries are using energy conservation promotional campaigns to help create a more favourable climate for energy conservation.

It appears that an effective energy conservation program combines the following ingredients:

(1) economic pricing of energy;
(2) financial incentives/disincentives;
(3) legislative reinforcement;
(4) research and development, incorporating the development of more energy efficient products; and
(5) continuing information, advice, promotion, and publicity programs (which are considered essential to the effective operation of the other programs).

Because of the wide differences among member countries in ethnic, economic, sociological, climatic, and media circumstances, there is no universal IEA promotional strategy. To illustrate this point, the concern for energy is much higher in non-energy-producing countries than in countries with big energy resources of their own. In Switzerland, for instance, a recent poll showed that 85 percent of the population saw energy as a main concern, whereas a similar poll in Australia revealed that less than ten percent saw problems with energy. In countries such as Germany and Switzerland that rely heavily upon market forces in their overall economic strategy, the main motivation for energy conservation is purely economic--save energy and save money! In other countries such as Sweden and the Netherlands environmental concern is a valid motive--less energy consumption is good for the environment!

While a number of member countries have tried conservation campaigns under the IECM umbrella, whether or not the IECM did help to create international awareness of the need to conserve energy is a debatable issue. In most countries, opinion is that IECM did not help much in this respect as far as the general public is concerned; only Denmark, Ireland, Japan, and to some extent Germany have noted any change at all. On the other hand, some countries have reported that the joint promotion was an advantage in creating a greater international awareness among opinion leaders, industrial experts, and other social groups.

SUMMARY AND CONCLUSIONS

Broadly speaking, the greatest improvement in overall energy efficiency, as measured by the TPE/GDP ratio, is found in those countries with the highest increases in real energy prices and the strongest measures of energy conservation. Conversely, those countries with lower price increases and weaker conservation programs ranked poorly in energy conservation performance.

Since 1973, consumption seems to have been influenced more by prices than by conservation measures like the retrofitting of existing houses which, by their nature, are often likely to have a long-term effect. The strong influences of prices on energy consumption is confirmed by analysis of demand sectors. Even allowing for other factors, energy efficiency in terms of the ratio of final sectoral demand to GDP has improved least in the transport sector, the sector in which price increases generally have been lowest.

Despite the incidence and importance of conservation programs, there is a poor understanding of energy demand and the effectiveness of energy conservation measures in place. There appears to be a very real need for researchers to document conservation results, if any, objectively from various financial and non-financial program types. Efficient allocation of resources devoted to conservation will be impeded until a "sort" can be made between effective and ineffective measures.

RELATED RESEARCH

International Energy Agency (1979), Energy Conservation in the International Energy Agency: 1978 Review, Paris, France: Organization for Economic Co-operation and Development.

PRICES AND CONTROLS

- Time-of-Day Electricity Pricing

- Increasing Gasoline Prices

- Progressive Rate Structure for Household
  Electricity

- Centralized Electricity Control

- Direct Control of Household Electricity

TIME-OF-DAY ELECTRICITY PRICING

Thomas A. Heberlein
Daniel Linz
Bonnie P. Ortiz

Two fundamental questions are asked about nontraditional electricity rates: Do they change consumption behavior and will the public accept them? This paper examines the second question based on residential customers' reactions to a two year time-of-day electricity rate experiment.

In the mid 1970s, the Federal Energy Administration (now part of the U.S. Department of Energy) began funding a set of demonstration projects around the United States. The focus of these was on the first question of effectiveness; the question of acceptance took a second place. Most of the experiments relied on volunteers: Arizona, California, New York, Ohio, Puerto Rico, and Vermont (Hill et al. 1979). In contrast, a mandatory experiment was designed by the Wisconsin Public Service Corporation and University of Wisconsin consultants with the cooperation of the Public Service Commission of Wisconsin and funded by the U.S. Department of Energy. This presented an opportunity to determine how a non-volunteer representative population felt about living with TOD electricity rates.

DESIGN OF THE WISCONSIN EXPERIMENT

The design of the Wisconsin experiment was a 3×3 ANOVA design, where three price ratios (2:1, 4:1, and 8:1) were fully crossed with three peak lengths (6, 9, and 12 hour). Cell sizes ranged from 37 to 43. The peak period ranged from six hours, which was the shortest peak period the utility felt would be likely to bracket a floating system peak, to a twelve hour period, which was believed to be the longest the customers could tolerate. The 12 hour peak, from 8 a.m. to 8 p.m. was the same

———
Partial support for this research was provided by the College of Agricultural and Life Sciences, University of Wisconsin-Madison. Additional support was provided by the Public Service Corporation, Green Bay, Wisconsin and the Department of Energy. We would like to thank Mr. Gary Grainger and Mr. Richard James of the Utility, Mr. Robert Malko, Dr. J. Stanley Black, and Mr. Dennis Ray of the Public Service Commission of Wisconsin, our colleagues Dr. Lauritis Christensen and his associates in the Economics Department, and Dr. Brian Joiner and his associates in the UW Statistical Laboratory for the major role they played in this experiment.

winter or summer. The six hour peak was from 9 a.m. to noon and
from 1 p.m. to 4 p.m. in the summer, and from 9 a.m. to noon and
from 5 p.m. to 8 p.m. in the winter. The 9 hour peak ran from 8
a.m. until 5 p.m. in the summer, and from 8 a.m. to noon and
from 4 p.m. to 9 p.m. in the winter.

Price Ratios

The price ratios represent the relationship between an off
peak energy charge and the on peak energy charge. For example,
in the 2:1 six hour cell, the off peak summer price of energy to
an urban customer was 3.6 cents per kwh, while the on peak was
two times this or 7.1 cents per kwh. In the 12 hour 2:1 cell,
summer off peak energy charges for the urban customers were 3.0
cents per kwh, and the on peak charges were 6.0 cents, twice as
much. These charges differ across peak lengths since a different proportion of energy is used in the 6, 9, or 12 peak hours.
In each cell, however, the ratio 2:1, 4:1, or 8:1 remains the
same. The most extreme pricing differences are found in the 6
hour 8:1 cell, where the off peak energy charge is 1.8 cents per
kwh and the on peak charge is 14.5 cents per kwh.

The customer was aware of the price signal each month based
on the information received on the electricity bill. One line
listed the fixed charge, a second line listed the kwh on peak
along with a total charge. A third line listed kwh off peak
along with a total charge. A small fuel adjustment clause was
pro-rated according to the on to off peak ratio. The bill also
listed the peak times each month and encouraged the customers to
shift.

Subjects

The subjects in the experiment were 413 residential customers drawn at random from the residential population served by
the Wisconsin Public Service corporation based in Green Bay,
Wisconsin. Customers were assigned to the 9 design cells using
a modified black-box technique. During the baseline and first
two years of the experiment, 50 cases were dropped. This was an
overall attrition of 12 percent or 4 percent a year over a one
year baseline and two year test period. Magnetic tape meters
were placed on the households during 1976 and the time-of-day
pricing began in May of 1977. In March of 1979 a 29 page mailed
questionnaire was sent to each address to be completed by the
family as a group, since all were involved in the household
consumption of electricity. A $5.00 incentive was used to
stimulate response. Of the 363 families, 329 or 90.6 percent
completed and returned a usable questionnaire after three
mailings.

FINDINGS

Overall satisfaction was measured, as well as the customer's perception of the fairness and reasonableness of the rates. A slight majority, or 52 percent of those in the nine design cells, indicated that they were satisfied with the rates. Another 17 percent were neutral, approximately 30 percent expressed overall dissatisfaction, and less than 10 percent of these were extremely dissatisfied.

Sixty-one percent felt the rates were more fair than their old rates. An additional 20 percent felt they were neither more nor less fair. Eighteen percent believe TOD pricing was less fair. Seventy-four percent agreed that it was reasonable to cope with TOD rates, the remainder disagreed.

Looking at the combined responses to these three items, 38 percent of responses were positive on all measures: fairness, reasonableness, and overall satisfaction. Almost 35 percent had positive responses to 2 of the 3, 21 percent felt positively about one, and less than 6 percent had negative responses to all three items.

In other words, 5.4 percent were dissatisfied and think TOD rates were unfair and unreasonable, a small group of hard core opposition. Another 20 percent felt more negative than positive. Three quarters felt more positive than negative, and two out of five families were completely satisfied with TOD rates. In addition, 64 percent of those in the experiment indicated that they would prefer to stay on TOD rates after the study was completed. Another 11 percent did not care one way or the other. When asked whether they felt all homes served by the utility should be placed on TOD pricing, almost 62 percent agreed that all residences should be billed on TOD, 17 percent were neutral. Satisfaction was not related to age, education, or the value of the house. Those with higher incomes were slightly more satisfied and those with larger households were slightly less satisfied.

Effects of Peak Length and Price Ratio on Satisfaction

Eight satisfaction items were put in a Likert scale with an α of .92 and a mean of 26.5. The range was from 10 to 38, with 38 representing the highest possible level of satisfaction. When considered across the three peak length periods, membership in the various price ratio groups had almost no impact of the level of satisfaction customers expressed with the rates. Mean scores for the three groups were 26.7, 26.4, and 26.6. In other words, people in the 8:1 group are just as satisfied as those on the 2:1 price ratio.

When comparisons were made between the peak-length groups, however, differences were apparent. Mean scores for the 9 hour and 12 hour groups were 27.1 and 26.8 respectively, but the score for the 6 hour group was lower, at 25.8. The probability

level of this difference failed to reach statistical significance at the conventional .05 level.

Nevertheless, the results of this analysis were surprising.
Prior expectations were that those on the longer 12 hour rather
than the 6 hour peak would be the least satisfied. The shorter
on peak periods of the 6 hour group should make adjusting
electricity usage to avoid higher changes easier. The range of
alternative times for using appliances would be much broader for
this group than for either of the others and yet the 6 hour
group tended to feel less satisfied than those on the longer
peak periods.

Perceived Savings

Customers in the survey were asked to indicate whether they
felt the efforts they had made to save on electricity costs with
TOD rates had paid off for them. Sixty-nine percent said they
considered their savings on TOD rates worthwhile, while 27
percent felt they had made efforts to save which had not paid
off. The remaining 4 percent of families reported they had not
tried to save on TOD rates. Almost half of the respondents, 44
percent, said their savings were greater than or about equal to
their expectations; 37 percent indicated they had saved less
than anticipated; and about 19 percent of families reported they
had experienced no savings or were unable to tell if they had
saved money. Most people, 70 percent, felt that savings possible to families under TOD pricing were worth the effort
required to reduce electricity consumption during on peak hours.
About 30 percent felt possible savings were probably not worth
the effort necessary to shift usage.

There was a strong relationship between scores on the
scales which measure satisfaction with TOD rates and a 4 item
perceived savings scale ($\alpha=.70$). People who felt their savings
were greater were more satisfied with the experimental rates
($r=.74$, $p<.001$). While the price ratio of on to off peak
charges seemed to have little effect on either of these indexes,
the length of the onpeak periods did seem to matter. Customers
who had a 6 hour peak perceived their savings as less than those
in other groups, and also scored lower on the measure of overall
satisfaction. This may help explain why people on the 6 hour
peak felt less satisfied. The correlation between being on the
6 hour peak and the perceived satisfaction was $-.123$ ($p<.03$),
but when perceived savings was controlled the 6 hour peak, the
satisfaction relationship dropped to zero. This means that the
slightly higher dissatisfaction in the 6 hour group was due to
their perception that they were saving less. Once the effect of
this belief was controlled, peak length had no additional effect
on satisfaction.

Customer Knowledge

A series of questions was designed to measure how well customers understood the pricing and hourly structure of the TOD program. The questions ranged from attempts to simply determine whether or not the customers knew they were on TOD rates to the identification of exact peak hours for summer and winter, as well as the ratio of on to off peak prices.

As hoped, nearly all customers, 93 percent, were aware they were being billed on TOD rates. Eighty percent also knew that weekends were always offpeak periods. Many customers did have a good grasp of the details of TOD pricing such as the fixed charge, onpeak hours, and the price ratios. Although all customers had a fixed charge listed on their bill each month, fewer than 40 percent of the families knew this. The remainder either claimed that they did not have a fixed charge or that they were unsure. Table 1 presents customer knowledge of winter peak hours which were in effect at the time of the survey.

TABLE 1

PERCENT OF CUSTOMERS KNOWING
THE PEAK HOURS

| | | Level of Knowledge | | |
| | | --- | --- | --- |
Treatment	N	Knew Exactly	Accurate within one hour	Don't Know or Inaccurate
6 hour	114	64 (73)	0 (0)	36 (41)
9 hour	113	53 (60)	10 (11)	37 (42)
12 hour	103	66 (68)	0 (0)	34 (35)

Price Ratio

In order for a unit price increase to induce a unit of electricity shifting, customers must accurately perceive the relative on peak to off peak differences. A lack of correspondence between perceived ratios and true ratios could result in differences between actual on peak consumption and predicted consumption for those customers who inaccurately perceived their ratios. Such confusion could accentuate the price signal for the inaccurate customers. To determine customer knowledge of the on peak to off peak ratio, a single item was included in the questionnaire which provided a list of ratios ranging from 2:1 to 12:1 from which the correct ratio was to be identified. The choice of no difference was also included.

Overall, from one-third to two-thirds of the families could not correctly identify the price ratio from the list presented. Those in the 2:1 cell were much more likely to be accurate. When the inaccuracies were examined (Table 2), it was seen that the higher price ratio customers were more likely to underestimate the ratio.

TABLE 2

PERCENT OF CUSTOMERS OVER- AND UNDERESTIMATING THE PRICE RATIO

Price Ratio	Under-Estimate	Accurate	Over-Estimate
2:1	10 (10)	68 (69)	22 (23)
4:1	27 (28)	57 (59)	16 (17)
8:1	40 (27)	35 (24)	25 (17)

$\chi^2 = 29.0$, p. $< .001$
df $= 4$

Commitment to Shifting Behavior

In general, families included in the experimental group were, or became, committed to adjusting to the new rate structure and to making it work for them. Almost 80 percent reported they were somewhat committed or strongly committed to reducing electricity usage during on peak periods. Another 14 percent said they felt only slightly committed to reducing usage on peak. In other words, 93 percent expressed some commitment to the experimental rates, and the remaining 7 percent reported no commitment. This commitment was more than just a general endorsement, it was also supported by reported behaviors (Heberlein et al. 1980). Ninety-five percent of the respondents said they had tried to reduce on peak usage: 38 percent said they had tried to reduce such usage a little, 56 percent reported attempts to cut their consumption a lot.

About 18 percent of the respondents said they used electricity whenever it was desired with no thought of peak periods. Forty-eight percent said electricity usage would be postponed until offpeak hours if it was convenient; another 19 percent said they would wait until offpeak even if it was inconvenient to do so; and 12 percent said their lifestyles had been completely reorganized to avoid on peak electricity usage.

Effects of Peak Length and Price on Commitment. A 6 item index (α=.85) was developed by combining the items just discussed with others measuring commitment to reducing electricity usage during on peak periods. Scores on this scale were very similar for all peak-length groups, ranging from 22.0 to 22.8. This indicated that the length of the on peak period had virtually no effect on the level of commitment to time-of-day rates.

Customers on the 2:1 ratio had a mean score on the commitment scale which was one standard deviation lower than the grand mean, significantly (F=4.44, p<.0125) lower than the other groups. Shifting electricity usage does result in less actual savings for this group than for those with the 4:1 or 8:1 ratios. Because of the smaller differential between the on peak and off peak rates, rearranging schedules to avoid the higher rates may not have appeared worth the effort required, and hence, the lower level of commitment.

Lasting Commitment to Time-of-Day Rates. Because the experiment covered a three year period, it is possible to determine whether customers made initial adjustments to TOD rates which were not sustained over time. The subjective perception of sustained adjustments in energy use was also of interest. Almost 60 percent of the customers reported they were trying as hard to reduce on peak usage of electricity in March 1979 as they did during the summer of 1977. One-fourth of the households said they tried harder during that first summer; 12 percent reported trying harder at the time of the survey. Most customers, then, seem to have maintained a constant level of effort to avoid electricity usage during on peak periods, with some back sliding after the first summer.

SUMMARY AND CONCLUSIONS

The findings indicated that even when TOD pricing is mandatory and on to off peak ratios were as high as 8:1 and peak periods as long as 12 hours, people were generally favorable to this non-traditional pricing of electricity. In fact, fewer than 10 percent of the families who responded could be classified as completely opposed.

It is easy to assume that consumers will be less satisfied with longer peak periods. This study disputes this assumption. If the choice were between a 6 hour and a 12 hour peak, the data would support a 12 hour peak since the shorter peak didn't produce as favorable a reaction. This may have been due to the difficulty of shifting enough appliance use off peak to save money when the family was on a short peak period. Only about 20 percent of the total household electricity was consumed in this 6 hour weekly peak period. There was less opportunity for the family on a short peak to shift consumption to off peak daily and weekend hours than there was for the family on a 12 hour daily peak rate. This obviously would not mean that 16 hour or 24 hour peak periods would be even are better, because longer on peaks naturally diminish the opportunity to shift at all.

Another common assumption is that the public will oppose extreme differences in on to off peak pricing. In one cell of our experiment the on peak energy charge was over 13 cents per kwh in contrast to less than 2 cents off peak; yet, the price ratio had no effect on satisfaction and willingness to continue. Extreme price ratios in our experiment did not alienate the public. In fact, the customers on the lower price ratio reported putting less effort into shifting consumption. This suggests negative aspects of low price ratios.

The data highlighted a problem with TOD pricing which also may be a problem with energy pricing in general. Substantial proportions of the customers in a mandatory experiment, although they knew they were on time-of-day rates, did not know either the peak hours (over one-third) or the price ratio (one-third to two-thirds). This general lack of knowledge is indicated by failure of over 60 percent of our respondents to know their bills contained a fixed charge. Clearly TOD pricing would have a greater chance of effectiveness if customers were better informed about prices and peak periods. The Wisconsin experiment did show significant changes in behavior over the two year period (Caves and Christensen 1979), but we expect that it would have seen even greater had more efforts had been made to inform the customers.

It was interesting to note that the customers on the 8:1 price ratio underestimated the ratio. It appeared that those people in the experiment were generally encoding the price differential simply as "more" during the peak periods and "less" during the off peak periods. Since their monthly bills did not shoot up dramatically after they went on time-of-day prices, or plummet when they made some shifts, it is possible that customers had a hard time comprehending that on peak electricity costs eight times as much as off peak energy. They seemed willing to believe two or four times as much, but not eight. This suggests that economic extrapolations to higher price ratios such as 10:1 or 12:1 can be safely made only if one ignores the psychological processes of distortion and leveling which seemed to be occuring.

RELATED RESEARCH

Bartell, T. (1974), "The Effects of the Energy Crisis on Attitudes and Life styles of Los Angeles Residents," paper presented at the Annual Meeting of the American Sociological Association, Montreal.

Blakley, E.J. (1976), "Energy, Public Opinion, and Public Policy--A Survey of Urban, Suburban, and Rural Communities," California Agriculture, 30, 8, 4-5.

Bowman, C.H. and Fishbein, M. (1978), "Understanding Public Reaction to Energy Proposals; An Application of the Fishbein Model," Journal of Applied Social Psychology, 8, 4, 319-340.

Bultena, G.L. (1976), "Public Response to the Energy Crisis: A Study of Citizens Attitudes and Adaptive Behaviors," Sociology Report no. 130, Iowa State University, Dept. of Sociology, Ames, Iowa.

Caves, D.M. and Christensen, L.R. (1979), "Residential substitution of off-peak for peak electricity usage under time-of-usage pricing; An Analysis of 1976 and 1977 summer data from the Wisconsin experience," unpublished manuscript, Dept. of Economics, University of Wisconsin, Madison, Wisconsin.

Connecticut Public Utilities Control Authority (1977), "Final Report: Connecticut Peak Load Pricing Test," Hartford, Connecticut.

Curtin, R.T. (1976), "Consumer Adaptation to Energy Shortages," Journal of Energy and Development, 2, 1, 38-59.

Doner, W.B. (1975), "Consumer Study: Energy Crisis and Attitudes and Awareness," W.B. Doner, Inc., Detroit.

Gollin, A.E. (1976) "Energy Consumers' Awareness and Preferences in New Hampshire: A Comparative Assessment," Bureau of Social Science Research, Inc., Washington, D.C.

Gottlieb, D. and Matre, M. (1975), "Conceptions of Energy Shortages and Energy Conserving Behavior," paper presented at the Annual Meeting of the American Sociological Association, San Francisco.

Harris, L. (1975), "A Survey of Public and Leadership Attitudes toward Nuclear Power Development in the United States," Ebasco Services, New York.

Heberlein, T.A., Ortiz, B.P., and Linz, D. (1980) "Attitudes and Reported Behaviors of Customers on a Mandatory Participation Time-of-Day Electricity Pricing Experiment," Preliminary Report, Department of Rural Sociology, University of Wisconsin, Madison.

Little, R.L. (1976), "Rural Industrialization: The Four Corners Region," in Social Implications of Energy Scarcity: Social and Technological Priorities in Steady State and Constricting Systems, National Science Foundation, Washington, D.C.

Lopreato, S.C. (1977), "Citizen Attitudes with Respect to Energy Exploration and Development in One Texas County," paper presented at Social and Behavioral Implications of the Energy Crisis: A Symposium, Woodlands, Texas.

Milstein, J.S. (1977), "Attitudes, Knowledge and Behavior of American Consumers Regarding Energy Conservation with Some Implications for Governmental Action," unpublished manuscript, Office of Energy Conservation, Federal Energy Administration.

Muchinsky, P.M. (1976), "Attitudes of Petroleum Company Executives and College Students toward Various Aspects of the Energy Crisis," Journal of Social Psychology, 98, 2, 293-294.

Olsen, M.E. (1977), "Public Acceptance of Energy Conservation," paper at Social and Behavioral Effects of the Energy Crisis: A Symposium, Woodlands.

Romano, J.C. and Elliott, C.A. (1977), "Investigations into the Effects of Rate Structure on Customer Electric Usage Patterns," State of Vermont Public Service Board, Montpelier, Vermont, and Green Mountains Power Corporation, Burlington, Vermont.

Smith, J.R. (1978), "Socio-Economic Impact of Peak Load Pricing Rates," Rates and Research Department, Georgia Power Company, Atlanta, Georgia.

Sundstrom, E.P. (1977), "Citizens' Views About the Proposed Hartsville Nuclear Power Plant: A Survey of Resident's Perceptions in August 1975," Oak Ridge National Laboratory, Oak Ridge, Tennessee.

Warkov, S. (1976), "Energy Conservation in the Houston-Galveston Area Complex," University of Houston Energy Institute, Houston, Texas.

Wascoe, N.E. (1976), "The Effect of Fear Appeals Upon Behavioral Interactions toward Energy Consumption: A Replication," Institute of Behavioral Science, University of Colorado, Colorado.

Zuiches, J.J. (1975), "Energy and the Family," Department of Agricultural Economics, Cooperative Extension Service Report No. 390, Michigan State University.

_____, (1976), "Acceptability of Energy Policies to Mid-Michigan Families," Michigan State University Agricultural Experiment Station Research Report No. 1976, East Lansing, Michigan.

INCREASING GASOLINE PRICES

Robert E. Pitts
John F. Willenborg
Daniel L. Sherrell

The major purpose of this study is to gain understanding of how people have reacted to the increasing price of gasoline in an environment of perceived energy shortages. Relative to the many possible factors influencing consumer decision-making in response to increasing transportation costs, this study has a narrow focus. Two categories of behavior were studied: annual change in the number of miles driven by all members of households, and modification of the household mix of automobiles over the period of the study.

The study was longitudinal with the same households responding to questions at periodic intervals for several consecutive years. As a result, behavior was monitored on a frequent basis during several periods of dramatic change in gasoline prices.

METHODS

Data Source

The University of South Carolina statewide consumer panel was the principal source of data. The panel is composed of over 700 households, randomly recruited and representative of urbanized area residents with annual household incomes in excess of $6,500. Data utilized in this study were obtained via 12 questionnaires administered from June, 1973 through November, 1979. The study's major focus is on behavior reports from 1975 through 1979.

Over the period, 260 panel members responded to all of the questionnaires, the results of which form the data base for the study. For some analyses, the data set was reduced by deleting respondents with incomplete demographic or personal value profiles and those who did not report auto driving behavior. There were 217 households who met all criteria for inclusion in all dimensions of the study.

Measurement Period and Variables

Data on actual miles driven and size of automobile inventory (measured by average number of cylinders in all cars maintained) were obtained annually for the time period January 1975 through November 1979. In addition, attitude measures were taken beginning in June 1973 and at regular intervals through November 1979.

The explanatory variables employed in the data analyses were both demographic and personal value-related. Demographic variables included: formal education of household head, the head's employment status (retired or employed), job classification (blue-collar or white-collar), age of household head, race, family size, employment status of spouse, and annual household income. Personality variables included a range of terminal values, as derived from administration of the Rokeach Value Scale.

Adaptive Behavior Framework

Households studied are classified into one of four groups based on their reported adaptive behavior relative to change in miles driven and in downsizing as reflected in the average cylinder change measure.

The four groups can be defined as: (1) households whose automobile inventory had been downsized and whose annual miles driven decreased from 1975 to 1979; (2) households who downsized auto inventory, but did not decrease miles driven; (3) households who decreased miles driven, but did not downsize automobile inventory; and (4) households who neither decreased miles driven nor downsized their auto inventory. Groups 1 and 4 exhibited intuitively consistent behavior--a high degree of adjustment to prices and no adjustment, respectively.

Downsizing in automobile inventory occurred when the average number of cylinders in automobiles maintained by a household decreased in 1979 from 1975. A mileage level decrease of at least 1,000 miles from 1975 to 1979 was necessary for grouping with households on the basis of fewer miles driven.

Data Analysis

Panel households were classified into adaptive behavior groups on the basis of data generated throughout the study period. Then, stepwise discriminant analysis procedures were employed to classify them on the basis of their change behavior, utilizing the wide range of explanatory variables described above. A holdout sample was used to validate the discrimination model.

Means of the explantory variables were analyzed to generate profiles of the group members (segments). The relative weights of the factors in the classification process were examined.

The analyses focused on three different time periods within the 1975 - 1979 interval: 1979 versus 1975, 1978 versus 1975, and 1979 versus 1978. The three periods were studied to draw conclusions about the types of adaptive behavior undertaken under different gasoline price conditions.

FINDINGS

There is considerable evidence from this study to support the view that the 1979 period of gasoline price increases and automobile industry turbulence did, indeed, lead to adaptive consumer behavior. When all 217 households are considered, total miles driven per household varied from 21,487 (1975) to 22,288 (1976), 22,845 (1977), and 23,119 (1978), and decreased significantly to 19,635 in 1979. The average cylinder size of automobile inventories for all households decreased gradually from 1975 (7.06) to 1978 (6.90), but exhibited the largest decrease in 1979 to 6.79.

The data relative to the adaptive behavior groups are more enlightening. In the period 1975 to 1978, only 11 percent of the households both downsized and cut back on miles driven, as per the group 1 definition (Table 1). In the 1978-1979 period, the proportion increased to 15 percent and from 1975 to 1979, the proportion was 25 percent of the panel households. In contrast, group 4 behavior (neither downsizing nor mileage reduction) was reported by 35 percent from 1975 to 1978, 19 percent from 1978 to 1979, and only 15 percent in the 1975 to 1979 interval. From 1975 to 1979, 85 percent either downsized, reduced mileage, or both as compared to 65 percent in the 1975 to 1978 period.

Mileage and average cylinder data relative to the four adaptive behavior groups are shown in Table 2. The contrasts between 1979 and 1975 are significant. In the group that both downsized and reduced driving mileage (Group 1), average cylinders maintained dropped from a peak of 7.16 in 1975 to a low of 5.83 in 1979. At the same time, total miles driven in 1979 were less than 50 percent of any other year. At the other end of the behavior spectrum (Group 4), total miles increased steadily over the five years of measurement and average cylinders increased each year until stabilizing in 1979.

The phenomenon of "compensatory" behavior was evident (Pitts, Willenborg, and Sherrell 1979). Significant numbers of households in groups 2 and 3 undertook behavior that seemed to imply a conservation motive, but took other action leading in the opposite direction. For example, group 3 households did not reduce average cylinders, either maintaining status quo or substituting a larger automobile for a smaller one, while decreasing total household miles traveled.

The discriminant analysis procedure provided correct classifications of households into adaptive groups 41.4 percent of the time (see Table 3). The most important classification factors were fairly consistent across groups. Of greatest importance were three demographic variables--race, size of family, and years of formal education of the household head. Three values also emerged as significant across all groups-- comfortable life, family security, and exciting life. Finally,

TABLE 1

HOUSEHOLD MEMBERSHIP IN BEHAVIOR GROUPS
FOR VARIOUS COMPARISON PERIODS

Adaptive Driving Behavior Groups[a]

Comparison Periods	Reduction in Average Cylinders per Household		No Reduction in Average Cylinders per Household	
	Reduction in Total Mileage	No Reduction in Total Mileage	Reduction in Total Mileage	No Reduction in Total Mileage
	Group 1	Group 2	Group 3	Group 4
1975–1978				
n[b]	24	44	73	76
%	.11	.20	.34	.35
1978–1979				
n[b]	32	14	130	41
%	.15	.06	.60	.19
1975–1979				
n[b]	55	26	103	33
%	.25	.12	.48	.15

a. Group membership was defined as in Exhibit 2 for all comparison periods.

b. Total sample size = 217.

TABLE 2

MILEAGE AND AVERAGE CYLINDERS FOR ADAPTIVE BEHAVIOR
GROUPS BY YEAR

	Year	Reduction in Total Annual Household Mileage (1975–1979)		No Reduction in Total Annual Household Mileage (1975–1979)	
		Total Household Mileage	Average Cylinders	Total Household Mileage	Average Cylinders
		Group 1		Group 2	
Reduction	1975	23,600	7.16	17,179	7.53
in Average	1976	24,931	6.85	24,484	7.12
Cylinders per	1977	25,866	6.54	33,593	6.98
Household	1978	24,272	6.30	24,663	6.60
(1975–1979)	1979	11,636	5.83	32,250	6.00
		n=55		n=26	
		Group 3		Group 4	
No Reduction	1975	23,074	7.00	13,000	6.79
in Average	1976	21,382	7.11	15,534	6.93
Cylinders per	1977	21,686	7.26	16,214	6.98
Household	1978	20,157	7.28	18,170	7.20
(1975–1979)	1979	9,564	7.41	23,200	7.16
		n=103		n=33	

TABLE 3

STANDARDIZED CLASSIFICATION COEFFICIENTS
AND (MEANS) OF ADAPTIVE BEHAVIOR GROUPS

Adaptive Driving Behavior Groups[a]

Independent[b] Variables	Reduction in Average Cylinders per Household		No Reduction in Average Cylinders per Household	
	Reduction in Total Mileage	No Reduction in Total Mileage	Reduction in Total Mileage	No Reduction in Total Mileage
	Group 1 n=55	Group 2 n=26	Group 3 n=103	Group 4 n=33
Race[c]	5.30 (0.98)	4.96 (0.92)	5.08 (0.96)	4.65 (0.84)
Number of Household Members	3.93 (3.58)	4.01 (3.76)	3.39 (3.00)	3.50 (3.15)
Education[d] of Head of Household	2.34 (11.85)	2.53 (12.61)	2.38 (11.94)	2.00 (10.00)
A Comfortable Life[e]	0.48 (-0.34)	0.47 (-0.29)	0.84 (-0.06)	0.25 (0.07)
Family Security	0.38 (0.68)	0.28 (0.99)	0.38 (0.70)	0.74 (0.23)
An Exciting Life	0.23 (-0.83)	0.29 (-0.76)	0.14 (-0.89)	0.22 (-0.55)
Spouse Employed[f]	0.08 (0.49)	0.31 (0.35)	0.11 (0.38)	0.12 (0.46)
Household Income	0.00 ($24,536)	0.14 ($26,000)	0.28 ($24,592)	0.28 ($19,454)
Percent Correctly Classified	.291	.346	.417	.667

Average Percentage Correctly Classified   .414

a. 1979 behavior relative to 1975 behavior.
b. All independent variables significant at .01 level or better.
c. Expressed as proportion of white to total respondents.
d. Expressed in years of education.
e. A terminal value from Rokeach's value scale.
f. Expressed as proportion of total spouses.

household income was shown to be a significant explanatory variable, but to a lesser degree.

Analysis of standardized classification coefficients and means of explanatory variables provides some indication of the nature of the groups or segments. For example, households in group 1 are characterized as predominantly white, a larger than average family size, greater than average education level achieved by the household head, and spouse employed. Household income is above average (but not as high as in some other groups). Values such as a comfortable and exciting life are not judged to be important by this group as compared to others, but family security is a strongly held value. By far the most important classification factor is race (1.3 times as important as size of family and 2.3 times as powerful as education).

An interesting contrast is provided by analyzing the characteristics of group 4. The same factors emerged as impor-tant in classifying these households, but their characteristics varied. They were more likely to be non-white, had fewer persons residing there, less household head education, and substantially less income. In terms of personal values, these households were somewhat less interested in family security and more interested in a comfortable life.

SUMMARY AND CONCLUSIONS

Given the high-priority goal of reducing American depen-dence on foreign oil and, coincidentally, reducing consumption of gasoline, a deeper understanding of consumer behavior and decision making is required. This study provides some useful insights for planners and policy-makers.

Although some consumers are sensitive to price increases, their sensitivity seems to become dulled quickly and is sharpen-ed only by very dramatic increases. The evidence indicates that demand for gasoline is very inelastic. Thus, public policy makers' reliance on the price mechanism to slow down consumption substantially probably is ill-advised. Certainly, small gaso-line tax increases offer little potential for conservation.

Since consumers seem willing to choose different adaptive behavior alternatives (decrease mileage, alter auto inventory), more alternatives should be offered by policy-makers. This recommendation is supported by the capability exhibited in this study to correctly classify adaptive behavior, pointing out the feasibility of a segmentation approach.

The segmentation evidence leads to several conclusions: policy cannot be applied uniformly to all segments with expec-tations of similar results; efforts aimed at persuasion must recognize segment differences and will be more effective when designed for specific segments where they can do the most good; new alternatives for energy conservation can be presented on a segment by segment basis.

Reduction of gasoline consumption will require extensive planning and both intermediate and long-term strategies. There is evidence that consumers are crisis-oriented and will not react significantly to gradual changes. Even 50 percent price increases have led to minimal behavior change. Yet, the ability to begin to explain decision making and behavior related to gasoline usage as shown in this study suggests that continued application of consumer behavior concepts to public policy problems should prove fruitful.

RELATED RESEARCH

Barnaby, David, Jr. and Reizenstein, Richard (1975), "Attitudes Toward Energy Consumption: Segmenting the Gasoline Market," Advances in Consumer Research, 2.

Feather, Norman T. (1975), Values in Education and Society, New York: The Free Press.

Henry, Walter A. (1976), "Cultural Values Do Correlate with Consumer Behavior," Journal of Marketing Research, 12, 121-127.

Hill, Daniel L. and Hill, Martha S. (1979), "Consumer Attitudes and Perceptions and Automobile Fuel Economy Standards," Economic Outlook USA, Spring 1979, 39-42.

Hollen, C. C. (1967), "The Stability of Values and Value Systems," unpublished dissertation, Michigan State University.

Milstein, Jeffrey S. (1977), "Consumer Behavior and Energy Conservation," Advances in Consumer Research, 4, 315-321.

_____, (1978), "Energy Conservation and Travel Behavior," Advances in Consumer Research, 5, 422-425.

Pitts, Robert E. (1977), "The Influence of Personal Value Systems on Product Class and Brand Preferences--A Segmentation Approach," unpublished dissertation, University of South Carolina.

_____, Willenborg, John F., and Sherrell, Daniel L. (1979), "Rising Energy Costs and Adaptive Consumer Behavior," Proceedings of the American Marketing Association, 121-124.

Shahabuddin, Syed and Chang, Yu Chi (1978), "Consumer Attitudes toward Fuel Consumption in the United States," Urban Systems, 3, 117-122.

Willenborg, John F. and Pitts, Robert E. (1977), "Gasoline Prices: Their Effect on Consumer Behavior and Attitudes," Journal of Marketing, 41, 24-31.

PROGRESSIVE RATE STRUCTURE
FOR HOUSEHOLD ELECTRICITY

G. Jan van Helden
Selie S. Weistra

This chapter illustrates how the rate structure of electricity can contribute to a policy of energy saving. More specifically, the relevance of a progressive rate structure for household electricity will be considered. The rate structure or tariff generally defines the several components of the total amount of money which must be paid for the electricity supplied, as well as the relationship between these components. An extensive treatment of the advantages and disadvantages of a progressive rate structure is beyond the scope of this chapter. A summary is included in the final section of the chapter.

ALTERNATIVE VARIANTS OF A PROGRESSIVE RATE STRUCTURE

A rate structure can be progressive, proportional or degressive. This means that the price per unit is higher, equal, or lower, respectively, when the yearly consumption per household is larger. If applicable there is differentiation of the price per kWh in relation to consumption by blocks instead of a continuous differentiation. Irrespective of a kWh price, often a fixed charge has to be paid per period, given a certain consumption block. This charge covers the consumer costs. Moreover kWh prices can be differentiated according to the period in which the consumption takes place, e.g., "peak load pricing." The latter component of the rate structure, although widely used, will not be considered in this paper.

There are two fundamental shapes of a progressive rate structure. Irrespective of the fixed charges, the two shapes are:

• The step tariff. When moving from, for example the first to the second block, the consumer has to pay the (higher) price per unit of the second block for all kWh's he uses.

• The block tariff. When moving to the next block, the consumer only has to pay a higher price per unit for his additional consumption.

The authors are indebted to Aart Bosman and Janny Hoekstra for giving helpful comments on an earlier draft of this paper and to Harrie Austie, Rob Makkinga, and Arie Smit for their research assistance.

The following four rate structures are examined:

1.   the proportional rate structure with a constant fixed charge;

2.   the progressive step tariff with a constant fixed charge for every consumption block;

3.   the progressive step tariff with degressive fixed charges;

4.   the progressive block tariff with a constant fixed charge.

The proportional rate structure (1) is in accordance with the current tariff for household electricity consumption in the Netherlands.   The kWh prices of rates 2, 3, and 4 had to be chosen in a way such that the total expenses of a representative consumer in the various blocks of each rate structure are the same as in the proportional tariff.   In the case of a step tariff with a constant fixed charge (2), there is an abrupt increase in expenditure at every block transition.   To counter this, the step tariff with degressive fixed charges (3) has been introduced.

In Table 1, a comparison has been made between the four tariff variants with respect to the total annual expenditure per household in each of the three distinguished blocks.   Only the block tariff (4) will be dealt with in the following sections of this chapter in order to limit the scope of the exposition.

OVERVIEW OF RESEARCH

In the following, use has been made of a study of households in Groningen, a town of about 160 thousand inhabitants in the north of the Netherlands (Van Helden 1978, Chapter 3; Van Helden 1979).

In constructing a progressive block tariff the following three variables are used:

   i. the number of blocks and the size of each block;
  ii. the price per kWh of every block, given the progressiveness;
 iii. the size of the fixed charge.

The values of the three variables are determined as follows:

a.   The number of blocks is placed at three or four.   Two blocks was considered too small, because a saving stimulus only occurs once.   In order to simplify the exposition and to reduce the amount of computation, five or more blocks were not considered.   The determination of the block sizes should ensure that both the number of consumers and the

TABLE 1

TOTAL EXPENDITURE FOR ELECTRICITY CONSUMPTION PER HOUSEHOLD PER YEAR WITH PROGRESSIVE BLOCK OR STEP TARIFF (THREE BLOCKS) AND WITH THE PROPORTIONAL TARIFF

	First block $(0 < X < X1)$	Second block $(X1 < X < X2)$	Third block $(X > X2)$
With the block tariff	$p_1^b X + f$	$p_1^b X_1 + p_2^b(X-X_1) + f$	$p_1^b X_1 + p_2^b(X_2-X_1) + p_3^b(X-X_2) + f$
With the step tariff (constant fixed charge)	$p_1^s X + f$	$p_2^s X + f$	$p_3^s X + f$
With the step tariff (degressive fixed charges)	$p_1^s X + f_1$	$p_2^s X + f_2$	$p_3^s X + f_3$
With the proportional tariff	$p^p X + f$	$p^p X + f$	$p^p X + f$
Comparison of kWh prices	$p_1^b = p_1^s < p^p$	$p_2^b > p_2^s = p^p$	$p_3^b > p_3^s > p^p$
Comparison of fixed charges	$f_1 > f$	$f_2 > f$	$f_3 < f$
Increase of expenditure at block transition with step tariff (constant fixed charge)	$f_1 - f_2$	$f_2 - f_3$	

X = total consumption (per household per year)

X_i = maximum consumption of i-th block, i=1,2: $0 < X_1 < X_2$.

p_i = price per kWh at the i-th block, i=1,2,3: $p_1 < p_2 < p_3$ (the indices b, s, and p refer to the block, step and proportional tariff, respectively).

f_i = fixed charge at the i-th block of the step tariff; $f_1 = f_2 + (p_2^s - p_1^s)X_1$; $f_2 = f_3 + (p_3^s - p_2^s)X_2$; $f_3 > 0$.

f = (constant) fixed charge.

consumption is distributed over the blocks in such a way that the relative frequencies per block do not differ too much. The results are shown in Table 2, columns (1) up to and including (4).

b.   In 1978 the price per kWh of the proportional tariff in Groningen was Dfl. 0,154. Assuming that the total revenues have to be the same as the current revenues (at the proportional tariff), with similar consumption, the prices per kWh of the progressive tariff were determined. The large and small differences in prices of a progressive rate structure (mentioned in Table 2) were chosen in a fairly arbitrary way, see Table 2, columns (5) and (6).

c.   The fixed charge stands at Dfl. 75,- per year and is the same as the fixed charge of the proportional rate structure in 1978 (this fixed charge is not shown in Table 2).

The determination of the values of the variables a, b, and c, as shown above, thus leads to four alternative rate structures: 2 (a.) × 2 (b.) × 1 (c.) = 4

EMPIRICAL RESULTS

The Effects on Electricity Consumption

Table 3 shows the effect of the different variants of the progressive block tariff, as introduced in Table 2, on electricity consumption. The consumption effects have been expressed as relative quantities or percentages of change where appropriate. These are computed in such a way that the only relevant influence concerns the turn-over of a proportional to a progressive rate structure. So, in these computations other factors which influence the consumption (e.g., the level of the tariff, the average welfare of the households, etc.) have been disregarded.

Table 3 shows that the decrease of consumption of the different variants of the progressive tariff are estimated at 1.5 percent, 2 percent, 4.3 percent, and 5.8 percent, respectively.

Generally speaking, Table 3 shows the following results:

• Irrespective of the considered variant, the turn-over of a proportional to a progressive rate structure causes a decrease of consumption. This effect occurs because households with a medium-large and large electricity consumption are more price sensitive than households with a low consumption.

• As the differences in price between the blocks are larger, the decrease of consumption will be larger. Compare the results of variant 1 and 2 with variant 3 and 4; see column (6).

TABLE 2

RELATIVE FREQUENCIES OF THE NUMBER OF CONSUMERS AND OF THE CONSUMPTION WITH
TWO DIVISIONS OF BLOCKS AS WELL AS THE PRICES PER kWh OF THOSE BLOCKS
(CHARACTERIZED BY SMALL AND LARGE DIFFERENCES IN PRICES RESPECTIVELY)

(1) Number of blocks	(2) Size of blocks (in kWh)	(3) Relative frequencies of the consumption	(4) Relative frequencies of the number of consumers	(5) Small differences in prices per kWh (cents)	(6) Large differences in prices per kWh (cents)
Three	0-1740	22.2	47.8	14.4	12.4
	1741-3400	48.7	39.6	17.0	20.0
	>3400	29.1	12.6	20.0	29.5
Four	0-1520	17.6	42.3	14.1	11.6
	1521-2300	25.0	25.2	16.2	17.6
	2301-3400	28.3	19.9	18.5	24.0
	>3400	29.1	12.6	20.0	29.5

TABLE 3

THE EFFECTS OF SOME VARIANTS OF A PROGRESSIVE BLOCK TARIFF
ON ELECTRICITY CONSUMPTION

(1) Tariff variant	(2) Consumption block (in kWh)	(3) Price per kWh (cents)	(4) Relative* change of consumption (pessimistic assumption)	(5) Relative* change of consumption (optimistic assumption)	(6) Relative* change of consumption (most probable assumption)
1	0-1740	14.4	+1.6	+1.6	+1.6
	1741-3400	17.0	+0.8	-4.7	-0.6
	>3400	20.0	-3.4	-12.0	-5.6
	"average"		-0.2	-5.5	-1.5
2	0-1520	14.1	+1.7	+1.7	+1.7
	1521-2300	16.2	+2.0	-1.8	+1.5
	2301-3400	18.5	0	-11.1	-2.8
	>3400	20.0	-4.2	-12.0	-6.2
	"average"		-0.4	-6.8	-2.0
3	0-1740	12.4	+4.9	+4.9	+4.9
	1741-3400	20.0	+2.9	-13.5	-1.2
	>3400	29.5	-10.1	-36.6	-16.7
	"average"		-0.4	-16.2	-4.3
4	0-1520	11.6	+4.5	+4.5	+4.5
	1521-2300	17.6	+6.0	-5.0	+3.3
	2301-3400	24.0	0.0	-30.7	-7.7
	>3400	29.5	-11.9	-36.6	-18.1
	"average"		-1.1	-19.8	-5.8
Current proportional tariff	all	15.4	0	0	0

* The underlying computations are explained in van Helden 1980.

A progressive block tariff with four blocks induces a larger decrease of consumption than a block tariff with three blocks. Compare the results of variant 1 with those of variant 2 and the results of variant 3 with variant 4; see column (6).

Side-Effects

Table 4 shows the magnitude of the yearly expenditure of electricity consumption, at each variant of a progressive block tariff and--for comparison--of the current proportional tariff. Obviously, there is an increase of expenditure for the large consumers and a decrease of expenditure for the small consumers. This effect can be logically deduced from the properties of a progressive rate structure; Table 4 shows the magnitude of this effect.

TABLE 4

THE YEARLY EXPENDITURE IN DUTCH GUILDERS (FIXED CHARGE EXCLUDED), WITH VARIOUS KINDS OF PROGRESSIVE BLOCK TARIFF AND WITH THE PROPORTIONAL TARIFF (ALWAYS REFERRING TO THE MIDDLE OF THE CLASSES OF EVERY CONSUMPTION BLOCK)

(1) Consumption block	(2) Progressive block tariff with large differences in prices*	(3) Progressive block tariff with small differences in prices**	(4) Proportional tariff***
0-1740	111.40	129.37	138.35
1741-3400	342.82	385.56	365.80
>3400	860.87	744.90	686.86
0-1520	93.96	113.48	123.94
1521-2300	245.66	278.45	294.76
2301-3400	423.11	425.09	424.47
>3400	890.55	756.26	686.86

  * c.f. tariff variant 3 and 4 in Table 3, respectively.
 ** c.f. tariff variant 1 and 2 in Table 3, respectively.
*** c.f. the last row in Table 3.

Next, the change of the distribution of expenditure over households with a low or a high income and over small and large households is considered. The difference between large and small households refers to the number of persons in a household (recall that the difference between large and small consumers concerns the size of the electricity consumption per household per period). Tables 5 and 6 show the relation between the consumption blocks on the one hand and income and the number of

TABLE 5

THE RELATION BETWEEN ELECTRICITY CONSUMPTION AND INCOME PER HOUSEHOLD*

Income in guilders per year

Consumption blocks (in kWh)	Smaller than 27.000	27.000 to 47.000	Larger than 47.000
0-1520	32 (59)	9 (24)	1 (11)
1521-2300	13 (24)	12 (32)	0 (0)
2301-3400	7 (13)	9 (24)	4 (44)
>3400	3 (4)	7 (19)	4 (44)

*This table shows the relative frequencies of the total per cell and the relative frequencies of the column total per cell in brackets. So, this means that all numbers not in brackets add up to 100, whereas the numbers in brackets add up to 100 for every column. To avoid misunderstanding it should be remarked that the numbers in brackets do not (necessarily) add up to 100 for every row.

The relation in this table is statistically significant. With six degrees of freedom and a reliability interval of 99% the critical chi-square value is 16.8 and the computed chi-square is 27.5.

persons per household on the other hand, respectively.   In Tables 5 and 6 only the results of a rate structure with four blocks are shown; a progressive rate structure with three blocks leads to comparable results.

The following can be concluded from the two tables. A progressive tariff means an increase of expenditure for the groups with a high income: for instance 88 percent of the households with an income larger than Dfl. 47.000 has a consumption larger than 2300 kWh. Similarly, it can be concluded that there will be a decrease of expenditure for the households with low incomes. With respect to large and small households there are comparable effects, although less strong: in 66 percent of the cases households of 5 or more persons have a consumption larger than 2300 kWh, whereas in 81 percent of the cases small households (1 or 2 persons) have consumption smaller than 2300 kWh.

The last side-effect of a progressive rate structure concerns the neutrality of revenues. A certain tariff alternative is revenue-neutral if it leads to the same revenues as in the current situation.   The neutrality of revenues is often related to the objective of many public utilities that the total costs must be covered by the total revenues. Table 3 shows that the variants of a progressive tariff, as presented, are not

TABLE 6

THE RELATION BETWEEN ELECTRICITY CONSUMPTION
AND NUMBER OF PERSONS PER HOUSEHOLD*

Number of persons

Consumption blocks	1 or 2	3 or 4	5 or more
0-1520	32 (60)	6 (15)	1 (17)
1521-2300	11 (21)	16 (39)	1 (17)
2301-3400	4 (8)	13 (32)	2 (33)
>3400	6 (11)	6 (15)	2 (33)

*See the first part of the note of Table 5.
The relation in this table is statistically significant. With
six degrees of freedom and a reliability interval of 99%, the
critical chi-square value is 16.8 and the computed chi-square
value is 25.9.
Ideally, there should not be any difference between the relative frequencies of the sum total for every consumption block,
when comparing Tables 5 and 6. However, the relative small
differences, which are actually present, result from the
circumstance that the non-response on the question for the
income per household (Table 5) and the question for the number
of persons per household (Table 6) differ.

revenue-neutral. There appears to be a decrease of consumption
and therefore a decrease of revenues. Given that an important
share of the total costs does not vary with the production (or
the consumption), the need to break even is in danger. In order
to break even in the short-term, assuming that this is the case
with the current proportional tariff, it is possible to introduce equal increases of kWh prices for all the consumption
blocks, or to diminish the price decrease per kWh for the first
block in respect of the proportional tariff. Of course, it is
also possible to drop the need for covering of the costs.
Probably, in the long-term, this need is not endangered, if the
fixed costs fall (proportionally) with the decrease in consumption. (For a discussion about the desirability of a progressive
rate structure for household electricity consumption in relation
to the empirical results presented above, see van Helden 1980).

SUMMARY AND CONCLUSIONS

If the introduction of a progressive rate structure for
household electricity consumption is considered, one has to
choose between a block tariff and a step tariff. Both being
progressive tariffs, the difference stems from the applicability
of the specific block price per kWh. While the use of a block

tariff means that the higher price only applies to the appropriate blocks, this price is also applicable to the intramarginal blocks in the case of a step tariff. In order to restrict the scope of the empirical research, only the progressive block tariff has been considered in the chapter.

The advantages of a progressive rate structure are:

a.   A progressive tariff stimulates the individual consumer to save, because he has to pay a relatively higher price for additional consumption.

b.   It leads to a decrease of consumption, because small consumers, as far as the size of electricity consumption is concerned, are relatively less price sensitive than medium-large and large consumers.

c.   It is fair to over-charge the consumers who contribute more to a coming energy shortage.

d.   A progressive tariff has an equalizing effect on the income distribution of the electricity consumers.

The disadvantages of a progressive rate structure are:

a.   This tariff disregards the responsibility of the consumers for the costs (of the electricity supply) they cause.

b.   It can lead to injustice with respect to households having comparatively high consumption.

c.   It brings about problems of substitution if, at the same time, a progressive rate structure for (partly competitive) gas will not be introduced.

In our opinion, the advantages are not always relevant. (See Van Helden 1980).

A progressive rate structure always leads to decrease of consumption in comparison with the current proportional tariff. This decrease of consumption varies only from 1 to 6 percent and appears to be larger as the differences in prices between the consumption blocks are larger and there are more tariff blocks.

A progressive rate structure induces increased expenses for large consumers and decreased expenses for small consumers. Side-effects are that households with a high income and large households have to pay higher charges, relative to households with a low income and small households.

It is impossible to cover the costs of the utility, at least at short notice, because of the decrease of consumption associated with a switch from the proportional to a progressive tariff. Thus, it might be necessary to increase the progressive kWh prices additionally to equilibrate revenues and costs. Of course it is also possible to relinquish the need of covering the costs connected with electricity pricing.

Complementary research is needed to formulate fully elaborated proposals of a progressive rate structure. It is also necessary to further investigate the relation between the level of consumption and price sensitivity. In this context, it is worthwhile considering experimental studies.

RELATED RESEARCH

Berg, S.V. and Herden, J.P. (1976), "Electricity Price Structures: Efficiency, Equity and the Composition of Demand," Land Economics, 52, 169-179.

_____, and Roth, W.E. (1977), "Some Remarks on Residential Electricity Consumption and Social Rate Restructuring," Bell Journal of Economics and Management Science, 8, 690-699.

Berg, J.P. van den (1975), "Energiebeleid en Tarieven van Gas en Electriciteit," Economisch-Statistische Berichten, 60, 313-317.

Burian, F. von (1978), "Überlegungen zur Reform der Stromtarife in Österreich," Österreichische Zeitschrift für Electrizitätswirtschaft, 31, 121-128.

Helden, G.J. van (1978), De Prijsgevoeligheid van het Huishoudelijke Electriciteitsverbruik, Leiden, Stenfert Kroese.

_____, (1979), "Measuring the Price Sensitivity of Household Electricity Consumption by Means of Interview Data," European Journal of Marketing, 13, 183-193.

_____, in collaboration with H. Austie, R. Makkinga, and A. Smit (1980), "Progressieve Electriciteitstarieven," Economisch-Statistische Berichten, 65, 144-151 and 176-183.

Hirst, E. and Carney, J. (1977), "Residential Energy Conservation: Analysis of US Federal Programmes," Energy Policy, 5, 211-222.

Miedema, S. (1975), "Energiebeleid en Aardgastarieven voor Huishoodelijk Gebruik," Economisch-Statistitische Berichten, 60, 574-577.

Mutzner, I. (1978), "Im Gerpräch: Degressive und Progressive Tarifsysteme," Bulletin SEV/VSE, 69, 119-123.

Nederlands Economisch Instituut (1979), De Merites van een Progressieve Gasprijs, Rotterdam, Stichting Het Nederlands Economisch Instituut.

Taylor, L.D. (1974), "The Demand for Electricity: A Survey," Bell Journal of Economics and Mangement Science, 5, 74-110.

Varkevisser, J. (1975), "Progressieve Energiebelasting," Economisch-Statistische Berichten, 60, 465.

Verenigning van Directeuren van Electriciteitsbedrijven in Nederland (1974), Enkele beschouwingen over elektriciteit-starieven die beogen de groei van het verbruik af te remmen, Arnhem.

Vereniging van Exploitanten van Elektriciteitbedrijven in Nederland (1979), Overzicht van de tarieven voor woningen per 1 maart 1979, Arnhem.

Vlieg, F. (1977), "Huishoudelijk elektriciteitsverbruik; besparingen en consequenties," Economisch-Statistische Berichten, 62, 537-542.

Waverman, L. (1977), "Estimating the Demand for Energy: Heat without Light," Energy Policy, 5, 2-11.

Yayima, A. (1975), "The New Electricity Tariff in Japan," in UNIPEDE Conference on Electricity Tariffs, Madrid.

CENTRALIZED ELECTRICITY CONTROL

William J. Corney
John E. Nixon
Betty Yantis

One problem faced by power companies is energy load management. Due to regional climatic conditions, extremely high peak loads may be encountered on a seasonal basis. As an alternative to high investments in auxiliary equipment, power companies are exploring energy management programs whereby they assist the customer to use energy more efficiently and thus assist the utility in controlling expenditures for additional equipment.

Under the Public Utilities Regulatory Act of 1978 (PURA), every utility is required to consider all possible approaches to energy load management: direct control by the utility; non-utility control; pricing methods; and customer education (Maczka 1979). Of these methods, direct control of customer load by the utility offers the most reliable procedure, from the utilities standpoint, for affecting consumer peak usage. The majority of load management systems using direct utility control have remote on-off switching of air conditioning or water heating units. For instance, an air conditioner cycles "on" and "off" as required to maintain a preset home temperature. In a managed program, the utility controls the "off" period to coincide with the "on" periods on other consuming units resulting in a lower overall peak load demand. The ultimate benefit of an energy management program would appear to be lower or at least stable electric rates, because the power company can defer installation of "peaking" generators which are very costly to buy and operate.

Energy management programs are initiated by a load survey in order to determine consumer use habits. In a load survey, the utility installs a metering cluster at the customer's residence to replace the standard house meter. Along with the measurement of overall usage, meters are connected to the air conditioning and hot water heater circuits to measure the load and the time of day it is used. Data are recorded on magnetic tape and are processed and printed showing usage for each 15 minute interval throughout the day.

The use of load management allows the utility to turn off, remotely, selected household power consuming devices during peak load periods. This can be affected on a city-wide basis in such a manner that individual consumers suffer little or no discomfort, while the power company is assured of a reduction in peak

---

This research was supported, both technically and financially, by the Nevada Power Company, Las Vegas, Nevada.

power usage. Cost for a load management system, including radio switches, transmitters and computerized control, is less than one hundred dollars per customer, an economically feasible alternative to the purchase of "peaking" generators (Reynolds 1976). It appears that the major problem with load management is neither technological nor financial, but that of public opinion and acceptance of the method (Hurlberg 1975).

An ongoing attitude measurement and experimental residential air conditioning load management program was planned and executed by the local power company. This chapter details the results of this major and continuing effort. Because of the insular geographic location of the study area and the diversity of its population with respect to age, income, and ethnic backgrounds (White, Malamud, and Nixon 1975), the results may reflect national findings.

METHODS

Phase I of this study was conducted in 1977. A sample of 270 single-family dwellings was surveyed by personal interview to determine residents' attitudes toward energy management, energy-use metering, energy-use patterns, and energy problems. Data on power company customer characteristics were also collected. As a result of this survey, 50 single-family residences were selected to participate in a load measurement program. Results of this program suggested that an energy management program would be a viable alternative to the construction and operation of peak load generators and an experimental program was initiated in mid-1979.

In 1979, a sample of 5000 power company residential customers was randomly selected from company billing files (approximately 3 percent of the residential population). Completed, usable questionnaires were returned by 911 customers, an 18 percent response rate. Of these, 479 agreed to participate in the program.

Phase II of the study consisted of attempts to contact each of the 479 "willing" respondents to verify that the home was a single-family dwelling and had an electric, roof-type air conditioning unit. Qualified respondents who agreed to participate in the survey and completed all requirements consisted of 161 residents.

A remote control device was attached to the thermostat control of each participant residence, allowing the power company to turn off the air conditioning units for periods of 7.5, 10.5, and 12.5 minutes per each half-hour. Disruption times were between 12 noon and 8 p.m. (July through August). Cut off periods applied to all residences for one week at a time, e.g., as indicated in Table 3.

Participants received a free initial inspection and repair on air conditioning units, free maintenance during the test period, and a rebate on their electric bill averaging $10.00 per month.

FINDINGS

Reasons for Entering the Program

Subsequent to entry into the program, participants were asked why they agreed to participate in the air conditioning control program. A summary of responses is shown in Table 1. Energy conservation is the primary reason mentioned by the respondents, followed by rebate. Air conditioning maintenance is the third most frequently mentioned reason.

TABLE 1

REASONS FOR PARTICIPATION*

(Why did you agree to participate in this program?)

Reason	No.
Rebate	74
A/C Maintenance	22
Energy Conservation	102
Curious	11
Good Idea	7
Other	12

* Does not sum to n = 161 because of
  multiple responses.

Participant Reactions to Energy Management

Participants were asked to specify the minimum condition under which they would agree to participate in similar future load management programs. Air conditioning maintenance, with a rebate, is the dominant condition (71 percent) followed by no incentive at all (11 percent). Data are summarized in Table 2. Participants were given postage paid, addressed cards and were asked to keep logs of any discomfort experiences. These cards were to be mailed to the local power company. A total of 26 cards were received. In the follow-up interviews, respondents were asked to specify periods of discomfort that they remembered or had noted. Of those responding to this question, the largest number identify the last two weeks of August as being periods of discomfort; however, statistically, there are no significant differences. September and October data are not included because the follow-up interviews were conducted in mid-September. Data are presented in Table 3. Variations in

TABLE 2

CONTINUED PARTICIPATION

(Under what conditions would you be willing
to continue participating in this program?)

Conditions	No.	Percent
Under present conditions (both rebate and a/c maintenance)?	115	71
With present rebate only (no a/c maintenance)?	10	6
With a/c maintenance only (no rebate)?	8	5
Without rebate and without a/c maintenance?	17	11
With additional rebate?	5	3
No response	6	4
Total	161	100

TABLE 3

TIME PERIODS OF DISCOMFORT

(When did you experience discomfort while participating in the
program?)

Mo.*	Week	No.	Percent	Average High Temperature Degrees F	Minutes A/C Off Per Half Hour
July	1	14	9	101	0.0
	2	15	9	111	7.5
	3	19	12	105	10.5
	4	17	11	108	12.5
August	1	15	9	110	7.5
	2	15	9	98	10.5
	3	11	7	90	12.5
	4	11	7	102	7.5

* September was not included due to interview time frame.

reported discomfort are <u>not</u> significantly different for the eight-week period.

It was hypothesized that whether or not a participant was at home during the control period would be a major factor in perceived discomfort. Data indicate that over 80 percent of the residences were occupied always or most of the time during the test period. Those respondents who spend the most time at home report discomfort most frequently. The difference of reported discomfort, however, was not statistically significant between the two groups.

Participants were asked how many times they called the power company for air conditioning service during the experimental period. Responses are shown in Table 4. Participants reported a total of 82 service calls. The local power company's records show a total of 71.

TABLE 4

SERVICE CALLS

(Did you have to call for service on your air conditioner during the experimental period?)

Frequency of Service Calls per Residence	No. of Responses	Total Calls
1	37	37
2	8	16
3	1	3
4	4	16
10	1	10
Total		82

Consumers were asked their opinion about the effect of the monitoring device on their air conditioning units (Table 5). Well over half (67 percent) say there was no effect. Three percent perceive it as harmful.

SUMMARY AND CONCLUSIONS

Energy management provides an alternative to continued purchase of expensive peak generating equipment. The present research has provided information concerning the practical viability of energy management for residential air conditioning systems.

Because energy management involves turning the customer's equipment on and off, voluntary participation is essential. If the method is to succeed on a system-wide basis, large numbers of volunteers are required. Results of the present study indicate that a substantial percentage of total residential

TABLE 5

PERCEIVED EFFECT OF MONITORING DEVICE

(In your opinion, what was the effect of the monitoring
device on your air conditioning unit?)

Perceived Effect	Responses	
	No.	Percent
No Effect	107	67
Harmful	4	3
Helpful	13	8
Don't Know	35	22
No Response	2	1
Total	161	101

customers could be expected to volunteer if an effort were made
to implement the program for all power customers.   The 1977
survey, which was preceded by very little publicity concerning
the reasons for or benefits of energy management, produced a 40
percent volunteer rate.   The 1979 study, after increased mass
media publicity about energy management, found a 53 percent
volunteer rate.

For an energy management program to be successful over the
long term, it is necessary to maintain participation in the
program. While 63 percent of participants indicated that energy
conservation was a reason for participation, it appears that
this reason alone may not be enough to keep a consumer in an
energy management program.   Seventy-one percent indicate that
they would continue only with a rebate and air conditioner
maintenance. Because the cost of air conditioner maintenance on
a system-wide basis would be prohibitive, a different incentive
approach will have to be developed to maintain necessary participation.

Reactions to the energy management program by participants
were essentially favorable with regard to perceived comfort.
During the period in which no energy management control was
effected, 9 percent of the participants felt discomfort; during
the maximum control on the hottest week, the percentage increased to 11 percent, a nonsignificant change.   Air conditioning control did not appear to affect perceived comfort
level.

Consumer attitudes toward the effect of the device on their
unit was also favorable.   Only 3 percent felt it had a harmful
effect, an important finding for sustained participation in the
program.

There are major issues that the present research does not address.   An effort to develop a system-wide program of air conditioner control may prompt objections from consumers or other special interest groups who may object to increased exercise of power by utilities. Pressure could be exerted on governmental entities as well as on the consumer themselves, making a comprehensive load management program impossible.   It also seems possible that other load leveling techniques may be operational soon, making the load management approach a cumbersome and costly alternative. Finally, since the permitted rates of return on utility operations are traditionally tied to asset values, there is little financial pressure to develop load management programs rapidly as opposed to other methods of meeting required capacity.

RELATED RESEARCH

Connor, J.T. (1975), "If the Energy Crisis is Over, Why Worry About Conservation?" Allied Chemical Conference Board Record, Vol. 12, p. 12.

Hurlberg, C.G. (1975), "Load Management: Total Systems Approach Used," Public Power, Vol. 33, p. 14.

Maczka, W.J. (1979), "Load Management is a Winner with No Direct Path to Success," Electric Light and Power, Vol. 57, No. 5, p. 28.

Reynolds, M. (1976), "Motorola's Ted Miller Sees Load Management as a Major Growth Area," Power Engineering, p. 68.

Roger, E. (1962), Diffusion of Innovation, New York: MacMillan.

Talarzyk, W.W. and Omura, G.S. (1974), "Consumer Attitudes toward and Perceptions of the Energy Crisis," American Marketing Association 1974 Combined Proceedings, Ronald Curhan (Ed.), pp. 316-322.

Tankersley, C.B. (1977), "Concern toward the Energy Crisis: Some Social-Psychological Correlates," Proceedings of the Conference of the American Institute of Decision Sciences, pp. 322-333.

Uhler, R.G. (1978), "Load Management: Strategy for Conservation," Public Power, Vol. 36, No. 3, p. 29.

White, W.T., Malamud, B., and Nixon, J.E. (1975), "Socio-Economic Characteristics of Las Vegas, Nevada," Centre for Business and Economics Research, University of Nevada, Las Vegas.

DIRECT CONTROL OF HOUSEHOLD ELECTRICITY

Robert F. Dyer

Governmental agencies and private sector energy suppliers have utilized a range of soft and hard alternative strategies in executing conservation programs. In order from soft to hard they are: communications programs, continuous feedback, residential energy audit programs, financial incentives, voluntary direct control programs (whereby customers agree to have major end use appliances), and mandatory direct control systems (employing either control of end use appliances, or rationing of energy supply, and similar approaches).

Some systematic research has examined both the consumption and customer acceptance impacts of the soft alternatives. Far less is known about the short and long run effects of hard strategies. One national study (Elrick and Lavidge 1977) suggested that the closer the strategy employed moves from the soft to the hard end of the policy spectrum, the lower the degree of public acceptance. Other evidence points to negligible long run demand conservation with the soft approaches (Kohlenberg, Phillips and Proctor 1976; Kagel, Battalio, Winkler, and Winet 1976; Booth undated; Palmer, Lloyd and Lloyd undated; Hayes and Cone 1975). What is known suggests that in a period of critical shortage, little assurance can be placed on the soft approaches to reduce a utility's system demand.

For the above reasons, this chapter is directed towards a hard approach. The results of a 1979 experimental study of residential direct load control (DLC) conducted by a large metropolitan electric utility are presented.

DIRECT LOAD CONTROL PROGRAMS AND
CUSTOMER ACCEPTANCE

Management of an electric utility's load curve has been a critical function since the Arab oil embargo. In order to avoid building costly generating facilities, deployment of less efficient generating plants, use of more expensive fuels, or wholesale purchase of additional power at prime rates to accommodate the "spike" in their daily or seasonal electricity demand charts, utilities have investigated a variety of load control alternatives.

Table 1 lists pilot projects where customers were actually involved in load management demonstration programs sponsored by the U.S. Department of Energy (EUS 1979). On close review it is apparent that these studies would serve as easy targets for criticism. Prepared by engineers and others unfamiliar with

TABLE 1

RESIDENTIAL LOAD MANAGEMENT DEMONSTRATION PROJECTS

Utility	Project Type	Participation	Sample Size
Arizona Power Service Company	Time-differentiated rates	Voluntary	78
Arkansas Power & Light Company	Time-differentiated and seasonal rates	Mandatory Mandatory	27 49
Dayton Power & Light Company	Time-differentiated and air conditioning	Voluntary Voluntary	25 25

research design considerations, it seems clear that the orientation was toward testing the equipment, metering devices, controls, and taking physical measures of energy consumption. In terms of either measuring customer acceptance, i.e., attitudes, or response, i.e., energy usage behavior, the studies share the obvious methodological drawback in experimental design, sampling and, measurement areas.

Table 2 summarizes the design aspects of DLC studies that reported customer acceptance results. Though only three of these studies used formal survey efforts, preliminary evidence suggests the following relationships between DLC and customer acceptance: (1) Residential participants possess a generally positive attitude toward DLC programs; (2) attitudes appear to be linked to motivations for participation, methods of recruiting volunteers, the incentives structure, and the degree of obtrusiveness of the controls; (3) very low levels of awareness, discomfort, and inconvenience are attributed to DLC and little direct linkage between the level of interruptions and level of obtrusiveness is suggested; and (4) intentions of subject to participate in future load control programs are, overall, very high.

RESEARCH DESIGN

Experimental Design

A 3 × 2 longitudinal (repeated measures) design was utilized to measure the impact of direct or mechanical controls used in this study. Three types of mechanical control treatments were utilized: (1) Radio-control air conditioning (AC) and hot water heating (HW), (2) radio-control AC only, (3) priority relay—HW heating controlled when AC was in operation. Test groups and matched sample control groups of households were formed to measure the impact of experimental treatments on home

TABLE 2

SUMMARY OF DIRECT LOAD CONTROL STUDIES
INCLUDING CUSTOMER ACCEPTANCE MEASURES

Utility	Experimental Treatment				Experimental Subjects			
	Control Functions	Incentives Employed	Duration	Time Period	Sample Size/ Participation Rate	Types of Residences	Data Collection Method	Customer Acceptance Measures
PEPCO	RC-AC/HW	$25/mo. 5 mo. Equip. maint.	10+13 min per 1/2 hr	Summer 78 50 mo. 26 signal days AC, 22 HW	47/50 contacts	Single housing Subdivision Volunteers	Telephone & Interviews	Customer awareness Discomfort (AC) HW Shortages
	RC-AC Only	$5/mo. Equip. maint.	7, 10 min per 1/2 hr		21/40 eligible contacts	Random selection of 200 homes to inquire about participation.	"hot line"	
	Priority relay HW only	$7/5 mo Equip. maint.			30 eligible contacts			

(continued)

TABLE 2 -- (Continued)

| | Experimental Treatment | | | | | Experimental Subjects | | |
Utility	Control Functions	Incentives Employed	Duration	Time Period	Sample Size/ Participation Rate	Types of Residences	Data Collection Method	Customer Acceptance Measures
Arkansas Power & Light	RCAC	Average $11/mo 13 mo. Equip. maint.	5-9 min Intervals 10-18	Summer 75 (3 mo.)	211/261	West Little Rock Res. Volunteers	Mail survey "hot line"	-overall attitude -experience temp. changes (awareness of controls) -equip. problems with AC system -complaint calls (discomfort) -willingness to have AC control device left on unit.
	RCAC Cent. AC	Avg. $11/mo 3 mo. Equip. maint.	7 min. per 1/2 hr	Summer 76 (3 mo.)	200/219	West Little Rock (Same volunteers in 1975)	Telephone survey "hot line"	-awareness of controls -discomfort -equip. problems -desire to be on permanent load management -willingness to participate next summer.
	RCAC Window units	Avg. $3/mo Equip. maint.	7 min. per 1/2 hr		41/102 contacts 53 agreed to participate	Single housing subdivision- volunteers		

(continued)

TABLE 2 -- (Continued)

| | Experimental Treatment | | | | Experimental Subjects | | | |
Utility	Control Functions	Incentives Employed	Duration	Time Period	Sample Size/ Participation Rate	Types of Residences	Data Collection Method	Customer Acceptance Measures
Detroit Edison	RCAC Cent. AC	% disc. Avg. saving $2/mo	10-20 min per hour	Summer 78 (3 mo) 70 signal days (350 interr.	285/offered to all cust. 1st. 500 would qualify	Entire sevice area - Volunteers	Mail survey 83% resp.	-interruption awareness -comfort level -satisfaction with rate -desire to extend interruption period to increase rate reduction.
Pioneer Rural Elec. Coop. (Ohio)	RC-HW	None	5-9 min per hour	Winter 73	150/985 coop.	One housing Subdivision Volunteers	Observation	N/A
	RC Elec.	None	6-9 pm 50% heating when temp. below 20°C		30/NA			
Cobb Elec. Membership Corp. (Georgia)	RCAC	% disc. rebate	7 min per 1/2 hr	Summer 76 20 signal days (89 interruptions	5000/12000+ customers	Volunteers- Entire service area contacted stratified mailing and telephone contact by kW/hr usage groups.	"hot line"	-complaint calls reviewed

energy consumption. Kilowatt (KW) demand data was monitored over the entire experimental program for both test and control groups. Customer acceptance data, however, was obtained from test homes only at four different intervals. The control group served the function as a benchmark for changes in electricity demand. "Before" comparisons of tests and control homes' energy use were also available. A series of analyses were conducted to assure the comparability of these tests and control groups on demographic and household energy use characteristics.

Sample

Voluntary homeowners were recruited from several housing subdivisions within the utility's service area. After contacting potential participants by telephone, the firm's customer service representatives made a personal visit to the homes to discuss the experiment and explain the nature of the controls and equipment that would be installed. Homeowners were offered rate discounts or heat pump services as an incentive to participate in the experiment. A total of 147 homeowners were finally recruited for the study. Cell sizes ranged from 16 to 33. The drop-out rate was very low.

Data Collection

Several data collection efforts were involved in the study. Personal interviews were conducted by customer service representatives in the participants' homes prior to and after the experiment. Preliminary interviews obtained data on physical, energy-use related characteristics of the residence; demographics; and knowledge of energy-related terms and topics. Final interviews (after the formal experiment) obtained information on participants' reaction to the controls in addition to their intentions to participate in a followup experiment. Three telephone interviews were conducted—one prior to the initiation of the experiment, the second after June/July operating period, and the third after the August/September operating period. Finally, metering devices allowed kilowatt energy consumption data to be monitored continuously for the housing unit and specific appliances within each unit.

Measurements

KW Demand. KW demand was the performance indicator for both the test and control groups. Energy consumption data was recorded by the entire home and specific end use appliances during the time periods where the system peak was exceeded and on a daily basis. Monitoring also enabled a determination of whether and when thermostat adjustments were made by household residents.

Customer Acceptance. Three measurements (T1-T3) were taken within the test groups only of the following variables: awareness of controls (AC and HW), discomfort experienced (AC), shortages experienced (HW), inconvenience attributed to controls (AC and HW), attitudes towards utility's control system (AC and HW).

The exit interview (T3) also measured participants' intentions to participate in followup load control studies conducted by the utility as well as their perceptions of appropriate incentives and modes of operation.

Measures of customer acceptance taken by telephone interviews in the baseline, first operating period, and second operating period included: Number of interruptions experienced (AC or HW), inconvenience due to controls (AC or HW), discomfort due to controls (AC only), HW shortages due to controls (HW only), and overall attitude toward control system (AC or HW). The personal exit interview used a nine point scale format with numerical scale values and verbal anchors on cards to generate measures of: Awareness of controls, discomfort, inconvenience, and intentions to participate in a permanent load control program.

ANALYSIS

Considering the average responses on each customer acceptance measure, the general trend suggested by the data is that very low, almost minimal levels of intrusiveness were experienced and that attitudes toward the control system were strongly positive.   Another notable finding is that intentions to participate in future load control programs were uniformly high across the test groups.   The fact that mean exit intentions were higher than any of the mean overall attitudinal ratings implies that the subjects were willing to endure at least moderate amounts of discomfort and inconvenience in order to participate.

Pearson correlation matrices indicate, for both the air conditioning control and hot water control measurements, moderate (e.g., $r=.20$) to strong (e.g., $r=.80$) positive correlations between the repeated measures of each intrusiveness variable—again suggesting a stable response pattern where attitudinal data from T2 is correlated with each of the exit measurements, the same pattern occurs for the AC and HW sets of variables.   No significant relationships occur between the intrusiveness measures and the attitudes or intentions.   The direction of the relationship between attitudes and intentions is, as expected, positive for both the data sets.   The relationship is nonsignificant for the AC groups whereas it is only moderately strong ($r=.43$) for the HW groups.   The implication is that future intentions to participate in load control are, at best, only weakly associated with experience-attitudes toward direct load control.   Furthermore, attitudes toward the program do not appear to be linked to awareness, discomfort, or inconvenience attributed to the controls.

Analyses of covariance tests (using various models of dependent and independent variables) were conducted to determine if significant differences existed between the attitudes and intentions ratings of the three test groups. The results of the various models that were tested indicate that: (1) Temporary shortages of hot water are likely to be far less obtrusive than both central AC and HW control, for example; (2) the more positive the opinion of the study, the greater the average intentions to participate; (3) only in the group where both AC and HW were being controlled were negative opinions about the study manifested in significantly lower intentions to partici- pate in a future DLC program; (4) attitudes and beliefs based on recent events increased the sensitivity of the models; (5) only in the RCAC/HW test group did weaker opinions result in signifi- cantly lower intentions (it is important to note that none of the intrusiveness covariates were significant for either model); (6) significantly higher intentions scores were held by the Priority Relay group and those subjects with highly positive attitudes; (7) only in the RCAC/HW group did poorer attitudes significantly decrease intentions; (8) higher perceptions of hot water shortages were associated with lower intentions.

Based on exit interview findings, the DLC program was a resounding success on several grounds: nearly 90 per cent of study participants utilized the "very probable" to "certain" response categories in describing their intentions to partici- pate in future DLC efforts. No significant variation existed in this bottom line measure across the three study groups. Levels of interruption awareness, inconvenience, temperature or humid- ity discomfort, or hot water shortages were consistently rated at the low end of the response scales.

Content analysis of test group response to questions about how they liked/disliked the program revealed that: (1) Only slightly more than 40 per cent of the participants were able to provide a single negative feature of the program; (2) the inconvenience and discomfort aspects, the intrusiveness (privacy invasion) aspects, and equipment aesthetic concerns loomed fairly large as disliked aspects. Further load experiment studies should provide initial briefings on the requirements-- equipment, interviews, etc.--of participation during the re- cruitment phase. Dealing with these aspects "up-front" may decrease the eventual degree of concern during the experiment. The aspects of the program that participants liked most are: (1) Monetary rebates, (2) saving energy, and (3) interest in the utility's study objectives and its concern for energy conserva- tion.

When subjects were asked to suggest modifications in the program that would be beneficial to the utility's customers, given the assumption that it would be made available permanent- ly, a fairly broad range of comments for improvement were given.

A considerable number could not suggest any changes ("no improvement needed," "don't know," or "conduct year round"). Some of the suggestions were oriented toward equipment aesthetics such as "placement outside." In addition, a fairly large proportion of the respondents offered comments oriented toward continued or improved incentives for participation ("continued heat pump maintenance," "more money"). Understandably, some participants wished to be able to "control the controls" or at least through warning lights or notification of results receive some feedback as to when the controls were in operation.

Many of the above suggestions may be impractical, overly expensive, or inconsistent with current technology. In a sense they suggest problems and opportunities for future load management programs. Equipment aesthetics and placement concerns could of course be minimized with centralized, mandatory radio controls. Continued or improved incentives is an anticipated response--people want a better deal. Responses relating to the interest in changing hours of control or providing override features indicate that some people want to have their energy usage patterns in their hands--not the utility's! This is also understandable. Although few in number, the responses relating to feedback (control warning lights, notify homeowners of results, and give conservation results) suggest some interesting possibilities for combined feedback and load management experiments. By far, the largest combined response categories (no improvement needed, do study year round) indicate a high level of satisfaction with the program.

An additional question was posed to determine customer perceptions of methods to encourage high participation in future DLC programs. The most popular suggestions fell into the incentives category.

SUMMARY AND CONCLUSIONS

The Elrick and Lavidge national survey suggested that consumers may react negatively to load management programs, particularly to DLC systems. These results are based on loose perceptions or opinions because the respondents had no familiarity with the attitude object. Customers involved in the Dayton Power and Light load management demonstration project who were actually involved in a DLC program expressed the view that DLC was a viable solution to the peak load problem.

Similarly, review of customer acceptance findings from utilities in Arkansas, Georgia, Michigan, and Ohio present a picture of very unobtrusive controls, low levels of inconvenience, discomfort, and hot water shortages. Attitudes towards the programs are generally very positive. Data from the DLC program presented in this report are very consistent with the above studies.

Clearly, no generalization can be made from existing research about customer acceptance of DLC. All the studies are flawed with the following series of weaknesses:

1. In all cases subjects have volunteered for the programs. Most given subjects are residents of the same housing subdividion, and subjects' interaction has not been controlled, therefore increasing the possibility of group norms generating a consensus response. In only one instance were customers randomly selected and then solicited for participation. Refusal rates and analysis of demographic housing characteristics and energy usage patterns of those who declined participation should be recorded as well as their reasons for refusal.

2. The treatments utilized in the DLC studies are confounded by several factors. It is impossible to determine if customer acceptance is a function of the type of control system utilized, the duration and frequency of control intervals, or the incentives employed. True experimental designs are critically needed to manipulate these factors systematically.

3. A variety of operational definitions of customer acceptance have been employed including: complaint calls, satisfaction with motive, obtrusiveness of controls (i.e., awareness of operation, inconvenience, discomfort, equipment problems), overall attitude toward DLC program, intentions to participate in the future, and signing up for another year's DLC program. Single (exit only) and multiple, repeated measurements have been taken with mail, telephone, and personal surveys.

The above comments suggest that existing DLC research can only be characterized as crude, at best. Despite all the limitations noted, what is known about DLC and customer acceptance from a very fragmented, preliminary review is positive. Evidence also suggests that if multiple end use appliances are controlled, the threshold of customer cooperativness may be reached with DLC. Participants in the RC AC/HW had the lowest intentions to participate ratings, and were significantly less prone to approve of mandatory DLC.

RELATED RESEARCH

Arkansas Power and Light Co. (1976), 1976 Peak Load Control Study, Little Rock, Arkansas.

Barrett, A. (1976), "An Evaluation of the Load Reduction Program for Central Airconditioning: Cobb Electric Membership Corporation".

Detroit Edison Company (1979), "Update on Customer Reaction to the Experimental Interruptible Airconditioning Rate," Detroit, Michigan.

Elrick and Lavidge, Inc. (1977), "Attitudes and Opinions of Electric Utility Customers toward Peak Load Conditions and Time-of-day Pricing," Electric Utility Rate Design Study, Electric Power Research Institute, Palo Alto, Calif.

EUS, Inc. (1979), Survey of Load Management and Energy Conservation Projects, Oak Ridge National Laboratory, Oak Ridge, Tenn.

Holtzinger, J. (1975), "Load Management by Radio Control," Arkansas Power and Light Study, paper presented at Missouri Valley Electric Association Engineering Conference, Kansas City, Missouri, April 7-9, 1976.

Kagel, J., Battalio, R., and Winkler, R. (Fall 1975), "Energy Conservation Strategies: An Evaluation of the Effectiveness of Price Changes and Information on Household Demand for Electricity"; Booth, L.R. (undated), "Energy Management Program," Pennsylvania Electric Company; Palmer, Lloyd and Lloyd, (undated), "An Experimental Analysis of Electricity Conservation Procedures," Drake University; Hayes, S., and Cone, J. (1975), "Reducing Residential Electrical Energy Use: Payments, Information and Feedback," West Virginia University, in Duggan, M. (1977) "Customer Acceptance-- Reporting Task Force No. 10," Electric Utility Rate Design Study, Electric Power Research Institute, Palo Alto, Calif.

Kohlenberg, R., Philips, T., and Proctor, W. (June 1974), "A Behavioral Analysis of Peaking in Residential Electrical Energy Customers," Journal of Applied Behavioral Analysis.

Potomac Electric Power Co. (1979), Customer Acceptance of Load Control Methods--Summer 1978. Washington, D.C.

Roberts, R. (May 1, 1973), "Load Factor Improvement through Radio Controlled Diversity (Pioneer Rural Elect. Coop. Study)," paper presented at the 1973 Rural Electric Power Conference, Minneapolis, Minn.

INFORMATION AND INCENTIVES

- Energy Labels for Appliances

- Effects of Consumption Feedback

- Minnesota Computerized Home Energy Audit Program

- Marketing Incentives and Energy Conservation

- U.S. Residential Energy Tax Credit

- Refrigerator Energy Labels

ENERGY LABELS FOR APPLIANCES

C. Dennis Anderson
John D. Claxton

Energy labeling programs for major appliances are in operation in the United States, Canada, France, and Switzerland and are under consideration in Great Britain, Germany, and a number of other countries of the European Economic Community. The details of the programs differ substantially from one country to another. For example, in France the labels are compulsory on ten appliances including hot water heaters and boilers (furnaces). The labels indicate energy consumption in kWh per cycle or per period and provide a comparison with other products of the same type (OECD 1976). In Canada the ENERGUIDE program began in 1978 with the compulsory labeling of refrigerators in kWh per month, and is currently expanding to include other major household appliances (Anderson and Claxton 1979). Some will have yearly dollar energy cost, others will have an energy effiency index.

The purpose of this chapter is to report on a major field experiment that assessed the impact on refrigerator sales of energy labels, and sales staff energy information emphasis.

ENERGY LABELING RESEARCH

There are three types of energy labeling research of interest: attitude surveys, lab experiments, and field experiments. Attitude surveys have been used to determine consumers' views regarding the usefulness of appliance energy labels. For example, a study in Great Britain found that 91 percent of consumers sampled favored energy labeling (Consumer Association 1978). In Canada 81 percent of a sample of refrigerator buyers in Western Canada believed consumers would find energy labels useful (Anderson and Claxton 1979).

A lab study was used to aid in the design of the U.S. labeling system (Response Analysis Corporation 1977). The conclusion reached was that only a subset of consumers sought and used energy information. Further, this subset preferred detailed information, and, therefore, labels providing detailed information were most desirable. The unanswered question is whether consumers would prefer the same type of label in a

---

The authors are pleased to acknowledge the financial support for this study that was provided by the Canadian Department of Consumer and Corporate Affairs.

retail setting as they do in a lab.   The range and sources of
information at point of sale are relatively complex.   In this
setting a simple label may be more appealing than in a lab
setting.   This issue is of particular concern in light of
research indicating the limited nature of consumers' cognitive
processing (summarized by Bettman 1979).

A second lab study focused on energy labeling is the work
reported by McNeill and Wilkie (1979).   The study was based on a
sample of 155 women in Gainesville, Florida, and was designed to
minimize demand effects associated with lab experimentation
(Sawyer 1975).   One of the tasks in this study required subjects
to "build" a refrigerator that would suit their needs and
budget.   Incremental costs of features available were provided,
but incremental impact on energy consumption was not provided to
avoid demand effects.   There was no statistical evidence that
consumers implicitly consider operating costs when building a
preferred refrigerator.   Other findings indicated that measurement units used to provide energy consumption had no impact, but
that energy information had somewhat greater impact if it
indicated model performance relative to other models rather than
on absolute consumption data.

A final paper of note is a review of the effects of information disclosure requirements (Day 1976).   Although the review
did not deal specifically with energy information, label impact
was a major concern.   First, Day concluded that label information will be relevant when retail outlets provide adequate
selection, when brand loyalty is low, and when attribute salience is high.   Second, he hypothesized that labels have low
impact on low income segments since information awareness and
use appear to be related to education and income.   Third, he
noted that labels can be expected to have little short run
impact, and finally, that indirect effects on producers and
retailers may be of substantial importance.

FIELD EXPERIMENT

The general purpose of the experiment was to assess the
initial impact of refrigerator energy labels on consumers'
purchase decisions with a view to improved information environment design.   In terms of the data reported in this chapter, the
specific concerns were:

- Will the presence of energy labels have an impact on consumers' refrigerator choice?
- Will emphasis of energy efficiency by retail sales people
  have further impact on consumers' refrigerator choice?
- Will the type of energy information supplied (kWh versus
  dollar) influence the impact of the information?

Experimental Design

A two-by-two design was used to manipulate information type (kilowatt hours versus dollars) and sales force emphasis (no emphasis versus emphasis). The four combinations of these, plus a no energy information (control) formed the five experimental conditions.

The treatment units were 18 stores of a major national department store chain located in 10 cities in western Canada. With the aid of a regional manager the stores were judgmentally clustered based on store size, geographic region, and local socio-economics. Twelve stores were then randomly assigned to the four information treatments and six stores to the control condition. A system of simulated shopping was used to unobtrusively monitor in-store treatment conditions.

Criterion Variables

Impact of energy information was assessed in terms of both behavioral and attitudinal variables. Assessment of behavioral impact was accomplished by compiling unit sales data by refrigerator model for each store during the six week experimental period. These data were used to develop the following three behavioral criterion variables:

- Manual/Frost-Free Defrost: Manual defrost refrigerators had lower energy consumption ratings than frost free models. However, since manual defrost was only available in 10 to 13 cubic foot sizes, it would not likely be considered an option except when buying a smaller refrigerator (possibly in the 10 to 14 cubic foot range). Thus, one criterion was the proportion of manual defrost in the 10 to 14 cubic foot size range.
- Refrigerator Size: Generally smaller refrigerators had lower energy consumption ratings. Thus, a second criterion was refrigerator size in cubic feet.
- Energy "Stars": Within the frost-free refrigerator group, some models were clearly superior in terms of energy efficiency. To reflect this models were compared within each size category with the most efficient being identified as a "star." A limited number of exceptions to this relative rule were made when a model's absolute level of energy consumption was either much better or much worse than models of other size categories. Thus, each frost-free refrigerator available for sale was identified "star/non-star," the third behavioral criterion.

Two attitudinal variables were also considered: awareness of energy information and salience of energy information in refrigerator choice.   These variables were obtained by a post-purchase mail question sent to each household buying a refrigerator from the treatment or control stores during the experiment. Awareness was measured by asking if the respondent had seen the energy label when buying his/her refrigerator.   Salience was measured by asking respondents to rate on a 5-point scale the importance of operating cost along with 18 other refrigerator characteristics.

Findings

A total of 720 refrigerators were purchased during the experimental period and were analysed in terms of the three behavioral criteria.   Mail questionnaires were subsequently received from 303 of the buyers (42 percent), and were used as the basis for developing the two attitudinal criteria.

The dummy variable regression model used to evaluate experimental effects is indicated in Table 1.   Two of the three behavioral criteria indicated significant effects, as did one of the two attitudinal criteria.   The energy information treatments had no impact of size of refrigerator purchased (the average size across the five conditions ranged from 15.58 to 15.98 cubic feet).

Analysis of the second behavioral variable, stars/non-stars, indicated that for buyers of frost-free refrigerators, the probability of choosing an energy efficient model was somewhat increased when kilowatt hour consumption data were present.   The probability of buying a "star" was 0.61 with kWh information and 0.54 otherwise.

The final behavioral criterion, manual/frost-free, was analysed using the same model.   For buyers of 10 to 14 cubic foot models, the probability of choosing manual defrost was markedly higher when energy information was present, 0.27 in control stores and 0.53 in energy information stores.   Incremental impacts of information types and sales staff emphasis were not significant.

It should be emphasized that this energy information impact, although substantial, was only associated with purchases in the small refrigerator segment.   During the experimental period approximately 17 percent of purchases were in this segment.

The same model was used to analyze the two attitudinal criteria.   The probability of noticing the energy labels was 0.28 if not emphasized by sales staff, and 0.39 if emphasized. That is, although the sales staff were instructed to emphasize energy, the majority of respondents did not remember seeing the labels.   Either sales staff did not provide uniformly strong emphasis, or low salience resulted in low recall.   Both explanations are feasible.

TABLE 1

ENERGY INFORMATION EXPERIMENTAL EFFECTS

General Model:

   Effect = f(kWh, \$, EMPH, \$-EMPH)

   where: kWh is 1 when labels provided kilowatt hour informa-
         tion, and 0 otherwise,

         \$ is 1 when labels provided dollar information, and 0
         otherwise,

         EMPH is 1 when sales staff emphasized energy, and 0
         otherwise,

         \$-EMPH is 1 when dollar information was emphasized,
         and 0 otherwise.

Behavioral Criteria[a]

   $p(STAR)$[b] = $0.54 + 0.07$ kWh $(\alpha=0.08)$
                 $F(1,567) = 3.001$: Signif at α of 0.08
                 \$, EMPH, \$-EMPH: not signif.

   $p(MANUAL)$[c] = $0.27 + 0.26$ kWh $(\alpha=0.02) + 0.21$ \$$(\alpha=0.001)$
                 $F(1,117) = 5.58$: Signif at α of 0.02
                 EMPH, \$-EMPH: not signif.

Attitudinal Criterion[d]

   $p(AWARE)$[e] = $0.07 + 0.21$ kWh $(\alpha=0.001) + 0.21$ \$$(\alpha=0.001)$
                 $+ 0.11$ EMPH $(\alpha=0.05)$
                 $F(2,295) = 12,56$: signif. at $\alpha < 0.001$
                 \$-EMPH: not signif.

---

a. There were no significant effects for the third behavioral criterion, refrigerator size.

b. The probability of buying a "star," conditional on buying a frost-free defrost refrigerator.

c. The probability of buying a manual, conditional on buying a 10 to 14 cu.ft. refrigerator.

d. There were no significant effects for the second attitudinal criterion, salience of energy information.

e. The probability of noticing the energy labels.

No significant differences across conditions were found in the second attitudinal criterion, stated salience of energy information. A possible explanation is the generally low salience of this attribute. Respondents rated 19 attributes on a 5-point importance scale. Averaged across all respondents "operating cost of electricity" ranked 15th.

SUMMARY AND CONCLUSIONS

The implications for future point of sale energy programs is considered in detail elsewhere (Claxton and Anderson 1980). The purpose here is to summarize the major findings of the field experiment and suggest future research directions.

The Bad News: Limited Energy Information Impact

From the perspective of implementing energy label programs, one discouraging finding was the limited impact that energy information appeared to have on the market segment interested in frost-free models, a substantial majority of refrigerator purchases. Although choices in this segment appeared· to be influenced by the presence of kilowatt hour consumption data, three factors suggest that these findings should be viewed with caution. First, the probability of choosing an energy efficient model was not greatly increased by presence of kWh information, 0.61 versus 0.54. Second, the probability of statistical significance for this model was modest (α of .08). Finally, it was hypothesized that dollar information would be more under-standable, and therefore have more impact than kWh information. The only explanation that has been identified for the counter intuitive finding is that with dollar information the differ-ences across frost-free models are understandable, and perceived to be minor; whereas, with kWh information these differences are less understandable and therefore perceived to be more signifi-cant. Clearly, further research is needed to help clarify this area.

The Good News: Energy Information Sensitive Purchases

Some limited encouragement can be gained from the findings regarding awareness of the energy information. Although the labels were entirely new to the retail setting and the experi-mental period was only six weeks, more than one quarter of refrigerator buyers recalled seeing the energy labels.

The most encouraging finding was the impact of energy information on the small size refrigerator segment. First, it should be noted that it is in this segment that energy savings were most substantial. That is, the difference in dollars operating costs was greatest when comparing manual with frost-free. Further, the energy cost savings relative to the purchase price was greatest in this low price segment. Second, it seems reasonable to assume that a major reason for choosing a manual defrost over a frost-free would be the lower price of the former. It is not surprising that the larger savings in energy operating cost would have more impact on this price sensitive segment. Notably, the probability of choosing a manual defrost doubled when energy information was present.

Directions for Future Research

An area for future research is the issue of energy information salience. Ongoing analysis of the questionnaire data will focus on the association between salience and perceived differences in operating costs, and between salience and energy efficient choice. Other research might pursue the suggestion by Day (1976) that the usage of disclosure information is related to education/income. Evidence in the present study indicated that energy information was most influencial in the low price segment. Since this segment might also be expected to be related to lower income consumers, a hypothesis contrary to Day's is suggested. Further research might clarify this apparent contradiction.

A second area for future research is further understanding consumer information processing in terms of attribute versus brand processing and in-store heuristic construction. An in-store experiment that manipulated the use of a matrix format shopper's aid and utilized both video recording and protocol measurements might prove fruitful in this area.

Finally, from the perspective of information program management, a research area that remains of concern is the assessment of indirect effects on producers and retailers. The ENERGUIDE program has taken initiatives in this direction in terms of longitudinal analysis of models offered for sale and interviews with both producers and retailers. Other information programs might consider a similar evaluation approach.

Clearly, interest in energy labeling is continuing. The findings of the present study indicate the importance of careful information program design. If this is not the case, the popularity of energy label programs will not likely be matched by effectiveness in terms of energy savings.

RELATED RESEARCH

Anderson, C. Dennis and Claxton, John D. (1979), "Impact on Consumer Refrigeration Purchases of Energy Consumption Information at Point of Sale," Ottawa: Consumer and Corporate Affairs Canada, Consumer Research and Evaluation Branch.

Arch, David C., Bettman, James R., and Kakkar, Pradeep (1978), "Subjects' Information Processing in Information Display Board Studies," in Advances in Consumer Research, Volume 5, ed. H. Keith Hunt, Chicago: Association for Consumer Research.

Bettman, James R. (1979), An Information Processing Theory of Consumer Choice, Reading, MA: Addison-Wesley, Inc.

Claxton, John D. and Anderson, C. Dennis (1980), "Energy Information at Point of Sale: A Field Experiment," in Advances in Consumer Research, Vol. 7, ed. Jerry C. Olson, San Francisco: Association for Consumer Research.

Consumer Association (1978), "Energy Efficiency Labelling," report prepared by the Consumers' Association for the Department of Energy, London.

Day, George S. (1976), "Assessing the Effects of Information Disclosure Requirements," Journal of Marketing, 40, 42-52.

McNeill, Dennis L. and Wilkie, William L. (1979), "Public Policy and Consumer Information: Impacts of the New Energy Labels," Journal of Consumer Research, 6, 1-11.

OECD (1976), "The Energy Label, a means of energy conservation," Paris: OECD.

Olshavsky, Richard W. (1973), "Consumer-Salesperson Interaction in Appliance Retailing," Journal of Marketing Research, 10, 208-212.

Pennington, Allen L. (1968), "Customer-Salesman Bargaining Behavior in Retail Transactions," Journal of Marketing Research, 5, 255-262.

Response Analysis Corporation (1977), "Communication Effectiveness of Energy Consumption Labels for Major Appliances," Washington, D.C.: Federal Trade Commission.

Sawyer, Alan G. (1975), "Demand Artifacts in Laboratory Experiments in Consumer Research," Journal of Consumer Research, 1, 20-30.

Willett, Ronald P. and Pennington, Allen L. (1966), "Customer and Salesman: The Anatomy of Choice and Influence in a Retail Setting," in Science Technology and Marketing, ed. Raymond M. Haas, Chicago: American Marketing Association.

EFFECTS OF CONSUMPTION FEEDBACK

G. Gaskell
P. Ellis
R. Pike

It is estimated that 15 percent of energy consumption in the domestic sector is wasted and that consumers could save this amount without reducing comfort levels by good housekeeping (Morris 1974). In order to use energy more efficiently, consumers need to be motivated to change their existing consumption patterns and knowledgeable about energy use in the home. We describe such a consumer as energy literate; literate to the extent that he has pro-conservation beliefs, understands energy use in the home and knows where savings can be made. Without such knowledge even the strongest motivation to conserve derived from persuasive appeals or higher prices cannot be effectively realized. Following mass media campaigns, many consumers hold positive beliefs about the general idea of energy conservation but research shows that few report trying to save themselves, or know how to do so. This is not surprising since the general information conveyed in such campaigns would be predicted to have little effect on behaviour (Fishbein & Ajzen 1975).

Positive general beliefs do not necessarily counter others which have behavioural relevance. Seligman et al. (1979) show that beliefs toward maintaining comfort are related to consumption of energy which suggests that while consumers may be pro-conservation, other beliefs, typical of those low on energy literacy may be obstacles to conservation behaviour. If changing behaviour is the objective, then communication should be directed toward those beliefs which are related to behaviour, e.g., comfort, or introducing new beliefs and knowledge which have behavioural significance, e.g., cutting out waste and how to achieve this. There is a need to investigate the relations between consumers' beliefs, knowledge, and behaviour, i.e., energy literacy, in order to understand the obstacles to conserving energy and formulate more effective campaigns.

A general problem with nationwide campaigns is that of giving advice on energy savings which is of relevance to the particular consumer's needs and personal situation. Additionally, there is the problem of convincing consumers that they can achieve something themselves and that it is worthwhile for them to do so. In the absence of normative pressures to change or clear examples of the potential benefits, few feel inclined to

This research was supported by grant number RB/18/12/3 from the Social Science Research Council (U.K.).

act upon the exhortations from above. One attempt to circumvent this problem has been the use of feedback on levels of consumption to individual consumers. Such consumption feedback is a very specific form of information about the results of using energy consuming appliances and, in some studies, has been found to lead to reductions in consumption of between 10 and 15 per cent (Becker 1977; Seligman and Darley 1977). In other studies no reductions have been observed (Seaver and Patterson 1976; Becker and Seligman 1977). A number of feedback strategies have been used, including raw consumption sometimes converted into monetary cost (Pallak and Cummings 1976; McClelland and Cook 1978), comparisons between past and present consumption (Hayes and Cone 1977; Winett et al. 1978), and a variety of ways which incorporate a correction factor for changes in consumption attributable to variations in outside air temperature (Seligman and Darley 1977; Becker 1977). Much of this research has been practical in orientation, with the objective of testing different feedback strategies rather than investigating the mechanisms which might account for its effect on consumers. But unless the mechanisms are understood, it is difficult to synthesize diverse results or evaluate consumption feedback as a potential contributor to energy conservation policy.

In Ellis and Gaskell (1978), hypotheses were suggested regarding the functional properties of feedback and the way in which this form of information influences the consumer. It was proposed that the energy literate consumer should be conceptualized as an active information processor operating a complex man/machine system. The term system was used to denote all energy relevant aspects of the dwelling and the appliances which consume energy. Use of space and water heating, lighting, and appliances were all inputs to the system in which the feedback was an output of the metered consumption.

Given this, a review of research on the learning of skills is relevant. According to Annett (1969) feedback, or knowledge of results, during task performance has two consequences. First, it acts to motivate the individual and encourages him to set new performance goals. Second, it facilitates learning by allowing the individual to compare predicted with actual outcomes. In the context of energy use, feedback could be expected to lead to reductions in consumption by motivating the consumer to change his overall consumption level, that is, setting a new goal, or by increasing his knowledge of the energy system enable him to use that system more efficiently. Pilot research pointed to the need to modify this general model. The motivating function of feedback was not found to lead to changes in consumption goals or targets; rather it gave the individual confidence that energy consumption was predictable and potentially controllable--a feeling of personal efficacy.

Given this new belief, feedback may lead to some limited system learning. Limited because in the average home the energy

system is complex and has many inputs with variable contributions to overall consumption.   By relating use of inputs to
total consumption, it is difficult to do more than identify the
relative contributions of certain inputs.   The varied use of
space, water heating, and large appliances, such as tumble
dryers and washing machines, create obvious peaks and troughs in
day-to-day consumption and can be easily identified as major
consumers. But learning the contribution of small appliances is
not possible unless the consumer experiments with the system.
Knowledge of the relative contribution of different inputs is
valuable since it suggests where the greatest potential for
savings exist.

But changes in use may occur only when the consumer is
motivated by other considerations such as the price of energy,
or a belief that something needs to be done about the energy
crisis and that the individual consumer has a role to play.
Some energy literate consumers may not have tried to reduce
consumption because they do not perceive the need to do so.

Research into skills learning also points to the characteristics of feedback which are necessary for learning to occur.
In general terms, it is the information value of the feedback
which is critical.   For system learning, the operator must be
able to relate his use of inputs to the output, so the feedback
must be specific and immediate.   Clearly a utility bill is one
form of feedback, but one which lacks both immediacy and speci-
ficity.   The use of daily feedback augmented by a parallel
record of appliance use could be suggested as an appropriate
form of feedback in the context of household energy.

The practical implications of this discussion for energy
conservation are as follows:

General appeals to save energy should not be expected
to change consumers' behaviour directly.

Specific information such as practical advice on
energy saving is necessary but not sufficient to
induce changes in patterns of energy consumption.   In
addition personal motivation is required on the part
of the consumer to set a goal to reduce consumption.
Such motivation might arise from the cost of energy or
the recognition that unnecessary consumption can be
cut without affecting comfort.

Feedback which enables the consumer to relate the use
of appliance (inputs) to total energy consumption
(output) promotes a feeling of personal efficacy, the
confidence that energy use is controllable, and may
lead to learning about the basic aspects of the system. Experimenting with appliances and monitoring the
effects can demonstrate how to use them economically.
However, as with any acquired knowledge, some external

motivation is required for translation into conservation behaviors.

The present experiment was designed to:

(1)   investigate the relations between beliefs, knowledge and report behavior, and overall consumption, and changes in consumption;

(2)   assess the effectiveness of three energy conservation strategies, namely specific information on energy savings, feedback on consumption, and feedback and information in combination;

(3)   explore the mechanisms which might account for changes in consumption as a result of the experimental treatments, and define the characteristics of consumers who make substantial savings.

THE DESIGN

Households were randomly assigned to one of four conditions in a three-phase field experiment conducted during the winter of 1979-80.

The Experimental Conditions

Information Condition. Householders were given a specially prepared leaflet which included both a motivating appeal and information on savings. The general theme was wasting energy down the "energy drain," and that worthwhile financial savings could be made without affecting comfort by more efficient use of energy. A five-star rating system identified the importance of particular appliances in the home, and specific and practical suggestions on energy savings were given.

Feedback Condition. On specially prepared charts, householders recorded their daily consumption of gas and electricity. The charts allowed for a graphical plotting of daily consumption and conversion into daily and weekly cost. An appliance use record was made in parallel with the consumption record. Here below or above average use of different appliances was recorded as well as an assessment of outside air temperature.

Information and Feedback Condition. This condition combined the above information and feedback conditions.

Control Condition. This condition provided base line data.

The Experimental Phases

Phase I   - preliminary interview

Phase II   - lasting 8 weeks, the 4 experimental conditions
                    1. Information (I)
                    2. Feedback (F)
                    3. Feedback and Information (F + I)
                    4. Control (C)

Phase IIa   - Post experimental interview

Phase III   - 12 weeks. Assessment of longer term effects
of the experimental treatments based on
consumption levels. Householders were not
aware that this follow-up would take place.

The Sample

A total of 160 households in the London Borough of Camden
agreed to participate: 42.4 per cent were private owners and 57
per cent lived in accommodation rented from the Local Authority.
All the houses were of the terrace type and fitted with gas-
fired space heating systems. In each condition, an even distribution of household size and tenure (public or private) was
achieved by random allocation from the different categories.

Procedure

The respondents were interviewed in the first week of the
experiment. The questionnaire covered basic socio-demographic
details, followed by an extensive set of attitudinal, belief,
and knowledge items. These included general attitudes concerning the energy situation and its solution, specific attitudes to
comfort and waste, as well as the value of individual efforts,
knowledge about energy use and savings in the home, and savings
measures which had been taken during the previous winter.
Households were then assigned to one of the four conditions. In the information condition, the interviewer went
through the leaflet, drawing the householder's attention to its
message and hints on savings. In the feedback condition, the
procedures were fully explained and a first meter reading was
taken with the householder. All the households were visited
weekly by the researchers to take readings of consumption, and
to check that no problems had arisen in the experimental conditions. After 8 weeks, a post-experimental questionnaire was
conducted in which many of the questions posed in the first
interview were repeated. The interviewers, all trained social
scientists, made extensive notes on each household and assessed
their degree of commitment and interest. Three months later,

the households were re-visited to obtain readings of consumption following the experiment to assess the longer term impact.

RESULTS

Energy Literacy: Beliefs, Knowledge, and Reported Behaviors

In the pre-experimental interview, householders were asked to register their agreement or disagreement with 20 belief statements related to various aspects of energy and its use. In addition, a series of 16 factual items were used to assess various aspects of the understanding of energy use in the home. The belief and knowledge (+ reported behavior) items were factor analyzed using an oblique rotation. Five belief and three knowledge (2 knowledge and 1 reported behavior) clusters emerged accounting for 54 percent of the total variance. A generic label for each factor and its percentage contribution to the 5 factor solution is summarized as follows:

Beliefs

Rationalized apathy (the extent to which the consumer sees the energy problem as external to him and beyond his control) 43%

Perceived scope for savings (the extent to which the consumer feels he can personally save energy) 21%

Belief in scientific solutions to the energy problem 13%

Importance of personal comfort 10%

Perceived effects of individual efforts to reduce consumption 8%

Knowledge and Reported Behaviors

Labelling knowledge: comparative levels of consumption of different appliances 52.5%

Reported behaviors: conservation measures taken in the past year 28.5%

Economical use and general knowledge: how to use appliance economically and broader aspects of the house as an energy system, e.g., the effects of insulation 19.2%

Factor scores were then derived from these eight factors. Since the concept of energy literacy is hypothesised to encompass beliefs, knowledge and behaviors, a correlation matrix was computed for the eight factor scores (5 beliefs, 2 knowledge, and 1 behavior). The pattern of correlations provided reasonable support for the assumptions underlying energy literacy. The direction of all correlations were as expected, and 12 of 28 correlations were significant at p<0.05.

Further analyses showed that social class as indexed by public tenure/private ownership was highly correlated with energy literacy. Those in the private sector were less inclined to rationalize apathy and showed more pro-conservation beliefs on science and comfort as well as being more knowledgeable (in both categories). There were no differences in reported savings behavior, largely due to the private sector failing to register behaviors which in reality would save energy, e.g., their thermostats were set on average at 66.4F while in the public sector 72.4F. This substantial social class effect acted to reduce the number of significant correlations for the various aspects of energy literacy within the entire sample.

The Effects of the Experimental Treatments

On Consumption Levels. For each household, levels of gas and electricity consumption were computed for week 2, week 6, and for the 12 weeks following the experimental period. Since the variance in consumption levels was high, the base used to assess changes in consumption was taken as the mean level for week 2 of the entire sample. Percentage changes in comparision to the control condition are presented in Table 1 for gas and Table 2 for electricity.

Table 1 indicates that all three experimental conditions made some savings during the experimental period the greatest being made in the F+I condition. In the post-experiment quarter the savings were maintained in the F+I and I but not in the F condition. With respect to electricity consumption, Table 2, conditions F+I and I showed reductions during the experimental period while there is an increase in consumption for F. Through the following quarter F+I and I showed increased savings while F maintained its higher level of consumption.

In producing longer-term reductions in energy consumption, feedback plus information was the most effective conservation strategy. On its own, the information leaflet, which emphasized the potential for energy savings by more efficient and economical use of central heating and appliances, had substantial effect on electricity consumption but only a small impact on gas consumption. The daily record of consumption and cost given by feedback appeared at worst to have increased consumption or at best to have had no impact.

On Reported Conservation Measures. The ways in which savings were achieved were suggested by analysis of open-ended questions in the pre- and post-test interviews about measures which householders had taken to reduce consumption during the previous winter and in the course of the experiment. Table 3

TABLE 1

CHANGES IN GAS CONSUMPTION AGAINST
THE CONTROL BY EXPERIMENTAL CONDITION

| | Period | |
| | | |
Condition	Week 2-6	Weeks 2-6 + following 12 weeks
Feedback and Information (F+I)	-22%	-24%
Feedback (F)	-5%	+5%
Information (I)	-9%	-10%

TABLE 2

CHANGES IN ELECTRICITY CONSUMPTION AGAINST
THE CONTROL BY EXPERIMENTAL CONDITION

| | Period | |
| | | |
Condition	Week 2-6	Weeks 2-6 + following 12 weeks
Feedback and Information	-11%	-24%
Feedback	+9%	+11%
Information	-8%	-22%

TABLE 3

MEAN NUMBER OF REPORTED SAVINGS MEASURES

	F+I	F	I	C	All Experimental Conditions
During the previous winter	0.9	1.1	1.0	0.9	1.0
Additional measures during the experiment	0.9	0.7	0.7	0.2	0.8

shows the mean numbers of reported savings measures taken during the previous winter and the number of additional measures taken during the experimental period.

It was interesting to note that the control group report some new measures, 0.2 on average, which were probably due to the sensitizing effect of participating in an energy conservation study. The three experimental conditions reported significantly more additional measures than the controls, 0.8 to 0.2 respectively (sig. P<.002), with F+I reporting the highest use of new measures. When behaviors reported as being taken during the experimental period were divided into gas- and electricity-related measures, the differential reductions in consumption between the conditions become clearer. The Feedback group reported fewer measures which would reduce either gas or electricity consumption than either F+I or I. Almost 40 percent of the measures reported by the Feedback condition involved experimenting with appliances and heating. However, either this activity did not result in learning about energy saving, or else the learning did not get translated into conservation behaviors.

Savings and Changes in Energy Literacy

The next question was whether reductions in consumption were accompanied by changes to more pre-conservation beliefs and by increased levels of knowledge. Since the post-experimental interview included a re-test on all the belief and knowledge items, scores for the five belief and two knowledge factors were computed and changes during the experiment calculated. Since actual savings in consumption were made by the F+I and I conditions, these were combined to form a group of "savers," and compared to the F and C conditions, "non-savers."

Again the direction of the findings were consistent the concept of energy literacy, however, for the most part the changes were not statistically significant. Savers indicated a reduced concern about comfort. Non-savers indicated an increased belief in the futility of individual efforts. Savers also indicated slight improvements in both categories of energy-related knowledge.

SUMMARY AND CONCLUSIONS

On the basis of this research, there appears to be considerable scope for energy savings in the domestic sector by the more efficient use of existing space heating systems and appliances. Substantial savings can be achieved by consumers who are motivated to cut back and know how to do so. While many consumers hold pro-conservation beliefs and are knowledgeable about domestic energy use, they seem unwilling to attempt to cut back largely because they lack the confidence that they can achieve anything by themselves. However, a strategy covering specific information and feedback on daily consumption was found to be successful in achieving long-term reductions in total energy use and in increasing levels of energy literacy. Drawing attention to the waste in daily consumption and emphasizing the financial savings that can be made by using energy more efficiently seemed to provide a strong incentive to try out suggested savings measures. On its own, feedback had limitations because of the complexity of the domestic energy system but, in the context of more literate consumers, it helped to reinforce the value of attempts to cut back by demonstrating the savings achieved. In this study the feedback and information, which implicitly involved a home energy audit, was delivered in a personal context. Olsen and Cluett (1979) found that such audits were the most effective instrument in producing reductions in energy consumption. Whether such an appeal would be effective in a mass media campaign cannot be determined from these results.

RELATED RESEARCH

Annett, J. (1969), Feedback and Human Behaviour, Penguin.

Becker, L.J. (1977), "Reducing residential energy consumption through feedback and goal setting," Princetown University, Center for Environmental Studies. Report PU/CES 55.

_____, and Seligman, C. (1977), "Reducing air conditioning waste by signalling it is cool outside," unpublished paper, Princetown University.

Ellis, P. and Gaskell, G. (1978), "A review of social research on the individual energy consumer," unpublished paper. Department of Social Psychology, London School of Economics.

Fishbein, M. and Ajzen, I. (1975), Belief, Attitude, Intention and Behaviour, Addison-Wesley.

Gaskell, B. and Ellis, P. (1981), "Energy conservation: A psychological perspective on a multidisciplinary phenomenon," in P. Stringer (Ed.) European Perspectives on the Application of Social Psychology, Vol. 1. Academic Press.

Hayes, S.C. and Cone, J.D. (1977), "Reducing residential electrical energy use: payments, information and feedback," Journal of Applied Behaviour Analysis, 10(3), 425-435.

McClelland, L. and Cook, S.W. (1978), "Energy conservation effects of continuous in-home feedback in all-electric homes," Institute of Behavioural Science, University of Colorado.

Morris, D.N. (1974) "Effects on energy shortages on the way we live," paper P-5377, Rand Corporation, Santa Monica, California, 90406.

Olsen, M. E. (1980), "Consumers' attitudes toward energy conservation," Journal of Social Issues, (in press).

_____, and Cluett, C. (1979), "Evaluation of the Seattle City Light neighborhood energy conservation programme," Battelle Human Affairs Research Centers.

Pallak, M.S. and Cummings, W. (1976), "Commitment and voluntary energy conservation," Personality and Social Psychology Bulletin, 2, 27-30.

Seaver, W.B. and Patterson, A.H. (1976), "Decreasing fuel oil consumption through feedback and social commendation," Journal of Applied Behaviour Analysis, 9(2), 147-152.

Seligman, C. and Darley, J.M (1977), "Feedback as a means of decreasing residential energy consumption," Journal of Applied Psychology, 62(4), 363-368.

_____, Kriss, M., Darley, J.M., Fazio, R.H., Becker, L.J. and Pryor, J.B. (1979), "Predicting residential energy consumption from Home Owners' attitudes," Journal of Applied Social Psychology, 9(1), 70-90.

Wicker, A.W. (1969) "Attitudes vs. Actions: The relationship of verbal and overt behavioural responses to attitudes objects," Journal of Social Issues, 25, 41-78.

Winnett, R.A., Kagel, H.H., Battalio, R.C. and Winkler, R.C. (1978) "The effects of monetary rebates, feedback and information on residential electricity conservation," Journal of Applied Psychology, 63, 73-80.

MINNESOTA COMPUTERIZED HOME ENERGY
AUDIT PROGRAM

Eric Hirst
Peter Lazare

In early 1979, Northern States Power Company (NSP) offered a computerized home energy audit called Project Conserve (PC) to all its 540 thousand residential customers in structures with 1-3 dwelling units. PC consists of a 67-question form completed by the household. The answers to these questions are then processed by an engineering analysis computer model that computes potential energy savings, dollar savings, initial costs, and payback periods for several retrofit measures.

The Minnesota Energy Agency and the Department of Public Service conducted a three-part evaluation of NSP's offer of PC. First, data collected and created for the 91 thousand PC participants were analyzed to determine the characteristics and energy conservation potentials of their homes. Second, a mail survey was distributed to 2,200 households in the NSP service area. The survey included questions on recent and planned conservation actions and the reasons for these actions. Half the households who received questionnaires had participated in PC and the other half were randomly selected. Third, visits were made to 312 homes in the NSP service area to complete the PC questionnaire. The auditors were students trained to inspect homes and to properly complete the form. About half the homes visited had participated in PC and half had not.

EVALUATION DESIGN

This evaluation deals with three issues related to PC:

(1) What specific actions were taken by NSP residential customers to reduce energy use?

(2) To what extent are these conservation actions induced by PC as distinct from the federal tax credit, other government and utility conservation programs, and the market forces of higher fuel prices?

(3) What specific characteristics of households (demographic characteristics of the occupants and structural characteristics of their homes) determine their participation?

Research sponsored by the Minnesota Energy Agency, the Department of Public Service, and the Office of Conservation and Solar Energy, U.S. Department of Energy, under contract W-7405-eng-26 with the Union Carbide Corporation.

A three-part evaluation of NSP's Project Conserve offer was conducted. The first element involved analysis of household responses to the 67-question PC form and the engineering outputs from the PC computer program. This data base (called the PC history file) provides a rich source of information on the characteristics of a portion of Minnesota's housing stock and on the potentials to reduce energy use for heating and cooling these homes. The results of this analysis are summarized in subsequent sections and detailed in Hirst and Haller (1980).

The second element in the evaluation was a pair of mail surveys conducted by DPS in October 1979 (Lazare 1980). Two questionnaires were developed, one each for PC participants and for a random sample of single-family homes in the NSP service area. The surveys included questions on the characteristics of the respondent's home, recent and planned conservation actions, the motivations for these actions, participation in Project Conserve, and the socio-economic status of the household.

A random sample of names was chosen from among the PC participants. The nonparticipant sample was randomly selected by NSP from its list of single-family residential customers. Altogether, 1,000 questionnaires were mailed to PC participants and 1,200 were mailed to the sample from NSP's list.

All surveys were mailed in early October. Within a month, more than 1,300 (60 percent) of the surveys were returned. The number of PC participants who returned questionnaires was 882 (720 who received the participants form and 162 who received the nonparticipant form), yielding a response rate of 74 percent. Altogether, 440 nonparticipants returned forms, yielding a response rate of 44 percent. See Lazare (1980) for additional information on the two mail surveys, their distribution, response rates, and other details.

The third element of this evaluation included on-site energy audits at 312 homes in St. Paul and its suburbs. The major purpose of these audits was to determine the accuracy with which PC participants completed the 67-question form. In addition, the on-site visits provided interesting comparisons between the homes of participants and nonparticipants.

Six students from the University of Minnesota volunteered to conduct these audits. They received a four-day training program in October 1979, which consisted of lectures on residential energy conservation and practice audits at individual homes. Each student completed the PC form at these homes and then compared answers with other students.

On-site audits were arranged by DPS staff who telephoned people to request their cooperation in allowing student auditors to visit their homes. PC participants were called from a randomly-generated list of 1,000 participants in the St. Paul area. Nonparticipants were selected at random from the St. Paul telephone directory. Approximately one-third of the PC participants agreed to the on-site inspection and 15 percent of the nonparticipants agreed. These low response rates may introduce a bias into the results; however, the comparisons discussed in a later section suggest that bias may not be an important problem (Hirst and Haller 1980; Lazare 1980). Altogether the students visited 153 participant homes and 159 nonparticipant homes.

HOUSEHOLD CONSERVATION ACTIONS

The mail surveys were designed to determine past and planned residential conservation actions. Fully 91 percent of the PC participants and 83 percent of the nonparticipants reported taking actions "to conserve energy in the past 12 months." Table 1 summarizes the types of actions taken by both groups. By far the most common conservation actions were reducing winter thermostat setting (a no-cost behavioral change) and caulking and weatherstripping (a low-cost retrofit measure). Adding attic insulation and installing storm windows and/or doors were actions taken by more than one-fourth of the respondents in both groups.

Comparison of the PC and non-PC actions shows that participants were more likely to adopt the inexpensive measures (thermostat settings, caulking, and weatherstripping). Differences between the two groups were slight for the more expensive measures.

Two questions were asked about conservation actions planned for the next 12 months. Overall, 77 percent of the PC participants and 71 percent of the nonparticipants reported plans to take action during the coming year. Thermostat settings and caulking/weatherstripping are again the most common responses (Table 1).

Questions were also asked about the reason(s) for taking and planning conservation actions. The strongest motivation for conservation was rising fuel costs: 72 percent of the participants and 69 percent of the nonparticipants rated this the most important reason for taking conservation actions in the past 12 months. Similarly, 69 percent of the participants and 63 percent of the nonparticipants cited rising fuel costs as the major reason for planning future conservation actions. Almost 16 percent of the participants and 13 percent of the nonparticipants cited "concern about decreasing energy supplies" as the major reason for taking action.

Only very small fractions of either group cited patriotic duty, the Project Conserve program, or other utility or government conservation programs as major determinants of either past or future actions. Specifically, fewer than 1 percent of the participants ranked PC as either the first or second most important reason for taking conservation action. Altogether, 24 percent of the participants cited PC as a reason for taking past action. About 29 percent of the PC participants cited PC as a reason for planning future action (generally the fourth or fifth reason given for both past and planned actions). To explore the influence of PC further, participants were asked specifically

TABLE 1

PAST AND PLANNED CONSERVATION ACTIONS
AND THE INFLUENCE OF PROJECT CONSERVE ON THESE ACTIONS
(PERCENTAGES)

	Participants[a]			Nonparticipants[b]	
	Past[c]	Planned[d]	PC influence	Past[c]	Planned[d]
Turn down thermostat in winter	82	54	21	74	54
Caulk and/or weatherstrip	55	33	15	45	28
Install attic insulation	34	18	12	35	20
Install storm windows/doors	27	15	7	28	12
Install wall insulation	14	8	–	18	7
Purchase efficient appliances	15	11	3	17	9
Install solar heating system	2	0	–	1	0

a. Based on responses from 882 PC participants.
b. Based on responses from 440 nonparticipants.
c. Taken during past 12 months.
d. Planned for next 12 months.

TABLE 2

ENERGY CONSERVATION ACTIONS TAKEN DURING PAST 12 MONTHS
BECAUSE OF NSP'S OFFER OF PROJECT CONSERVE

Conservation action	Lifetime of action (years)	Percent who took action because of PC	Percent energy saving due to action[a,b]	Cost of action ($)[a]
Turn down thermostat in winter	2	21	8	0
Caulk and/or weatherstrip	3	15	5	40
Install attic insulation	10	12	10	400
Install storm windows and/or doors	10	7	7	600

a. The percent annual energy saving and cost of action are from Hirst and Haller (1980) and Hirst, Maier and Patton (1980).
b. The estimated annual cost for space heating is $750 = 15 Btu/ft^2-HDD x (1740 ft^2) x (8140 HDD) x $3.54/million Btu. This fuel price is a weighted average of natural gas and fuel oil prices in late 1979. HDD = heating degree days (65°F base).

whether PC motivated them to conserve energy. Almost 24 percent said yes, 18 percent said no, and the rest either were unsure or did not answer the question.

A question was also asked on the specific actions taken because of PC. The ranking of actions influenced by participation in PC is almost identical with the ranking of actions taken in general. These responses suggest that Project Conserve played a limited role in motivating participants to take conservation actions.

Another important consideration was to estimate the cost-effectiveness of the Minnesota Project Conserve. This was done by computing a benefit/cost ratio for the measures taken by PC participants that they credit to their participation. Two measures were developed: one for the participants and one that includes the costs of offering PC. Table 2 summarizes the elements that were used in these benefit/cost calculations.

The estimated annual reduction in space heating fuel use because of past actions influenced by participation in Project Conserve totaled 4.1 percent. The present value of the lifetime savings in fuel bills for these actions was $169. The cost to implement these actions was $96. Thus the benefit/cost ratio, from the perspective of the typical PC participant, was 1.8 ($169/$96). Because the ratio was greater than one, these actions were cost-effective for participating households. When the cost of offering Project Conserve (about $2 per participant) was included, the ratio dropped very slightly to 1.7 ($169/[$96 + $2]).

The benefit/cost ratio for all the actions taken by PC participants was 1.6 ($685/$427). The ratio for all actions taken by nonparticipants was 1.5 ($709/$462). Thus, participants, by differentially adopting the no-and low-cost actions, obtained greater economic benefits. The estimated reduction in annual energy use for both groups was 16 percent.

Because of uncertainties in household responses, benefit/cost ratios were computed in two other ways. First, differences between participant and nonparticipant past actions were compared (Table 1) and all increased conservation activity for participants (thermostat settings and caulk/weatherstrip) were attributed to PC. This yielded higher B/C ratios, 5.2 for program participants and 3.5 for NSP ratepayers. Second, credit was assigned to PC for only those households who claimed they would not have taken action without PC (0.7 percent of all participants). The B/C ratio for these participants was assumed to be the same as for all participants, 1.6. The B/C ratio for NSP ratepayers was much lower, about 1.0 ($685/[$427 + $2 / 0.007]). Further details regarding benefit/cost calculations can be obtained from the authors.

The mail survey asked nonparticipants why they had not completed the PC form. Almost 80 percent of the respondents claimed that they "did not receive the form." Assuming that the forms were received (they were sent with the monthly utility bill from NSP) this response suggests that many people do not look at bill stuffers. We assume that many customers simply ignore the cards and brochures that come with their monthly bill. The response rates to NSP's June 1978 pilot test support this hypothesis. Most of the remaining 20 percent (of the responding nonparticipants) said they did not return the form because they "already took conservation actions." A few indicated that they were "too busy," that the form was "long and confusing," or that the project was "not worthwhile."

ENERGY-RELATED CHARACTERISTICS OF HOMES

All three elements of this evaluation (analysis of PC data tapes, mail survey, and on-site visits) provided information concerning the thermal and structural characteristics of single-family homes in NSP's service area. These evaluation efforts also yielded information on heating and cooling equipment, appliance ownership, and demographic characteristics of these households.

Analysis of the PC history files provided considerable information concerning the thermal characteristics of PC participant homes. The average reported thickness of attic insulation is 7 inches. A surprisingly high 12 percent report having no insulation at all. The recommended optimum insulation is R-30 or R-38, equivalent to 10"-15" of insulation depending on insulation type.

Almost all the windows (94 percent) and slightly more than half the doors (56 percent) are protected by storms. From an energy conservation perspective, this difference is reasonable: storm windows provide larger energy savings per unit area than do storm doors.

About 40 percent of the homes need weatherstripping on some or all their windows and doors. Slightly more than 20 percent report that their windows rattle when opened or closed. About half the households report getting shocked in winter when touching light switches and door knobs. These responses suggest that at least 25 percent of the homes have problems with infiltration of outside air and might be considered "leaky."

Winter daytime temperature settings average 67F, suggesting only a small potential for savings due to lower temperatures. However, 60 percent of the respondents indicated a nighttime setting of above 65F; this suggests a substantial conservation potential through night setbacks.

These results suggested considerable conservation potentials in existing single-family homes. Specifically, the PC data showed the need for additional attic insulation, caulking and weatherstripping, other measures to reduce infiltration, and reductions in nighttime winter thermostat settings. Because Project Conserve dealt with only a few conservation actions, information is not available on the energy saving potentials for wall insulation, rim joist insulation, improved heating equipment, and other conservation practices and measures.

COMPARISON OF PC AND NON-PC RESPONSES

One issue complicated interpretation of the PC results: biases introduced because of self-selection. NSP offered PC to all its 540 thousand Minnesota customers living in structures with 1-3 dwelling units. About 91 thousand (17 percent) participated. How different (and in what ways) were the PC participants from the full population of 540 thousand households?

Fortunately, data from the mail surveys, the on-site audits, and published statistics on Minnesota's housing stock, i.e., from NSP (1979 and 1980), the U.S. Bureau of the Census (1976), and the Minnesota Planning Agency (1978); and Hirst and Haller (1980), were available to examine these differences.

Comparison of the two groups indicated a remarkable similarity between PC and non-PC households in terms of demographic characteristics. While participants had higher incomes, were better educated, had larger households, and were younger than nonparticipants, these differences were small. Comparison of the structural characteristics of the two groups' homes showed additional similarities. Based on the mail survey results, the average size of the houses was almost identical. However, the PC average was about 30 percent larger than an estimate from the NSP Business Research Department (NSP 1978). The average year of construction for participant and nonparticipant homes was almost identical. Gas was by far the predominant fuel choice for both space and water heating for both participants and nonparticipants.

The on-site audits included measurements of attic insulation thickness. The average thickness was almost the same for both participants and nonparticipants. Interestingly, the average thickness reported by particpants on the 67-question PC form is more than an inch greater than the average measured by the student auditors. Finally, the fraction of homes with all their windows and doors fully weatherstripped was nearly identical for the two groups. Again, the participant answers on the PC form were higher than the values measured by the student auditors.

The data presented here indicate that PC participants cannot be easily categorized on the basis of the energy efficiency of their homes. As a group, PC participants represented neither the customers who stand to gain the most from an energy audit nor the most energy-conscious households. Instead, PC participants seem to be representative of all single-family homes in the NSP Minnesota service area.

SUMMARY AND CONCLUSIONS

The evaluation findings were somewhat ambiguous because they rely primarily on self-reports. This problem has two aspects. First, household responses to the 67-question PC form contained errors. Second, reports of past and planned conservation actions and the influence of PC probably suffer from the "halo" effect; because conservation is socially-desirable, self-reports of conservation actions are likely to contain a positive bias. The Department of Public Service plans to collect and analyze fuel consumption records from samples of participants and nonparticipants. This should yield an alternative measure of the energy-saving effects of PC and of its cost-effectiveness. In addition, a similar evaluation effort is underway in Michigan (Keith 1979); comparison of the Michigan and Minnesota findings might reduce the uncertainty in our present conclusions concerning the cost-effectiveness of Project Conserve.

Comparison of the Project Conserve participants with random samples of households who did not participate shows considerable similarity. The two groups are very much alike in terms of demographic characteristics, structural characteristics of their homes, types of equipment in their homes, winter thermostat settings, and annual fuel bills. Only with respect to reports of past and planned conservation actions did the two groups differ. Even here, however, participants and nonparticipants differed primarily with respect to adoption of no- and low-cost actions. These comparisons suggest that those who took advantage of the PC offer are very much like those who did not.

Benefits to households were computed in terms of reduced fuel bills, the costs to households to implement conservation actions, and the cost to NSP to offer Project Conserve. The resultant benefit/cost ratios were generally greater than one (1.8 to 5.2 for participants, 1.0 to 3.5 for all ratepayers). These findings occur partly because participants were particularly likely to implement inexpensive conservation practices and measures.

Because Project Conserve was an inexpensive mass-produced service, both its costs and benefits were small per participant. It is therefore difficult to credit PC unambiguously with particular benefits because so many other factors also influence household conservation actions (climate, fuel prices, fuel availability problems, other conservation programs). In particular, there is uncertainty whether the actions taken by participants that they credit to PC would have been taken even without participation.

RELATED RESEARCH

Bureau of the Census (September 1976), Annual Housing Survey: 1974, Minnesota-St. Paul, Minnesota SMSA, Series H-170-74-9, U.S. Department of Commerce.

Business Research Department (September 1978), Residential Electric Load Characteristics Study, August 1977 - July 1978, Northern States Power Company.

_____, (June 1979a), Residential Electrical Use Study, Minnesota, Northern States Power Company.

_____, (June 1979b), Residential Gas Use vs Income Study, Minnesota, Northern States Power Company.

Hirst E. and Haller, M. (January 1980), Analysis of Single-Family Home Characteristics and Energy Use in Minnesota, Minnesota Energy Agency.

_____, Maier, R., and Patton, M. (1980), "Evaluation of Telephone Energy Conservation Information Centers in Minnesota," Journal of Environmental Systems, 10(3).

Jensen, R.C. (October 1979), personal communication, Business Research Department, Northern States Power Company.

Keith, J.G. (September 1979), First Annual Report on the Development and Operation of a Statewide Computerized Home Energy Program, Michigan State University, for the Michigan Energy Administration.

Lawrence Berkeley Laboratory (May 1978), Updated Project Conserve Audit System, Volumes 1 and 2, LBL-W7818.

Lazare, P. (September 1980), Evaluation of the Minnesota Home Energy Audit Program, Department of Public Service.

Minnesota Energy Agency (1978), Energy Policy and Conservation Report.

Minnesota State Planning Agency (June 1978), Housing in Minnesota 1977.

95th Congress, National Energy Conservation Policy Act (November 9, 1978), PL 950619.

Norris, C., Sickle, K.V. and Easley, R. (January 1978), "Residential Energy Audits--The Working Experience and Criteria for Evaluation," Proceedings of the 1978 National Conference on Technology for Energy Conservation.

U.S. Department of Energy (November 7, 1979), "Residential Conservation Service Program," Federal Register, 44(217), p. 64602-64760.

MARKETING INCENTIVES AND ENERGY CONSERVATION

Dennis L. McNeill
R. Bruce Hutton

The recognition of the savings potential in the household sector has led to several innovative conservation efforts on the part of U.S. policymakers. Some have been a voluntary relationship with the private sector such as the Energy Cost of Ownership Program (U.S. Department of Energy 1978) and Project Payback Program (U.S. Department of Energy 1980). Other programs have resulted from legislation including appliance labeling (Energy Policy and Conservation Act 1975) and the Residential Conservation Service Program (National Energy Conservation Policy Act). The results of these efforts have brought about recognition that an integrated systematic approach to motivate and inform the consumer market is necessary to achieve conservation objectives.

While marketing provides guidance to developing and implementing appropriate strategies for conservation, it also points out the necessity of research support in both program development and evaluation. The importance of consumer research in conservation is gaining increasing attention from the policymaker (Hutton and Collins 1978). Of particular importance to the policymaker is the design and implementation of both effective and efficient programs. To accomplish these objectives, research designed to measure the end-results of the program and to provide diagnostic guidance as to what dimensions contributed to the impact is necessary.

This chapter reports the results of the Deparment of Energy's (DOE) most recent effort in motivating household energy conservation--the Low Cost/No Cost Energy Conservation Program (LC/NC) (Hutton and McNeill 1980; U.S. Department of Energy 1980). This program represented a new thrust in consumer conservation effort by DOE. It was designed to motivate the New England population to implement a series of inexpensive or no

This research was supported under contract DE-AM18C521366 for the U.S. Department of Energy, Office of Buildings and Community Systems, Marketing Programs Branch to Booz-Allen & Hamilton, Inc. The authors wish to thank Dr. Lynn D. Collins, Market Development Branch and Joseph L. Barrow, Head of the Office of Commercialization of the Department of Energy for their support and assistance in this evaluation. In addition, the authors wish to acknowledge the important contribution of Roy Roberts, National Analysts, and the assistance of Min Kantrowitz and Paul Ackerman, Booz-Allen & Hamilton, Inc.

cost energy conservation measures in their homes.   The program was an integrated marketing and communications campaign with several innovative features.

THE LOW COST/NO COST ENERGY CONSERVATION PROGRAM

The LC/NC program in six New England states (Massachusetts, Vermont, Connecticut, Rhode Island, Maine, New Hampshire) was developed to inform and motivate homeowners to implement eleven free or inexpensive conservation actions that could result in saving up to 25 per cent on their residential energy bills.   In order to accomplish this objective, the program was developed with the following components: direct distribution, through the U.S. Post Office, of the LC/NC booklet to 4.5 million households, direct distribution of a shower flow control device along with the LC/NC Booklet, a paid advertising campaign including television, radio, and newspaper, and strong public relations activities including public service announcements for radio and television, press conferences, talk shows, and newspaper articles and editorials.

The focus of the program was the LC/NC Booklet.   This professionally designed booklet contained eleven categories of free or inexpensive energy conservation measures.   Within each category there was an explanation, including graphics, of how to do the tip, how much would be saved, and appropriate cautionary statements concerning installation.   It was stressed that implementation of all measures would result in a fuel bill savings of 25 per cent.

Packaged with the booklet was a plastic shower flow control device the combination of which acted as an incentive package to motivate households to do the energy conservation behaviors. The direct mail portion of the campaign was backed by radio, television, and newspaper advertising as well as a strong public relations effort.   The media campaign began November 8, 1979 and ended December 2, 1979.

METHODS

The evaluation plan for the LC/NC program involved the following major research questions.   What were the impacts on the energy conservation behaviors recommended by the LC/NC program?   What were the contributions of the specific components of the program to the overall effects?

Research Design

In order to assess the overall program effects and determine the contribution of the incentives package, a field experiment was used.   The design was a post-test only matched group design (Campbell and Stanley 1963) (Table 1).   The treatment

TABLE 1

DESIGN FOR THE LC/NC EVALUATIONS

		Urban Sample	Non-Metropolitan	Total
LC/NC Treatment (New England)	Boston & Hartford	604	603	1,207
Control (New York)	Buffalo & Rochester	453	151	604
TOTAL		1,057	754	1,811

condition consisted of the six New England states exposed to the LC/NC program.   The control condition consisted of selected (matched) counties from upstate New York.

A telephone survey of 1207 New England households and 604 from New York was conductecd to measure overall impact.   The sample was stratified at two levels, big city (e.g., Boston, Hartford vs. Rochester, Buffalo), and small town and rural areas.

The questionnaire had four major components:

Screening.   Questions were asked to determine dwelling type and readership of the booklet.

Reported Behavior.   Respondents were first sep-arated into readers and non-readers.   Readers were asked questions regarding their attitudes toward the booklet and non-readers why they did not read it.   All readers were asked sequentially if they were able to and did complete each con-servation tip, if not whether they intended to complete the tip in the future.   Non-readers were asked if they completed each measure and when it was done.

Attitudes toward the LC/NC advertising.   Respon-dents in New England were asked recall questions on the LC/NC advertising and to evaluate the perceived quality of the ads.

Demographics.   Standard demographic questions were asked including fuel type for heating and cooling, age of house, family size, amount of annual utility bills, education, age, marital status, and income (Department of Energy 1980).

The interviewing was conducted simultaneously in New England and New York during the period from December 15 to December 28, 1979. A validity check of 180 households showed 96 per cent accuracy in reporting the LC/NC behaviors.

RESULTS

The results of the evaluation will be summarized briefly discussed in two sections. First, overall differences between treatment and control conditions will be examined with attention to the impact of the incentives. Second, differences between readers and non-readers of the booklet will be reported to determine the impact of the booklet itself.

Overall Effectiveness: New England versus New York

Total Conservation Tips Implemented.   This provides the first test of the effectiveness. The important finding here is that while New York had completed significantly more tips prior to the program (2.77 vs. 2.00) New England completed significantly more tips both since the program (2.63 vs. 1.19) and in terms of the average total number of tips completed (4.63 vs. 3.96) (Table 2). This finding indicates a positive impact of

TABLE 2

AVERAGE NUMBER OF LC/NC ACTIONS TAKEN

Average Number of Actions Taken	New England	New York
Prior to the LC/NC Program:		
Total[a]	2.00	2.77
Readers	1.79	
Non-readers	2.41	
Since the LC/NC Program:		
Total[b]	2.63	1.19
Readers	3.15	
Non-readers	1.36	
Total Actions		
Total[a]	4.63	3.96
Readers	4.94	
Non-readers	3.77	

[a] $t = 9.17$, $p < .000$; [b] $t = 8.00$, $p < .001$; [c] $t = 8.00$, $p < .000$

the LC/NC program in overcoming the strong prior conservation efforts in New York.

Penetration of Individual Tips. The LC/NC program resulted in significant behavioral changes on four of the recommended actions:

1. Acceptance of the shower flow device incentive.   (48.1 percent of the population in New England reported installation versus 25.8 percent in New York; this difference was carried over to installations accomplished since the program as well—32.5 percent vs. 2.0 percent). Note: Of those that read the booklet but did not install the device since the program (n=466) 41 percent intended to do so later; of those that did not intend to, 45.2 percent already had one installed, 26.8 percent "tried one and didn't like it" and 22.1 percent stated "shower wouldn't work as well."

2. Acceptance of fireplace tips. (New England, 67.5 percent vs. New York, 60.8 percent); an even larger percentage was found to have engaged in this behavior since the media effort—34.9 percent vs. 7.6 percent, respectively.

3. Insulating ductwork. (New England, 42.5 percent versus New York, 30.8 percent); this significant difference is carried through on a since-the-program basis as well—New England, 3.2 percent vs. New York, 1.4 percent.

4. Improving efficiency of furnace. (New England, 64.3 percent versus New York, 51.9 percent); this difference is further evidenced by the level of activity since the program—New England, 23.8 percent vs. New York, 3.9 percent.

Finally, those subjects in both New England and New York that installed the shower flow device did significantly more tips than those subjects who did not install the device.

Impact of the Booklet on Program Effects:
Readers versus Non-Readers

Results indicate that 71.1 percent of the population in New England reported reading the booklet. Once the booklet was read, the material was expected to act as an incentive, so that readers would do significantly more tips than non-readers.

Total Number of Tips Completed: Readers versus Non-Readers. As in the previous analysis, readers did more conservation actions than non-readers both in actions taken since the program (3.15 vs. 1.36) and the total average number of actions taken (4.94 vs. 3.77). The non-readers lack of response to this program means a different strategy must be used to reach them, for the incentives used in this program did not motivate this group's response to the LC/NC program.

In an evaluation of the differences between readers and non-readers, readers had significantly higher penetration of six of the LC/NC conservation actions.

Penetration of Individual Tips: Readers versus Non-Readers. The following summarizes the significant differences for readers and non-readers for the individual conservation tips:

Readers reported a significantly higher percentage of installations than non-readers of the shower flow device (58.1 percent vs. 21.9 percent). This difference was reinforced by the level of activity occurring since the program where 43 percent of the readers reported installation versus only 5.1 percent of non-readers.

A significantly greater percentage of readers reported turning down the thermostat on their hot water heater (67.2 percent vs. 54.7 percent). The percentage differences were somewhat larger for the action taking place since the program (39.7 percent vs. 12.5 percent).

Checking for gaps around the damper in the fireplace represents the third significant difference between readers (70.7 percent) and non-readers. The difference is further reflected in the amount of activity since the media campaign (readers, 44.6 percent vs. non-readers, 6.9 percent). Of the readers that checked and found gaps, 85.7 percent actually sealed them compare to 76.9 percent for non-readers.

Significantly more readers (59.9 percent) than non-readers (47.4 percent) checked for gaps in their attics. In addition significantly more readers (38.7 percent) than non-readers (8.2 percent) checked for gaps since the media campaign.

Readers evidenced a significantly higher percentage checking for outside openings or cracks (70.2 percent) when compared to non-readers (57.0 percent). Readers also reported being more active since the program (57.9 percent vs. 9.7 percent). In both reader and non-reader cases, approximately 88 percent of the sample finding cracks went ahead and sealed them.

A significantly higher percentage of readers (68.9 percent) made adjustments to their furnace compared to

non-readers (53.5 percent). The percentage difference
was even greater for activity since the program (31.4
percent vs. 5.4 percent).

Finally, a significant difference existed between readers
who had installed the device (5.53) and non-readers who had
installed the device (4.17) in terms of the total average number
of tips completed, 5.53 versus 4.17 respectively.

Relationship of the Booklet Readership to Perception of Ads

Finally, one of the purposes of incentives is to produce a
synergism between the incentive package and related advertising.
A higher level of hearing or reading the LC/NC ads was reported
by readers (59.9 percent vs. 35.0 percent).   They reported
higher recall of the television ads (63.8 percent vs. 48.5
percent) and newspaper ads (49.1 percent vs. 38.0 percent), but
there was no difference in recall of radio spots (25.3 percent
vs. 27.8 percent).   Readers were able to recall the 25 percent
savings message somewhat better (31.1 percent vs. 25.6 percent).
However, they were more skeptical about the likelihood of
achieving the savings.

SUMMARY AND CONCLUSIONS

The program examination exhibited the following major
results:

There was a significant behavioral change in New
England on the LC/NC conservation measures.

The shower flow device incentive played a major
role in the program effects and was one of four
tips which exhibited significant behavioral
change.

The strength of this incentive is shown by the
fact that those installing the shower flow device
installed a significantly greater number of the
other conservation measures described in the
LC/NC booklet.

71.1 percent of the New England sample reported
reading the LC/NC booklet and this readership was
positively related to program effects.   These
effects were found for both the conservation
behaviors and perceptions of the LC/NC ads.

This evaluation yielded some additional findings relevant
to future efforts. First, choosing a control condition based on

matching criteria was a difficult task.   The research methodology must insure that analysis can rule out alternative hypotheses for program results when matching is not completely
achieved.   Second, there appeared to be segment difference in
response to the program.   Those households electing not to
respond to the LC/NC program had performed significantly more
conservation behaviors prior to the program.   However, these
households were still capable of benefiting from the LC/NC
program.   In the future, care should be taken to develop incentives for the various segments to which programs are targeted.
Finally, the results indicated that the use of incentives and an
integrated program were necessary for achieving program results.
The baseline control condition for this study provided a stringent test since virtually all LC/NC measures were already
available to the population.   However, the use of the incentives
and other program components resulted in significant behavior
change within just two week of the cessation of the LC/NC
program efforts.

The results indicate that inexpensive and small scale
conservation measures performed by households have worthwhile
potential for energy saving.   When these behaviors are coupled
with the emerging technological home improvements, they significantly add to the arsenal used to combat the country's energy
crisis.

RELATED RESEARCH

Campbell, Donald T. and Stanley, Julian C. (1963), Experimental
    and Quasi-Experimental Designs for Research.   Chicago,
    Illinois: Rand-McNally.

Energy Policy and Conservation Act (1975), Public Law 94-163.

Hutton, R. Bruce and Collins, Lynn D. (1978), "Consumer Research
    in the Department of Energy," Proceedings, American Psycho-
    logical Association Conference, Division 23, Toronto,
    Canada.

_____, and McNeill, Dennis L. (1980).   "An Empirical Evaluation
    of the Low Cost/No Cost Energy Conservation Program," Draft
    Report, Office of Conservation and Solar Applications, U.S.
    Department of Energy, Washington, D.C.

U.S. Department of Energy (1980), "An Evaluation of the Low
    Cost/No Cost Energy Conservation Program in New England,"
    Draft Report, prepared by Booz, Allen, and Hamilton, Office
    of Conservation and Solar Applications, Washington, D.C.

_____, (1978) "Evaluation of a Marketing Program Designed to Increase Consumer Consideration of Energy Efficient Products in Denver, Colorado," Report prepared by National Demographics LTD for the Office of Conservation and Solar Applications.

U.S. RESIDENTIAL ENERGY TAX CREDIT

Robert E. Pitts
James L. Wittenbach

Home energy use accounts for 10 percent of the national total and appears to be a particularly fruitful area for conservation in that the addition of insulation in homes without adequate insulation can reduce household energy consumption by 30 percent to 40 percent (Congressional Budget Office 1977, p. 82-83). The Residential Energy Conservation Tax Credit of 1978 was passed as a means of achieving the public policy goal of insulating 90 percent of the homes needing insulation over the life of the credit. The credit for "energy conservation" is 15 percent of the first $2000 of qualified expenditures or a maximum credit of $300 on a cumulative basis. Qualified expenditures include insulation, storm or thermal windows or doors, replacement burners, furnace ignition systems, clock thermostat, caulking or weather-stripping or exterior doors or walls, and other similar energy conserving devices.

The purpose of this chapter is to examine the merits of tax credits as a means of stimulating behavior and to report the results of a study measuring the impact of the energy tax credit on the decision of consumers to insulate their homes.

PROS AND CONS OF TAX CREDITS

Tax credits promote individual rather than governmental choice as to how money will be spent to accomplish public policy objectives (Weidenbaum 1974). As opposed to most governmental subsidies, a tax credit is given directly to the citizen from which the desired behavior is elicited after the behavior is accomplished. Tax credits appear to be public policy expedients that may serve as incentives in areas where direct expenditure by the government would be difficult (Hyatt 1977). Tax credits are perceived as a "costless form of subsidy" because the government merely refrains from collecting taxes from eligible individuals rather than redistributing funds.

The tax credit form of public policy implementation is not without its problems. One congressional study contends that the Energy Conservation credit would "merely add to the impetus" of individuals buying insulation as a result of fuel cost increases--current and expected. The study stated that "... a large share of any tax credit would be a windfall payment to people

The authors wish to express their appreciation to the Peat, Marwick, Mitchell Foundation for funding this research.

who have already decided to add insulation" (Congressional
Budget Office 1977, p. 85). In fact, increasing energy costs
appear to have already motivated a number of consumers to
purchase insulation products. In 1975, 9.1 million or 22
percent of the occupied, single-family, detached houses added
some form of insulation.

Critics contend that many credits are subsidies for the
middle class (Surrey 1973). It may be argued that subsidies
should not be given to people sufficiently motivated by environmental factors to engage in the desired behaviors regardless of
the credit (Hyatt 1977). The credit as implemented appears to
do little to help those consumers least able to afford insulation investment. Today the poor spend 15 percent of their
income on energy and in general have been less likely to make
energy conservation purchases. More than 50 percent of the
homes of the poor do not have insulation compared to only 5
percent of the homes of more well-to-do citizens (Hyatt 1977).
Yet, credits are available only to taxpayers whose tax liabili-
ties are sufficient to cover the credit claim. Further, the
after-the-fact nature of the credit requires that recipients
bear the entire initial cost of the desired expenditure. This
represents an almost intolerable situation for lower income
families who spend most, if not all, of their take-home pay on
consumption items and consequently have little to spend on
capital expenditures (Hyatt 1977, p. 314).

METHODS

A study of the impact of the residential energy consumption
tax credit on consumer behavior was conducted in the spring of
1979 (approximately 24 months after the tax credit became
effective) in a middle-sized midwestern "snowbelt" city. A
telephone survey was utilized to collect data for the study.
Lists of families making insulation and/or other energy conservation purchases since passage of the Energy Tax Act on November
9, 1978, were procured from the major insulation firms in the
city.

Two hundred purchasers of residential energy conserving
products were contacted by mail with a pre-study notification
letter. The purpose of the study was described in the letter
and recipients were requested to cooperate with interviewers who
would be contacting them by phone. The following week, study
participants were interviewed by telephone by a professional
interviewing service.

Respondents were asked a series of questions concerning the
importance of the energy tax credit in their decision to purchase insulation, their knowledge of the credit, and the acquisition of this information. Detailed information concerning the
value of the credit, the cost of the insulation, value of their
home, income, education, and occupation were also collected.

RESULTS

Of the 200 individuals contacted by phone, 146 agreed to provide all of the information requested for a response rate of 73 percent. Information collected concerning family income, education of the head of the household, and residence value indicated that insulation purchasers were generally "upscale" in nature. One-half of the respondents reported post high school education or college. Mean family income was reported at $23,500 with a median income of $19,500. Mean reported residence valuation was approximately $47,000 with a median of approximately $40,000.

Attic insulation was by far the principal energy conserving product/service purchased by the respondents, with 86 percent making this purchase. Thirty-three percent of the respondents purchased wall insulation, while 13 percent had purchased floor insulation. Only 4 percent of the respondents had purchased any of the mechanical devices eligible for the credit. The mean amount spent on energy conserving products by respondents was $428 with a range of from $50 to $2,000 and a median of approximately $315.

Two basic groups of individuals were identified in the study. The first group consisted of those taxpayers who made eligible energy conservation purchases after November 8, 1978 and prior to January 11, 1979 and thus any credit claimed was reported on their 1978 tax return (112 respondents or 73 percent). The second group consisted of taxpayers who made purchases after December 31, 1978, and would not be claiming available credits until after completion of their 1979 tax bill (34 respondents, 27 percent). The study was fixed so that respondents were contacted several weeks after the April 15, 1979 tax deadline for the 1978 filings.

The average credit taken in 1978 was $66 for the 112 respondents eligible for the credit in 1978. However, 20 respondents, or 18 percent, of those taxpayers making eligible 1978 purchases claimed no credit on their tax returns. Analysis indicated that even those citizens who had claimed the credit did not understand it fully. Several respondents reported simply taking a credit equal to the amount of the purchase while several others ignored the $300 maximum. For those taxpayers taking any credit, the mean credit was $84.

Forty-two percent of the study respondents reported that the credit was important in their decision to purchase insulation products. There was a significant relationship between reported importance and receiving the credit. As would be expected, taxpayers who did not or could not take the credit against their tax bill generally indicated the credit to be of little importance. Further, 62 percent of those respondents who purchased insulation products this year and have yet to compute their 1979 tax bill considered the credit unimportant.

Energy costs were ranked as the most important factor in the purchase decision by 95 percent of the respondents, while only 5 percent ranked concern over the national energy crisis as most important. Desire to take advantage of the tax credit received no "most important" ratings and only 14 percent of the "second most important" ratings. When asked if they would "have made the purchase if the credit had not been offered" not one of the 146 respondents indicated no. Every respondent stated that they would have made the same insulation purchase regardless of the credit. Thus, while the credit might be perceived as important by some respondents, it does not appear to be the deciding factor in the purchase decision.

Fifty-three percent of the respondents learned of the credit before considering purchase, while another 8 percent reported that they learned at the time of purchase. Thirty-nine percent, however, reported that they learned of the credit from various sources after purchase. Sixty-five percent of the respondents who knew of the credit prior to the study learned of it from television, radio, or newspaper. Eleven percent learned of it from a friend and another 12 percent learned of the credit during tax computation. It is surprising, however, that only 7 percent of the respondents learned of the credit from salesmen or sales aids.

The question of the social equity of the tax credit subsidy was examined in terms of income level and on the basis of those respondents unable or unwilling to use the credit. The impact of income on the tax credit was examined through the formulation of a low income group of respondents. A cut-off point of $10,000 in family income was selected, with 12 percent of the respondents falling into the "low income" category.

The average expenditure for respondents with incomes equal to or less than $10,000 did not vary significantly from the $474 reported by respondents with incomes above $10,000. But as was hypothesized, the credit and hence price reduction and subsidy realized did vary significantly between the two groups ($p < .0001$). Families with incomes less than $10,000 received credits which averaged only $16 with a maximum credit of just $45 for the group. The mean credit of those over $10,000 was $78 with a number of respondents utilizing the allowable maximum of $300. Further examination indicated that neither the understanding variable nor knowledge of the credit before purchase varied between the two income classifications.

SUMMARY AND CONCLUSIONS

The findings of this study indicate that the residential energy tax credit has had minimal effect on major insulation purchase decisions. Not one respondent considered the tax credit so important that the purchase would not have been made without its existence. It should be emphasized that the study population is not representative of all insulation purchasers in that only those making major purchases through full service channels were surveyed. This group, however, does have the most to gain in absolute dollar terms through the tax credit. It would appear that the study group would thus be more likely to know of the credit and more likely to be influenced by the subsidy than individuals making small dollar value purchases.

The overall impact of any subsidy type of public policy mechanism such as a tax credit is bounded by consumer knowledge of the subsidy. In the case of the Residential Energy Tax Credit such knowledge appears very limited. Despite the size of the expenditures in the study population, an average of $428, only 61 percent of the study respondents had acquired any information about the credit prior to the final purchase decision. Yet, by the very nature of the purchase and by the group from which the sample was drawn, higher levels of knowledge than that of the general public might be expected. Thus, the credit would appear to be a windfall to at least 39 percent of the respondents who learned of the credit only after purchase.

That the amount spent on insulation was not significantly different, whether the insulation purchasers had knowledge of the credit or not, is particularly important. The purchase decision would appear to be such that the amount of consumer purchase is dictated by need and the ability to make the necessary purchase. In that the credit provides no means of facilitating a purchase, the tax credit does not appear to be a salient factor in the purchase decision on the basis of future "price reduction" alone.

This study supports the contention that tax credits do not equally benefit lower income families. Since lower income families spend virtually all of their disposable income on consumption items, they are unable to save the necessary funds needed to retrofit their homes. Furthermore, these same families cannot benefit from the credit because they have little or no tax liability. This problem could be largely resolved by making the energy credit refundable.

RELATED RESEARCH

Bandy, D. and Hardman, C. (January 1976), "Accountants Will Juggle 15 Different Tax Credits During Tax Season," Taxation for Accountants, p. 38-43.

Dyer, Robert F. and Shimp, Terrance A. (January 1977), "Enhancing The Role of Marketing Research in Public Policy Decision Making," Journal of Marketing, Vol. 41, No. 1, 63-67.

Eisner, Robert and Lawler, Patrick J. (March 1975), "Tax Policy and Investment: An Analysis of Survey Responses," the American Economic Review, Vol. 65, No. 1, 206-212.

Heinhold, James C., A two-page letter dated August 24, 1979 responding to information requested by the authors to Senator Russell B. Long, Chairman of the Committee on Finance.

Hyatt, Sherry V. (1977), "Thermal Efficiency and Taxes: The Residential Energy Conservation Tax Credit," Harvard Journal on Legislation, Vol. 14:281, 281-326.

Internal Revenue Code of 1954, (January 1, 1979), Englewood Cliffs, NJ: Prentice-Hall.

President Carter's Energy Proposals: A Perspective. (June 1977) The Congress of the United States Congressional Budget Office.

Surrey, Stanley S. (1973), Pathways to Tax Reform: The Concept of Tax Expenditures, Harvard University Press.

Weidenbaum, Murray L. (March 1974), "The Advantages of Credits on the Personal Income Tax," George Washington Law Review, Vol. 42, No. 3, 516-525.

REFRIGERATOR ENERGY LABELS

Robert Redinger
Richard Staelin

The initial hypothesis, formulated on a model of economic rationality, was that when a consumer was confronted with the choice between a slightly higher priced, energy efficient refrigerator and an otherwise identical but lower priced and less energy efficient refrigerator, the consumer would view the energy saving-price increase tradeoff as an investment decision. In other words, consumers would view the increased initial costs as an investment in future savings and would select the energy efficient model if it was a good investment.

The primary goals of this study were two-fold: to test the validity of the payback model in a controlled task as similar as possible to the actual shopping environment, and to estimate the effects of various market variables on the consumer's decision process and on the probability of purchasing an energy efficient appliance.

While the measure of payback may be a good "as if" model of how consumers trade off between an increased price and operating cost savings, it probably does not depict the actual process most consumers use when making a decision about a complex product that includes these two factors. However, it is possible to test the adequacy of payback as a model of choice. If, in the process of selecting an appliance, a consumer makes an investment type decision when comparing price differences with operating cost differences, then this price-cost comparison should be independent of normal market forces except those that would facilitate the price-cost tradeoff. Thus, product characteristics such as features, color, or size should have no impact on the decision to buy energy efficiency, while market forces which may provide information to the consumer regarding operating costs (e.g., advertising, sales people, government labels) should increase (in the aggregate) consumers' use of an investment type decision.

If the payback is merely an "as if" model of the decision process (i.e., it predicts well at the aggregate level but not at the individual level) the stability of estimates based on such a model would be suspect over both time and changes in the

The authors would like to thank the members of the marketing project at GSIA for their assistance in the data collection of the study. This study was funded in part by a grant from the Department of Energy and in part by White Westinghouse, a division of White Consolidated.

market place. As an alternative, consider the product as a bundle of attributes, price and operating costs being two. Rather than trading off price and cost via payback, the consumer may trade off energy efficiency among all other attributes. For example, rather than viewing energy efficiency as an investment to be traded against price, he may hold price constant and trade energy for deluxe features or size or some other product characteristic. As with the investment model of choice, the importance of energy efficiency relative to other product characteristics can be estimated and, under controlled conditions, the effects of market forces on this "importance" determined.

THE EXPERIMENT

The experiment took place in the showrooms of the corporate offices of White-Westinghouse. The sample was a convenience sample of 123 people obtained from 3 civic/social groups in Pittsburgh and from the Blaunox plant offices of White Consolidated. The task facing each consumer was to "buy" a refrigerator from among a set of 12 alternatives which in fact consisted of six pairs, each pair identical except for differences in stated operating costs and prices. The six models differed by size (18 or 21 cubic feet), freezer location (top mounted or side by side) and type of features (standard--wire shelves, etc.--or deluxe--glass shelves, etc.). The prices and operating costs of each refrigerator pair were set so as to provide a wide range of paybacks.

The experiment was designed to estimate the effects of three market variables--government energy labels, energy communications, and energy sales push--on the decision to "buy" energy. Due to time and cost constraints only four treatment cells of the full 2 × 2 × 2 factorial experiment were chosen with subjects randomly assigned to each. Cell I was a control group to typify conditions if the energy models were available but with no other market impetus. This group provides the baseline measures for the other treatment groups. Because government labeling was to become mandatory in 1980, the remaining three treatment cells all had government labels on the upper right corner of each refrigerator.

To assess the effects of promotional material on the energy decision, subjects in cells I and III were given promotional material emphasizing traditional characteristics such as deluxe features while subjects in cells II and IV were given promotional material that included an energy efficiency push. The material was presented as being representative of the type of material they might obtain were they actually to engage in buying a refrigerator, and was introduced prior to the shopping activity.

The final aspect of the experimental design is the inclusion of the sales people into the shopping task. For the subjects in cells I and II the sales people were directed to push product characteristics such as deluxe features or freezer location. That is, they were to try to get the people to trade up in price but not at the cost of a sale. For the customers in cells III and IV the sales people were instructed to "sell" energy--to convince the subject to select the energy efficient model of whatever type of refrigerator the customer seemed most likely to buy. A summary of the design is provided in Table 1.

TABLE 1

EXPERIMENTAL DESIGN

Cell	Energy Information in Pre-shopping Ads	FTC Energy Labels	Sales Force Emphasis
I	No	No	Non-energy features
II	Yes	Yes	Non-energy features
III	No	Yes	Energy efficiency
IV	Yes	Yes	Energy efficiency

RESULTS

Payback Model

There are two aspects of this study that address the usefulness of payback as a model of choice. The first is whether or not the estimated distribution of paybacks across the population will predict aggregate choices in a buying situation. Specifically, do either (a) previously derived distributions of payback (e.g., Redinger and Staelin 1980) or (b) distributions of payback specific to this sample predict market shares for energy efficiency across a range of paybacks in a buying situation. The second aspect is whether or not people tend to actually use a payback decision rule in the shopping task. Thus, payback may predict well at the aggregate level but not at the individual level.

Four separate estimates of each individual's payback were derived from the study: three from direct questions in the final questionnaire and one from their top three choices in the shopping task. An additional estimate was obtained for 81 of the subjects who provided preference rankings of 12 refrigerators after the shopping task via conjoint analysis.

The overriding conclusion was that although the direct measures of payback provide market share estimates that behave properly (i.e., go down as payback increases) the measures are not reliable at either the individual or aggregate level.

However, measures derived from preference rankings yield estimates that predict well at both the individual and aggregate level.

Inferences about each individual's payback were also made from the top three choices in the buying task. As can be seen in Table 2, respondents in the label conditions acted more consistently with the payback model than respondents without the labels or than can be expected from chance alone. This does not imply that people use a payback decision rule but that when presented with the cost information are more likely to behave in a manner that is consistent with a payback model.

TABLE 2

PERCENTAGE OF RESPONDENTS SELECTING PRODUCTS
IN A MANNER INCONSISTENT WITH A PAYBACK MODEL

	Cell I	Cells II, III & IV
Expected Percentage Inconsistent (P_E)	25.0%	29.5%
Actual Percentage Inconsistent (P_A)	13.8%	5.3%
H_0: $P_E = P_A$	$z=1.517$ $\alpha= .1286$	$z=5.145$ $\alpha= .000$
H_0: $P_{A_I} = P_{A_2}$		$z=2.088$ $\alpha= .0366$

Finally, when other factors are introduced into the marketplace (especially the salesperon's push of energy efficiency) payback does not seem to provide a good indication of the choices people will make. Further details of this analysis are available from the authors.

The Effects of Marketing Variables on Energy Choice

Because the shopping task was a simulated task and customers did not actually purchase the refrigerator they selected, there was some concern that they would trade-up or select a more expensive model than if they were actually buying one. To help reduce this tendency to trade-up, customers were first asked which model they liked best and then they were asked which model they would buy if they really had to pay for it. This precaution partially worked in that 82 percent of the people selected a deluxe model as the one they liked best while only 70 percent actually purchased the deluxe model, 80 percent preferred a 21 cubic foot model while 67 percent actually purchased one, and 56 percent preferred a side by side model while only 35 percent purchased one.   However, based on a comparison of experimental market shares with actual market shares there still seemed to be some trading up.   Additionally, prior to the shopping task people expected to pay $650 on average for a refrigerator while the actual average price paid was $740 with approximately 63 percent of the respondents selecting a refrigerator costing over $50 more than what they had expected to pay.   This price differential may be due to a misperception of the actual market prices of refrigerators and/or to trading up in the experimental situation.

Of the three major manipulations (labels, advertisements, and sales push) only the sales person had a significant effect on the consumers' probability of purchasing energy (Table 3) and that effect was dramatic.   The chance that the customer would buy energy increased from 48 percent to over 90 percent when the salesperson was "pushing" energy.

TABLE 3

TREATMENT EFFECTS ON THE PURCHASE
OF ENERGY EFFICIENCY

Treatment	Coefficient	t-Statistic
(Constant)	.4827	
Sales push	.4820	4.720
Energy ad	.1106	1.025
Government label	-.1076	0.720

It is important to note that even though the effects of the labels were not significant, the manipulations did in fact work. Twice as many people in the label conditions recalled energy labels being present as in the non-label condition.   The labels also had an effect on the respondent's knowledge of operating costs but did not affect the rated importance of any of the product attributes (including energy-related attributes)   in making the purchase decision.

The advertisement manipulations also worked since approximately 80 percent of the people who saw the energy ads listed energy on the pre-shopping questionnaire as one of their concerns while only 24 percent mentioned it in the non-energy ad condition. Advertising had only a minimal effect on increasing consumers knowledge of actual operating costs, but it did serve to increase the rated importance of energy after the shopping task. The ads also had the effect of focusing the subjects attention on the government labels (60 percent in non-energy ad condition, 76 percent in energy ad condition). Thus, while the ads had no significant direct effect on the choice of energy, they may have had an indirect effect by increasing the importance of energy to the consumer.

Salespeoples' Effect on Energy Choice. As mentioned previously, the salespeople had a significant effect on energy choice, an effect that is even more dramatic when the first three choices are examined. After the customer selected the refrigerator he would buy, he was asked what his second and third choices would be if the specific model had not been available. When energy was pushed everyone included at least 1 energy model among their first 3 choices while 30 percent in the non-energy push condition failed to include at least one energy model among their first three choices. Further, about 37 percent of the subjects in the energy push condition selected an energy efficient model for each of their three choices while only 5 percent in the non-energy push conditions did.

Interestingly, the salespeople had a significant effect on knowledge of operating costs, but they had no effect on the customers' retrospective importance rankings. In fact, the subjects in both treatment conditions felt the salesperson had very little influence in their product selection, and additionally, there are very low correlations between what the people rated as important to them and what the salesperson ascribed as important to them (average correlation of about .16 for 17 different attributes).

SUMMARY AND CONCLUSIONS

It does not appear that the presence of government energy labels will have a significant effect in expanding the market for energy efficient appliances unless this information is supplemented with a heuristic on how to use the information to trade off price differences. One source which is capable of providing such strategy information is the retail store sales personnel.

One of the most significant findings was the fact that the salesperson had such a large influence on the purchase decision to buy energy efficient appliances. This influence can be attributed in part to the fact that the salesperson often showed the consumer how to trade energy savings and price. This was especially true when the labels were on each appliance. Consequently if manufacturers want to push the sales of more efficient appliances, they must enlist the cooperation of the retail store sales force. This enlistment will probably require some education about how to sell energy efficiency as well as financial incentives (spiffs) for taking the time to show the consumers how to make the tradeoff.

RELATED RESEARCH

Ferguson, C.E., and Gould J.P. (1975), _Microeconomic Theory_, Irwin.

Hausman, J.A. (Spring 1979), "Individual Discount Rates and the Purchasers and Utilization of Energy Using Durables," _Bell Journal of Economics_.

Redinger, R., and Staelin, R. (1980), "Individual Preferences for Energy Efficient Appliances," Carnegie Mellon University Working Paper.

EPILOGUE

A recent report, published by the National Geographic Society (1981), suggests a possible (maybe probable) future scenario:

> Violent uprisings have shaken Saudi Arabia ... oil no longer flows from rich Saudi fields. Critical elements of the oil distribution system, systematically wrecked, lie in ruins. The giant terminal at Ras Tanura, which once sent half a dozen tankers a day down the Persian Gulf and out to the global oil routes, rusts silently under a scorching sun.
>
> The free world has lost a fifth of its oil supply--some ten million barrels a day ....
>
> The oil glut of 1980, which cushioned the world's losses at the outbreak of the Iraqi-Iranian war, has long since evaporated. Bid up by the worst panic buying in history, prices on the spot market in Rotterdam are skyrocketing--$80, $100 a barrel. Official prices of the oil cartel are heading for similar levels, if more slowly.
>
> The 21-nation International Energy Agency has called on its members to fulfill an agreement signed in 1975: In the event of a major cutoff, they are to share their oil. Honoring that promise is costing the United States nearly three million barrels a day for Western Europe and Japan are far more heavily hit. The total U.S. loss equals more than half of all the oil consumed by its 160 million motor vehicles.
>
> Domestically the effects are disastrous. Critical gasoline shortages have brought endless lines at filling stations, even though prices have reached painful levels. Violence frequently erupts when the pumps reach empty, and thefts from gas tanks are epidemic. Gasoline-rationing plans are invoked, but will be months getting into operation.
>
> Meanwhile, transportation is hamstrung. Many workers cannot get to their jobs; productivity drops. Businesses dependent on gasoline, such as shopping centers, resorts, motels, are suffering heavy losses. All economic indicators are flying red flags. Unemployment is climbing. The stock market drops daily. Inflation has passed 30 percent.
>
> And all for the want of imported oil.

Scenarios such as this one help reinforce the significance of the energy problem, and accordingly, reinforce the relevance of the conservation solution being pursued by consumer energy research.

The National Geographic report goes on to describe many aspects of the energy problem. The section that directly relates to the papers in this volume is a section titled, "Conservation: Can We Live Better on Less?" Clearly, this fundamental issue is the stimulus for the preceeding studies. The purpose at this point is to reflect on these studies with a view to drawing conclusions for future consumer energy research and future conservation program options.

Consumer Energy Research

Review of the studies in this volume suggests a number of implications for future research. The first is the importance of collecting actual consumption data. Self-reports of energy consumption appear to be highly questionable with consumers being poor "guessers" when estimating monthly or yearly energy expenditures. Consequently, actual consumption data must be obtained from utilities by means of release forms from respondents, or in the case of the family automobile by using diaries which allow respondents to complete a form each time the car is refueled.

A second implication is the need to monitor consumption on a longitudinal basis. Cross-sectional studies cannot capture the dynamics of energy situations, and yet few studies have examined changes in consumption over time.

A third implication is the need for further creative research to improve the understanding of attitudinal-behavioral links. Although strong relationships have been found in homogeneous samples, greater generalization via national samples has not been particularly successful. Two options can be suggested. It seems possible that the modeling approach, attitude factors related to energy consumption, may be too simplistic. An alternative approach that structurally relates attitudes to specific energy consuming activities and subsequently to energy consumption may be more successful. The second option is the application of alternative methods of analysis. Although structuring conservation attitudes via factor analysis of attitude items has been widely adopted, greater attention to specific attitude items with the possibility of item cluster typologies may prove more useful.

A fourth research implication is the value of increased use of experimentation. Studies, such as the research done by Gaskell and colleagues and by Heberlein and colleagues, indicate the value of carefully designed experiments. This is particularly true in terms of evaluating the impact of energy conservation programs, the focus of discussion in the next section.

Conservation Program Options

    The conservation programs evaluated in this volume repre-
sent a small subset of the range of programs that could be
implemented. A framework for identifying program options is
presented in Table 1 (McDougall and Ritchie 1979). The framework has two major dimensions, policy type and intervention
focus. Policy type refers to primary thrust: financial versus
non-financial, and within each of these categories sub-cate-
gories based on degree of coerciveness, regulatory versus
persuasive.
    The second major dimension, intervention focus, is divided
into three main categories: availability of energy supply and
energy consuming products, choice of products at time of purchase, and use behavior associated with energy consumption.
Each of these categories is further subdivided based on three
areas of consumption: in-home, work and maintenance, and
leisure.
    In total this framework identifies 36 types of conservation
programs. For each type many options could be identified; Table
1 also provides a number of examples.
    Reviewing the studies in Part II in terms of this framework
indicates that the programs discussed provide examples of all
four major policy types. However, in terms of intervention
focus, almost all of the studies evaluated programs concerned
with in-home energy consumption.
    Other sources can provide a wider range of program options.
For example, an annotated directory of energy conservation
programs (Claxton, McDougall, and Ritchie 1980) describes
several dozen programs, and an annotated bibliography of consumer energy studies (Anderson and McDougall 1980) suggests many
others. However, although these sources help to identify many
conservation program options, unfortunately most have not had
the benefit of the careful evaluation characteristic of the
studies in Part II.
    In summary, this discussion of conservation program options
leads to three conclusions. First, a large number of program
options can be identified and should be reviewed when conservation efforts are being initiated. Second, there is a world-
wide increase in the number and types of conservation programs
being implemented. New programs will be well served by efforts
to collect and evaluate information on the many existing programs in other jurisdictions. Third, effective allocation of
future conservation efforts depends upon the careful analysis of
ongoing programs. The papers presented in Part II provide
examples of programs that have been subject to careful evaluation. To the extent that this example is pursued for a broad
range of programs, the conservation solution in aggregate will
benefit.

TABLE 1
CONSERVATION POLICY FRAMEWORK

Focus	Financial Policies		Non-Financial Policies	
	Regulatory	Persuasive	Regulatory	Persuasive
Availability:				
•Home activities	•Building codes •Appliance standards	•Direct utility load control	•Heat-fuel rationing	•Encourage switch from oil to natural gas
•Work/maintenance activities	•Design restrictions on autos	•Incentives for manufacture of small autos	•Gasoline rationing	
•Leisure activities	•Increase air tariffs to resorts	•Free entry to campgrounds for locals	•Limit resort developments	
Choice (purchase decisions):				
•Home activities	•Tax energy inefficient appliances	•Tax rebate on insulation •Subsidy for solar water heaters	•Appliance energy labels	•Promotion of solar heating hot water
•Work/maintenance activities	•Surtax on air conditioned autos	•Reduce licence fee for efficient autos	•Fuel consumption labels on autos	
•Leisure activities				•Promote low energy-use recreation
Use Behavior:				
•Home activities	•Time-of-day utility rates •Progessive utility rates	•Subsidize furnace retrofit	•Mandate fireplace dampers	•Information feedback •Energy audits •Media campaigns to cut energy use
•Work/maintenance activities	•Gasoline tax increases	•Reward for carpooling	•Reduce speed limits •Lanes for carpools/busses	•Promote correct driving habits and carpools
•Leisure activities				•Appeals for vacationing near home

REFERENCES

Anderson, C. Dennis and McDougall, Gordon H.G. (1980). Consumer
    Energy Research: An Annotated Bibliography,   Vancouver,
    B.C.: Behavioral Energy Research Group, University of
    British Columbia.

Claxton, John D., McDougall, Gordon, H.G., and Ritchie, J.R.
    Brent (1980). Annotated Directory of Energy Conservation
    Programs, Vancouver, B.C.: Behavioral Energy Research
    Group, University of British Columbia.

McDougall, Gordon H.G. and Ritchie, J.R. Brent (1979). "Con-
    sumer Energy Conservation: A Framework for Policy Re-
    search," in Jerry C. Olson (ed.), Advances in Consumer
    Research Vol. VII. Proceedings of the Tenth Annual Con-
    ference of the Association for Consumer Research, San
    Francisco, Ca., 272-6.

National Geographic Society (1981), "Energy: Facing up to the
    Problem, Getting down to Solutions," Special Report,
    Washington, D.C.

ABOUT THE EDITORS

C. Dennis Anderson is Associate Professor of Marketing, Faculty of Administrative Studies, University of Manitoba. He has conducted and published a number of empirical studies in the area of consumer behavior and energy use and has consulted with the federal government and utilities on energy consumption programs and research approaches. His current research and publication activities involve updating Consumer Energy Research: An Annotated Bibliography, analyzing consumer in-home energy use patterns, and evaluating the impact of two federal government energy conservation programs.

John D. Claxton is Associate Professor and Director of Masters' Programs, Faculty of Commerce and Business Administration, University of British Columbia. His academic interests have resulted in research publications in the Journal of Consumer Research, tthe Journal of Marketing, the Journal of Marketing Research, the Journal of the Marketing Research Society, and the Journal of Retailing. In addition to his continuing interest in household energy consumption patterns, he is currently involved in a study of leisure energy consumption, and initiating work in the area of energy technology adoption.

Gordon H.G. McDougall is Professor, School of Business and Economics, Wilfrid Laurier University. He has conducted a number of studies in the consumer behavior and energy field including an annual national survey of consumer attitudes towards energy, surveys of energy consumption patterns and the effects of alternative energy conservation messages. This and his previous research have been published in the Journal of Marketing, the Journal of Retailing, and a number of American Marketing Association Proceedings. His research interests in the energy field include the preparation of a revised annotated bibliography of consumer energy research and a study of the effects of a energy audit on energy conserving behaviors.

J.R. Brent Ritchie is Professor and Associate Dean in the Faculty of Management at the University of Calgary. He is also Director of the Division of Travel and Tourism in the Institute of Transportation Studies at the same University. His research activities have focused on the study of consumer behavior in the area of leisure and tourism as well as energy consumption and conservation. The results of these activities have appeared in numerous scholarly publications including the Journal of Travel Research, the Journal of Leisure Research, the Journal of Consumer Research, the Journal of Marketing, the Journal of Marketing Research, and Canadian Public Policy. Dr. Ritchie currently serves as Associate Editor of the Journal of Travel Research and as a member of the Editorial Advisory Board of several scholarly journals.

299

CONTRIBUTORS

Chris T. Allen, Assistant Professor of Marketing, University of Massachusetts, Amherst, Massachusetts

C. Dennis Anderson, Associate Professor, Faculty of Administrative Studies, University of Manitoba, Winnipeg, Manitoba

Laurel Andrews, Mathematical Sciences Northwest, Bellevue, Washington

M.K. Berkowitz, Associate Professor, Department of Political Economy, University of Toronto, Toronto, Ontario

Stephen P.A. Brown, Brookhaven National Laboratory, Upton, Long Island, New York

John M. Callaway, Pacific Northwest Laboratory, Richland, Washington

Lisa Cannon, Program Analyst, Office of Policy and Evaluation, U.S. Department of Energy, Washington, DC

Lynda T. Carlson, Senior Project Leader, Office of the Consumption Data System, Energy Information Administration, U.S. Department of Energy, Washington, DC

John D. Claxton, Associate Professor, Faculty of Commerce and Business Administration, University of British Columbia, Vancouver, British Columbia

William J. Corney, Associate Professor of Management, University of Nevada, Las Vegas, Nevada

Kenton R. Corum, Oak Ridge Laboratory, Oak Ridge, Tennessee

Mihaly Csikszenthmihalyi, Professor and Chairman, Committee on Human Development, Department of Behavioral Sciences, University of Chicago, Chicago, Illinois

Robert F. Dyer, Professor and Director of Marketing, George Washington University, Washington, DC

P. Ellis, Department of Social Psychology, London School of Economics, London, UK

George Gaskell, Department of Social Psychology, London School of Economics, London, UK

Susan McManama Gianinno, Research Supervisor, Needham, Harper and Steers, Chicago, Illinois

Rolf Gradin, Head, Energy Conservation Division, International Energy Agency, Paris, France

Ronald Graef, Research Associate, Department of Behavioral Sciences, University of Chicago, Chicago, Illinois

G.H. Haines, Jr., Professor, Faculty of Management Studies and Erindale College, University of Toronto, Toronto, Ontario

Thomas A. Heberlein, Associate Professor of Sociology, University of Wisconsin-Madison, Madison, Wisconsin

G. Jan van Helden, Lecturer, Economic Faculty, University of Groningen, The Netherlands

Eric Hirst, Energy Division, Oak Ridge National Laboratory, Oak Ridge, Tennessee

R. Bruce Hutton, Associate Professor of Marketing, University of Denver, Denver, Colorado

John Jeppesen, Evaluation Specialist, Energy Administration, Michigan Department of Commerce, Lansing, Michigan

Andrea Ketoff, Policy Analysis Group, Lawrence Berkeley Laboratory, Berkeley, California

Thomas C. Kinnear, Professor, Graduate School of Business Administration, University of Michigan, Ann Arbor, Michigan

Martin Kushler, Education Projects Evaluation Coordinator, Energy Administration, Michigan Department of Commerce, Lansing, Michigan

Duncan LaBay, Assistant Professor, The Whittemore School of Business and Economics, University of New Hampshire, Durham, New Hampshire

Peter Lazare, Department of Public Service, St. Paul, Minnesota

Dorothy Leonard-Barton, Assistant Professor, Alfred P. Sloan School of Management, Massachusetts Institute of Technology, Cambridge, Massachusetts

Mark D. Levine, Lawrence Berkeley Laboratory, Berkeley, California

Bertil Liander, Associate Professor of Marketing, University of Massachusetts, Amherst, Massachusetts

Daniel L. Linz, Graduate Assistant, Department of Rural Sociology, University of Wisconsin-Madison, Madison, Wisconsin

Gordon H.G. McDougall, Professor, School of Business and Economics, Wilfrid Laurier University, Waterloo, Ontario

James E. McMahon, Lawrence Berkeley Laboratory, Berkeley, California

Dennis L. McNeill, Associate Professor of Marketing, University of Denver, Denver, Colorado

John E. Nixon, Associate Professor of Management, University of Nevada, Las Vegas, Nevada

Dennis L. O'Neal, Oak Ridge National Laboratory, Oak Ridge, Tennessee

Bonnie P. Ortiz, Graduate Assistant, Department of Rural Sociology, University of Wisconsin-Madison, Madison, Wisconsin

Lynn D. Patinkin, Project Manager, Commerical Surveys, Office of the Consumption Data Systems, Energy Information Administration, U.S. Department of Energy, Washington, DC

Terry Petherick, Methodologist, Census and Household Surveys, Method Division, Statistics Canada, Ottawa, Ontario

R. Pike, Department of Social Psychology, London School of Economics, London, UK

Robert E. Pitts, University of Mississippi, Mississippi State, Mississippi

W. Fred van Raaij, Professor, Department of Economics, Erasmus University, Rotterdam, The Netherlands

Robert Redinger, Assistant Professor of Marketing, Graduate School of Industrial Administration, Carnegie-Mellon University, Pittsburgh, Pennsylvania

Fred A. Reid, Private Consultant

J.R. Brent Ritchie, Professor, Faculty of Management, University of Calgary, Calgary, Alberta

Chris Ruhm, Lawrence Berkeley Laboratory, Berkeley, California

Charles D. Schewe, Associate Professor of Marketing, University of Massachusetts, Amherst, Massachusetts

Lee Schipper, Policy Analysis Group, Lawrence Berkeley Laboratory, Berkeley, California

Kish Sharma, Private Consultant

Daniel L. Sherrell, Louisiana State University, Baton Rouge, Louisiana

K. Sorrenti, Project Manager, Special Surveys Group, Statistics Canada, Ottawa, Ontario

Robert H. Spencer, Jr., Loan and Market Research Supervisor, Puget Sound and Light, Bellevue, Washington

Richard Staelin, Professor, Australian Graduate School of Management, University of New South Wales, Kensington, Australia

Wendel L. Thompson, Project Manager, Residential Surveys, Office of the Consumption Data Systems, Energy Information Administration, U.S. Department of Energy, Washington, DC

Kenneth A. Vagts, Director, Office of the Consumption Data System, Energy Information Administration, U.S. Department of Energy, Washington, DC

Theo M.M. Verhallen, Assistant Professor, Department of Economic Psychology, Tilburg University, Tilburg, The Netherlands

Seymour Warkov, Professor of Sociology, University of Connecticut, Storrs, Connecticut

G. Keith Warriner, Graduate Student, Department of Sociology, University of Wisconsin-Madison, Wisconsin

Selie S. Weistra, Research Assistant, Economics Faculty, University of Groningen, The Netherlands

John F. Willenborg, Professor and Director of Marketing, University of South Carolina, Columbia, South Carolina

James L. Wittenbach, Professor, College of Business Administration, University of Notre Dame, Notre Dame, Indiana

Betty Yantis, Director, Centre for Business and Economic Research, University of Nevada, Las Vegas, Nevada

Carol A. Zimmerman, Doctoral Candidate, School of Forestry and Environmental Studies, Yale University, New Haven, Connecticut

Date Due